NOBLER THAN THE ANGELS, LOWER THAN A WORM

The Pietist View of the Individual in the Writings of Heinrich Müller and August Hermann Francke

Gary R. Sattler

UNIVERSITY
PRESS OF
AMERICA

Lanham • New York • London

Copyright © 1989 by

University Press of America,® Inc.

4720 Boston Way
Lanham, MD 20706

3 Henrietta Street
London WC2E 8LU England

British Cataloging in Publication Information Available

Library of Congress Cataloging-in-Publication Data

Sattler, Gary R.
Nobler than the angels, lower than a worm : the pietist view of the individual in
the writings of Heinrich Müller and August Hermann Francke / Gary R. Sattler.
p.   cm.
Bibliography: p.
1. Man (Christian theology)—History of doctrines—17th century.   2. Pietism—
History—17th century.   3. Francke, August Hermann, 1663–1727.
4. Müller, Heinrich, 1631–1675.   I. Title.
BT701.2.S25   1989   233'.5'09032—dc20   89–14657 CIP

ISBN 0–8191–7518–8 (alk. paper)

To Joyce

Acknowledgements

The Christian Church is by no means monolithic. It is certainly the one Body of Christ, but within that body has appeared all manner of understandings of just what it means to be, and to be within, the Church. Pietism is one manifestation of a particular way of seeing the Christian life.

My interest in Pietism goes back to my upbringing in an ethnic German denomination in Pennsylvania, the German Evangelical and Reformed Church, which has at least some of its roots in the Pietist tradition. In fact, a number of modern denominations owe more than a small debt to Pietism.

This book is a revision of my doctoral dissertation accepted by the theological faculty of the University of Marburg (Philipps-Universität). I wish to thank Professor Dr. Erich Geldbach, my Doktorvater, for encouragement and guidance in pursuing my interest in the Pietist movement and for being so helpful in enabling me to take up this pursuit. I am also grateful to Dr. Martin Kraatz and Frau Iris Hartje at the Religionskundliche Sammlung, the University of Marburg. Their help and support were both gracious and necessary as I explored the Bibliothek Wittgenstein housed there. To the late Prof. Dr. Winfried Zeller and his wife goes my deepest gratitude as well. Mr. Larry Russell deserves special mention for his great effort in seeing to it that the dissertation and this book could come to be. He and Pat were only a little lower than the angels. Finally, many thanks to Joyce Babb, who deserves better than simply having a book dedicated to her.

TABLE OF CONTENTS

INTRODUCTION

There has always existed in Christianity that way of thinking and speaking which places major attention on the person and his or her relationships—with God and others and self—rather than upon creedal statements (although these are by no means seen as unimportant) and on how one should respond to these documents and doctrines. This is true of that cluster of theologians severally known as Puritans, Precisianists, Arndtians, Lutheran Reform orthodox and Pietists of all confessions. Because their thought is so thoroughly impregnated with those Church Fathers who were also primarily concerned with the divine–human relationship, and with the mystics, for whom the person (read self) was a major preoccupation, these thinkers, too, tended to dwell upon the nature, behavior and fate of the individual—but always as over against the living God. Because for these theologians Christ is not only *for*, but is also *in* the individual, God-talk and anthropology are inseparable. What is the point of talking about God unless one somehow relates it to the current situation of humanity? How is it even possible to speak of human beings apart from the one who created, sustains, interacts with and awaits them? Our interests here, then, are what a human being is, the conditions of human life, how one is to act in society, and to what a person ultimately may look forward.

We shall explore the nature of the individual from the perspective of that group of theologians active in the Brandenburg-Prussia area of Germany between 1650 and 1727, particularly Heinrich Müller[1] and August Hermann Francke.

---

[1] Because Francke's life is so minutely recorded and because it is so illustrative of Pietist anthropology, I have used it extensively to introduce the systematic analysis of Pietism's view of the individual. Some data on Müller are important by way of introduction. There are a number of personal similarities between Francke and Müller which will appear. These should not be construed as indicating the connection of these men as concerns their view of the person. Perhaps it simply reflects the basic Pietist personality.

Müller was born on 18. October, 1631 in Lübeck, the place of Francke's birth some 32 years later. His parents, who soon moved back to Rostock, planned from early on for him to enter the service of the Church. He entered the University of Rostock at thirteen years of age, and lived and studied with the Arndtian Lutheran theologian, Joachim Lütkemann.

At the age of twenty he was called to preach in St. Mary's Church in Rostock. He, like Francke, found this a difficult assignment, but for different

In his *Pietismus Studien*, Horst Weigelt cites Reform orthodoxy as one of the major influences on the thought of Francke.
This opinion was also stated to me in 1980 by Prof. Dr. Winfried
Zeller (University of Marburg) during one of our many conversations about Pietism and spirituality. While similarity of
thought, and even of expression, is not proof-positive of direct
influence, when we consider: 1) the similarity of Müller's and
Francke's thought and choice of words, 2) that despite the fact

---

reasons: he felt too unskilled. After a time of prayer, however, he felt assured
by the Lord that he should go on with it. In 1653 Müller received his
doctorate in theology from the University of Helmstädt, and was named
Professor of Greek at the University of Rostock. In 1662 he was named
Professor of Theology there as well. At that time he was called as Pastor of
St. Mary's, and in spite of many calls from churches throughout Germany he
remained in Rostock, apparently quite content. He was well-known for his
concern for the needy, the sick, widows, and orphans. At his funeral it was
said that Müller had worked himself to death in the care of souls.

In 1671 he became Superintendent of Rostock (in charge of the
ministerium of the city), and continued in his Pietistic ways. By this time he
had written a number of increasingly popular devotional works and hymns,
and had befriended a number of leading lights in the Reform orthodox
movement, among them Scriver, Fritsch and Spener, to whom he had once
written of the Lutheran Church, "We shall heal Babylon. Oh, that it only
wanted to be healed."

Müller also attacked the hardened doctrinal and institutional attitudes
current in the Lutheran Church, styling the baptismal font, the pulpit, the
confessional and the altar (the celebration of the Lord's Supper) as "*die vier
stummen Kirchengötzen*" (the four dumb idols of the Church) because people
had come to feel that the simple observance of churchly customs was
sufficient for salvation. Such statements, plus his rejection of the
Beichtpfennig (money given to a pastor for hearing a confession), and his
constant criticism of the mere "outward faith" of most baptized people caused
him to be suspected of holding Anabaptist sentiments. He also encouraged,
appearing more Reformed than Lutheran, the disciplining of sinners and
backsliders, albeit with gentleness and sensitivity.

In poor health from childhood on, Müller became increasingly ill and
died at the age of forty-three, an influential churchman, a much-loved
composer of hymns, and a renowned author of devotional works. His
emphasis on the importance of the inner person, repentance and a holy life,
as well as his rejection of things worldly, puts him solidly in the pious
tradition of Perkins, Arndt, Lütkemann and the like. He left his wife and
children with a typically Pietist statement, recorded at the end of our section
on death. *AP*, pp. v–xvii; *GE*, pp. iii–viii; *Evangelische Volksbibnlithek*,
hrsg. von Dr. Klaiber, Band 3, (Stuttgart, 1864), pp. 225–239.

that Müller died when Francke was just a lad they both shared friendship with and/or were acquainted with Spener, Christian Kortholt, Caspar Sandhagen, Ahasverus Fritsch, Christian Scriver and others of that ilk, 3) that Müller was widely read, especially in northern Germany, and 4) that both relied upon the same sources and stressed the same themes, it seems foolish to consider them members of distinct movements.

Müller and Francke were members of that movement with roots deep in Arndtian spirituality which sought to complete in life and devotion Luther's Reformation, the so-called Lutheran orthodox theologians having already carried Luther's ideas to their logical ends doctrinally. Here we will examine the writings of Müller and Francke, utilizing as well some works of others such as Arndt, Scriver and Fritsch, and attempt to construct a Pietist view of the human being. Francke's own life will play a helpful role by serving as an introduction to some, if not all, of the basic elements of Pietist anthropology. Heinrich Müller (1631–1675) and August Hermann Francke (1663–1727) were in thought, method and concerns, citizens of the 17th century. That is, neither was unaware of the current trends of thought, the growing threat of atheism (both philosophical and "practical"), or the aridity and increasing irrelevance of Lutheran orthodoxy in the life of the average German, and they addressed these issues from the human perspective, a perspective in which the human being was definitely in need of God's help, indeed was nothing but, or was even lower than, a worm. Intellectually they were children of the 17th century because this is when their education occurred, before the Enlightenment had entered the schools of Germany. Methodologically they followed the traditional spiritualistic and mystic approach: sermons, prodigious amounts of devotional material (rather than doctrinal statements[2]), personal sharing through correspondence and edifying conversations (in fact, Ritschl numbers Müller among the leaders in establishing Pietist small groups[3]), teaching the catechism and other pastoral activities, all this being done in deep reliance upon the power of

---

[2] As Ritschl points out, or rather laments and accuses, in his epochal work on Pietism, "The principal element of true Christianity, *pure doctrine*, he [Arndt, although this applies equally to Müller] did not wish to treat at all, rather only the Christian life, how it is to be distinguished as inner transformation of the heart through repentance, and as outward behavior." Albrecht Ritschl, *Geschichte des Pietismus*, Band 2, (Bonn, 1884), p. 37. (Emphasis mine)

[3] Ibid., p. 137.

the Holy Spirit. There were innovations as well, the most notable being the deservedly-famous *Stiftungen* at Halle, but even these had many roots in the pious soil of the programs of Duke Ernst the Pious in Gotha.[4]

While Francke lived to see the irruption of the Enlightenment into the intellectual life of Germany, and Müller did not, the continuity of thought, method and concern between the two is striking and, to anyone who has read their material, virtually impossible to overlook. There are clear lines running from the Puritans, Philipp Nicolai's *Freudenspiegel des ewigen Lebens*, and Johann Arndt through Joachim Lütkemann, Christian Scriver, Ahasverus Fritsch and Müller (as main representatives of Reform orthodoxy) and directly on to the likes of Francke. We must also remember the close contact these theologians tended to maintain. Not even distant North America was beyond the lines of communication, as is shown by the busy correspondence between the American Puritan Cotton Mather and the German Pietist Francke.[5] We must not overlook the very extensive circulation of devotional materials (which were frequently translated within months or even weeks of their appearance) wherever Pietistic Christians travelled and relocated (the Bible, the hymnbook and Arndt's *Wahres Christenthum*, for example, graced many German homes in 17th and 18th century North America).

William Perkins (1558–1602) has been nominated as "the actual father of Pietism,"[6] as "the very center of this early group of Pietistic Puritans,"[7] and the like. How could a 16th century Englishman be called the father of Pietism? His writings were widely distributed and were avidly read throughout Protestant Europe. We are concerned here, however, not to make a case for Perkin's right to the title "father of Pietism," but rather to illustrate the location of the German Pietism of August Hermann Francke in a broad wave of remarkably similar Pietistic movements within European Protestantism. A huge amount of devo-

---

[4] See particularly Lowell C. Green, "Duke Ernest the Pious of Saxe-Gotha and his relationship to Pietism", in *Der Pietismus in Gestalten und Wirkungen*, hrsg. von H. Bornkamm, u.a., (Bielefeld, 1975), pp. 179ff.

[5] See Ernst Benz, "Ecumenical Relations between Boston Puritanism and German Pietism: Cotton Mather and August Hermann Francke", *The Harvard Theological Review*, Vol. LIV, No. 3, July 1961, pp. 159–193.

[6] *RGG*, Band IV, (Tübingen, 1930[2]), p. 1251.

[7] F. Ernest Stoeffler, *The Rise of Evangelical Pietism*, (Leiden, 1965), p. 50.

tional material in which the similarities far outweigh the differences, the differences generally arising from local contingencies rather than fundamental theological and/or pastoral disagreement, was circulated throughout Europe.[8]

In Francke's case, not only was he in an area of Germany in which Müller himself had been important and his writings very popular, he also lived and studied in an atmosphere saturated with Reform orthodox ideas. As we shall see, in his formative student years at Kiel, Francke was surrounded morning, noon and night by Reform orthodoxy. Like any movement, Reform orthodoxy was not monolithic. It was, however, saturated with the world-view of mysticism and Arndtian spirituality. Reform orthodox/Pietist statesman and lay theologian Ahasverus Fritsch (1629–1701) cites several rather significant devotional writers in his book *Gottlobs hundert...Züfallige Andachten*, among them Arndt, Lütkemann and Müller.[9] Perhaps were it not for the appearance of the word Pietist at a particularly acute moment in history, we would be more inclined to speak of Scriver, Müller, Spener (although he was originally a Strassburger) and Francke in one breath and as members of one movement. Indeed, it is not surprising that Klaiber, in his *Evangelische Volksbibliothek*, brings together these four theologians and pastors in the same volume. While Müller and Francke certainly differ (one of Müller's central themes, for example, in discussing the divine–human relationship was God's love for humanity and how one can and should return that love), we shall see that they not only concern themselves with the same basic issues and from the same theological/anthropological point of view, but they frequently use the same words and concepts to make the same points. That Francke's form of Pietism is *mutatis mutandis* a continuation of Reform orthodox thought is evident from the historical and literary data, and is attested to by the likes of K. D. Schmidt, W. Elert and K. Holl.[10] Some historians have protested the use of

---

[8] Francke, for example, in his *Lebenslauf* mentions his early awareness of the works of Arndt, Daniel Dyke, Emanuel Sonthom, and Christian Kortholt, among others. *WIA*, p. 22; H. Leube writes, "Unmistakable is the connection of the ideal of the religious life: practice of piety, practycke der godzaligheit, Uebung der Gottseligkeit, praxis pietatis, the same in all three lands." *RGG*, (2), p. 1251.

[9] *Gottlob*, p. 130.

[10] K. D. Schmidt, *Grundriss der Kirchengeschichte*, (Göttingen, 1960[7]), regrets the "tasteless" language of Müller (p. 421), but writes of the similarity of his and Francke's understanding of the "emotional manner of

the term "Reform orthodox," particularly because it generally is used to denote the vibrant, active Christian "good guys," as opposed to the Lutheran orthodox camp made up of spiritually dead, bitter polemicists.[11] It seems clear to me that within Lutheranism there were in fact those of a more activist, pastoral bent, and that they tended to hang together. If we need to defend Lutheran orthodoxy at all (which, in my opinion we need not do), we may simply read Hans Leube's *Orthodoxie und Pietismus* to find a stirring testimony to the strength and vitality of Lutheran orthodox pastors. On the other hand, without separating them out, Leube refers to the particularly *"seelsörgerlich"* (pastoral care oriented) pastors and tends to cite those commonly placed by others in the Reform orthodox camp. Here I am not trying to argue for the goodness of the Lutheran Reform orthodox or the wickedness of the Lutheran orthodox. Rather I am trying to explore the anthropology of those easily identified Pietistic Lutherans who make up the Reform orthodox/Pietist camp. Indeed, were it not for such terms one could call many of the Lutheran Pietists orthodox as well, but would, because of their easily identifiable traits need to come up with some term for them, or else name them all every time the group was mentioned.

For the purpose of this study and from this point on we shall use the terms Pietism and Pietist to denote the Reform orthodox/Pietist complex of thought and its adherents, except for purposes of clarification when more specific terms shall be used. We shall draw particularly from Müller and Francke with occa-

---

Piety". (p. 421) It is not unremarkable that in *Pietismus und Neuzeit*, volume 4, Müller is referred to four times in reference to his immediate connection with Pietism. (pp. 21, 46f., 219, 237). Erhard Peschke stresses the theological similarities between Christian Kortholt and Francke. While differentiating between their respective views of the mystical-spiritual tradition, he coincidentally mentions that Francke's high evaluation of the mystical elements in Lutheranism is precisely that of Müller as well. *Bekehrung und Reform*, (Bielefeld, 1977), p. 64. American Church historian F. E. Stoeffler places Müller in the "Arndt-Spener line", and calls him "the second person in the trio of great Arndtian Pietists." *Evangelical Pietism*, pp. 181, 221.

[11] Green, "Duke Ernest", pp. 190, 191. Here, however, Green, uses as an example of a "later Pietist", Heinrich Müller who is usually considered in the Reform orthodox camp. He also cites Johannes Wallmann, "Pietismus und Othodoxie: Überlegungen und Fragen der Pietismus Forschung" in *Geist und Geschichte der Reformation. Festgabe Hanna Rückert zum 65. Geburtstag*, (Berlin, 1966), pp. 426–431.

sional references as well to Arndt, Scriver, Fritsch, *et al.* in order to develop a comprehensive picture of the individual from the Pietist perspective. This approach will demonstrate the unity of the anthropological perspective of these men and, more importantly, is necessary if we are to gain a complete picture—a picture which currently is incomplete. On the one hand, for example, nothing is said in the 380 pages of Peschke's salient *Studien zur Theologie August Hermann Franckes* (2 vols.) of Francke's understanding of death. This seems at first an odd omission, given the Pietist preoccupation with that subject. In reading through Francke's sermons and devotional material, however, one discovers what are essentially indirect references to death, and then usually in connection with other, overriding concerns. A sermon on "A Departure in Peace/or The Blessed Death," for example, has much more to do with how one should prepare for death, with what it means to "see Christ," etc., than with death *per se.* Thus what can be selected in bits and pieces from Francke's works can be placed alongside Müller's more detailed and comprehensive treatment of death. On the other hand, Müller has less than Francke to say about the place of work in human life. This "bits and pieces" approach is in one sense rather unsatisfying in that it risks distortion. To concentrate on only a few individual sermons or devotional writings, however, would be to ensure distortion by presenting an analysis, however detailed it may be, of what is certainly an inadequate presentation of a preacher's or writer's thought on a subject.

It is my hope that this study will not only inform, but will be helpful as a tool, in that I have included in the text and particularly in the endnotes many, and occasionally lengthy, quotes— mainly from primary sources which are difficult to obtain. These serve not only to illustrate statements in the main body of the study, but provide the reader with some source material as well. I am fully responsible for the translations.

In preparation for this study I worked through more than 5,000 pages of sermons, devotional works, accounts and correspondence of Francke's and approximately 2,500 pages of material by Müller, as well as several thousand by Perkins, Baxter, Arndt, Scriver and Fritsch in particular. Despite their geographical and chronological differences, I was struck by the signal congruence of thought, language, theology, anthropology and pastoral concerns of these men. What began for me as an investigation of contrasts and developments ended as an affirmation of the unity of thought, with surprisingly little actual development (as distinct from divergence), of what must be seen as basically one movement and school of thought in the history of the Church, and which is manifested in ways of speaking, views of life and humanity, and pastoral concerns which are quite consistent.

Finally, it is important that we remember throughout this study that the Pietist's audiences and readership were made up of "christianized" people, that is, of people who for the most part were baptized, catechized, and more or less regularly attended confession, church, and the Lord's Supper. They were people to whom the God-talk of the Pietists would not come as a (totally) foreign language. Thus the lines blur a bit between pagan, nominal (or "mouth") Christian and "true" Christian, and the reader would do well to allow for some flexibility in how the Pietists use language. For them, Christian society was the new but yet old Israel. That is, as Israel was God's people yet did not follow God's commands and rejected God's son, the Messiah, so are all those baptized into the new covenant also God's people, but they, like the old Israel, are an errant, disobedient and unseeing people—until, of course, they are born again. "There is a difference between Christians/just as there was in the Jewish people."[12] That is, there were disciples, Pharisees and Scribes, tax collectors and sinners. Yet all were "good Jews" and "true Israelites" until John the Baptist appeared, called them to repentance and baptism, thus making the essential and crucial differences apparent and spawning discord, faith, rejection, obedience, division—all manner of responses and consequences. This was exacerbated by Jesus' preaching and is precisely what occurs in "Christian" society when "God's word is preached in earnest" (presumably by Pietists); some become scoffers while others follow the light (read Pietist ways of thinking, believing and living).[13] Thus one can be, as it were, a Christian *and* a *Weltkind*

---

[12] *SFA*, II, p. 232, Marginal note.

[13] "This [John the Baptizer's calling people to repentance] caused a separation and division/among all those/who would be called the people of GOd. Thus as our Savior/*Jesus Christ*/carried forth such preaching of repentance and the Gospel/such a difference was all the more apparent....So it always goes. Where the Word of God is taught and preached in the demonstration of the Spirit and of power/there it causes a division among the people. As long as one drones on in the old way/and flatters the people/calls them all dear children of God and dear fellow Christians/so long are they all good Christians in a city/in a congregation/or wherever it is: but as soon as GOd's Word is preached in earnest/there light and darkness separate/in that

(child of the world) at the same time, or one can be a Christian and a *Kind Gottes* (child of God), just as, depending upon their response to John the Baptist or, later, to Jesus, the Jews were God's people yet were in either a state of unrepentance or a state of obedient faithfulness. The goal, then, of Pietist preaching and writing was the rebirth of the *Weltkinder* and the edification of the *Gotteskinder*. And the Pietists had very clear ideas of to whom it was they were preaching and writing.

---

some receive the word of repentance/but others scorn/laugh at/despise and declare it heresy." *SFA*, III, p. 232. One can see how preaching of this sort would give rise to hostility between the Pietists, who considered themselves to be on the side of the light, and the Lutheran orthodox, who knew the Pietists considered them to be on the side of the darkness. For a rather harsh sermon on non-Pietist preachers, see Francke's "*Von den falschen Propheten*" ("On the False Prophets") in *SFA*, II, pp. 277–329.

CHAPTER 1

FRANCKE'S LIFE BEFORE HIS CONVERSION EXPERIENCE

Much has already been written concerning Francke's life.[1] This account and the following chapter, then, will present Francke as a "living model," as it were, of the Pietist view of the individual. Francke's report of his personal struggles, defeats, and eventual victory, through the grace of God, over his worldly ways and atheistic mind encapsulates Pietist anthropology. Thus through his personal story we gain a picture of what we shall subsequently investigate systematically and in depth. In Francke one sees the story of the Pietist everyperson.

Francke's life spanned the period of both the 17th and 18th centuries. While his major accomplishments took place at the turn of the century, intellectually he was, and remained, a child of the 17th century. The city of his birth, Lübeck, was so staunchly Lutheran that later in life Francke "could [gain permission to] preach in his home town only with difficulty."[2] His father, Johannes Francke, rose from being the son of a baker to the position of a successful jurist in Lübeck. His mother, Anna Gloxin, was the daughter of David Gloxin, Lübeck's Councilor and Mayor, and Anna Schabbel whose family foundation subsidized the theological education of many Lutheran Reform orthodox theologians[3] and Pietists, including that of August

---

[1] A standard biography in German is Erich Beyreuther, *August Hermann Francke: Zeuge des lebendigen Gottes*, (Marburg/Lahn, 1969³), hereafter called *AHF*. The most recent biography in English is Gary R. Sattler, *God's Glory, Neighbor's Good*, (Chicago, 1982).

[2] RGG², Band III, p. 1741.

[3] I use the term Reform orthodox for those otherwise solidly Lutheran theologians and laypersons such as Theophilus Grossgebauer, Joachim Lütkemann, Christian Scriver, and, of course, Heinrich Müller who did not reject the basic tenets of Lutheranism, but hoped to rejuvenate the Lutheran Church and Christianity through an invigorated laity and a revitalized devotional life centered on Scripture and the living Christ who dwells in the believer, rather than on the current church methodologies and the traditional creedal statements and loyalties of Lutheranism. Despite arguments that there was never a "Reform orthodox" group or movement *per se*, the very fact that the above-mentioned theologians stand out and are identifiable as representing specific sentiments and tendencies—if not a movement *per se*—within

Hermann Francke. As a result there was some degree of wealth, and certainly no lack of social connections, in the Francke household.

The entry in the *Taufbuch* of St. Aegidien's Church indicates that Francke was baptized at home. While we have no evidence that this was due to the unprecedented class consciousness in Germany to which F.E. Stoeffler refers,[4] it is significant that there were in attendance a number of members of Lübeck's high society. Francke's membership in the upper class did lend him a certain familiarity with the customs and manners of the ruling class which would stand him in good stead in later years in his numerous dealings with kings and members of courts. More significant for this study, however, is the fact that it also assured him of access to personal tutoring early in life and to higher education later on. Early on, Francke was introduced to the world of books, especially devotional books. He was frequently read to by members of his family—in fact his sister Anna read to him daily from Scripture, Arndt's works, and other devotional writings.[5] Johannes Francke's position and education enabled him to form friendships which simply would not have been possible had he remained in the bakery. "Johannes Francke had many friends among theologians. The longing for a true Christianity free of hypocrisy bound them together."[6] Contrary to the opinion of Horst Weigelt,[7] Francke makes it apparent that from the beginning his parents provided a pious atmosphere in the home and had pointed him toward the ministry.[8]

Lutheranism indicates that they are not particularly representative of Lutheran orthodoxy in general. We need not deny the existence of this group (or these groups) within Lutheranism in order to defend the piety and warmth of the (often unjustly maligned) Lutheran orthodox.

In subsequent chapters I will use the term Pietist to cover both the Reform orthodox theologians and those traditionally considered among the Pietists.

[4] Stoeffler, *Evangelical Pietism*, p. 181. He continues, "We are told that some of the noble families of Saxony, for instance, would not have their children baptized in church because this would involve baptism with the same water used for other children."

[5] Horst Weigelt, *Pietismus-Studien*, Band. 1, (Stuttgart, 1965), p. 48.

[6] *AHF*, p. 15.

[7] Weigelt, *Studien*, p. 48.

[8] "God had placed in my heart from childhood on a love for the Word of God, and particularly for the holy preaching office, that such manifested itself outwardly in many expressions, and thus my parents on both sides, as far as

When Francke was three years old, his father was called to Gotha as court councilor to Duke Ernst the Pious of Saxe-Gotha and Francke was plunged into an entire society characterized by an atmosphere of Arndtian piety, deep concern for the poor, and an acute moralism. After Johannes Francke died on 30. April 1670, the family remained in Gotha where August Hermann continued his education. We may safely assume that the rigorous catechetical program instituted by Duke Ernst[9] brought to the young Francke the strongly Lutheran yet Arndtian/Pietist orientation of the Duke. In statements of Duke Ernst's we encounter sentiments remarkably similar to those of Müller and, later, of Francke. Concerning the teachings of the pastors in his territories, the Duke wished to know "if he often stresses [*treibt*, drives] the elements of repentance and of the doctrine of good works, and describes well the wicked, hypocritical ways and warns against them?"[10] Elsewhere we find:

> By the grace of GOD we ERNST, Duke of Saxony...confess that he [a person] should consider every hour as the last, and not only get his house in order at the last moment, but remain steadfast and be ready by means of true repentance if he would be called out of this temporality to follow his Redeemer in true trust.[11]
>
> [God forgives us...] indeed [forgives] all with an earnest resolve to better one's life, to strive more and more against the devil, the sinful world, and our corrupt flesh, and, as said, to live in daily contrition and repentance.[12]

We see, then, that from childhood on, Francke's family and community environment was stamped with the insignia of

---

I know, never had any other intention than to dedicate me to the study of theology. I was supported diligently by my father in such a plan, to which his careful oversight contributed greatly during his life." *WIA*, p.6; Beyreuther points out that the strong paternal influence in Francke's life was an exception to the normal family situation of that time when women were the dominant family figures as far as children were concerned. *AHF*, p. 22.

[9] Green, "Duke Ernest", p. 184.

[10] Johann Heinrich Gelbke, *Herzog Ernst der Erste genannt der Fromme zu Gotha als Mensch und Regent*, Band 3, p. 61, quoted in Green, "Duke Ernest", p. 185.

[11] Ibid.

[12] Ibid.

Lutheran doctrine and the Pietist understanding of that doctrine and the Christian life. Francke recalls a period after his father's death in which he apparently lost his spiritual enthusiasm, or "backslid". This condition was not to last long, however, for when he was about eleven years old Anna, who had read to him daily, brought him back to true Christianity. He writes that at that time he

> was awakened anew through a most beautiful example of my right Christian and God-loving, blessed sister Anna Francke, now resting in God; I had her daily before my eyes, and recognized in her her sincere [*ungeheuchelt*] fear of God, love, humility, love and desire for the Word of God, longing for eternal life and much other good; and beyond this was attracted to all goodness by her through good, edifying speech. This was so piercing that I soon began earnestly to hate the idle ways of youth which I had come to love and into which I had plunged due to the bad example of other children, so that I almost no longer even considered them to be sins (because, being a child, people had put up with me, as is the way of the world),[13] [I began to] avoid worthless company, games, and other wastes of time, and to seek something more profitable and better.[14]

This account is particularly significant for us because here we see emerging in Francke those tensions and disciplines basic to the Pietist understanding of life. Remembering that this autobiographical account is also something of a confession and that it was written from the born-again side of Francke's conversion experience, we must allow for some degree of redactional and eisegetical activity on the writer's part. Letters written by Francke around the time of this experience, however, demonstrate that this account is nonetheless quite accurate. In any case, Francke's description of his life, be it totally accurate or not, is reflective of the Pietist view of the individual.

Assuming even a minimal amount of accuracy, we can see that in the very young Francke there appeared the conflictual elements that constitute the basic human condition: godliness vs. wicked and worldly ways characterized by "worthless company,

---

[13] "(because...the world) is a marginal note. *WIA*, p. 7, n. 15.
[14] *WIA*, pp. 6,7.

games and other wastes of time." We see, too, that one source of Francke's problems was, in his opinion, a lack of discipline, chastisement, and correction—people had simply put up with his wicked ways because he was a child. His will had gone unchallenged and remained unbroken. This perception undergirded a programmatic approach to the education and upbringing of children at what would become the Halle *Stiftungen*. Such inherent wickedness must be done away with and replaced by all those virtues which Francke saw in his "right Christian and God-loving" sister, the model of the ideal Christian (read ideal human). Already in childhood the lines had been drawn, behaviors labeled and evaluated. World vs. God, child of the world vs. child of God: these were the basic categories of inner (and outer) conflict and tension from Puritanism to late Pietism. These were the categories of thought used by Müller and Francke.

Francke's response to the "awakening" wrought in him by the life and instruction of his sister is also significant because it reveals the discipline necessary for true Christianity. He rejects his former ways, separates himself from the bad influences which seek to dominate him and which threaten to ruin his life, and tries to turn to something "more profitable and better". Strikingly, this means an almost eremitic separation in which he offers up his "whole life" to the service and glory of God.

> So my family gave over to me a room in which I
> daily cultivated in earnest my devotions and prayer, and
> already at that time promised to offer up my whole life
> to God, to his service and to his h[oly] honor.[15]

This, then, is the acceptable sacrifice: nothing less than one's whole life. Following this, then, is a manifestation of the dynamic, responsive divine–human relationship.

> The more I held fast to God and the less I stained
> my soul [*Gemüth*] with love of the world, the more
> God allowed me to experience and perceive his grace
> and blessing in all things, and particularly in my
> studies.[16]

This rather short statement contains two basic elements of Pietist thought: divine reward for sincerity and action, and, due

---

[15] *WIA*, p. 7.
[16] *WIA*, p. 7.

to the persistence of sin for all of one's life, be he or she a believer or a non-believer, the constant option and need to choose between God and world. We see that the more Francke turns away from the world and to God, he is blessed "in all things," including his studies. This grace and broad blessing apparently comes as a divine response to Francke's good behavior and is not limited to spiritual matters. He goes on to report that the more he would turn from God, the less he would accomplish, even with greater effort.[17] This tension between the roles of human merit (that is, that which elicits a favorable response from God) and divine initiative and grace remains throughout Pietism. While any Lutheran, the Pietist included, would hardly attribute any blessings to human merit, the language of Pietists such as Müller and Francke certainly lends itself to such an interpretation.[18]

The other element, the persistence of sin in the individual, plays a major role in the manner of disciplines expected of the Christian: struggle, charity, perseverance and self-examination. As we shall see, human beings are by nature so corrupt that even the believer is not free of the sin which the Pietists call by such names as corruption, depravity, the old Adam, and the like, and against which one must struggle all one's life.[19] This persistence of sin requires that the preacher keep busy describing, and warning against, the horrors of the wicked world and the dangers that lurk within all people. Thus every moment presents the opportunity for one to turn either to God or to "the world."

---

[17] "To the contrary, the more I turned my heart from God and became worldly-minded, the more I was led about in error and the less I accomplished with greater effort..." *WIA*, p. 7.

[18] Perhaps an appropriate question would be to what extent does the underlying perspective influence the language as well? We encounter here a vicious circle in which language about divine reward and punishment would certainly seem to reinforce the anticipation of a human-instigated response from God and an interpretation of events which is articulated in terms of a gracious or chastening divine response to human action. Nonetheless, through it all the Lutheran Pietists staunchly defended the doctrine that the initiative is God's.

[19] In *AWC*, for example, Francke warns the believer against "evil desires" which "stir and rise up in his flesh and blood." *AWC*, p. 27; He also says, "O! one thinks, one can happily enter the Kingdom of God. But such a view is not sure. He will soon be humbled and experience/how this is the time of struggle/and that such struggle must continue to the end...Behold/this is indeed a deep corruption/against which such a great/such a heavy struggle is required..." *SFA*, II, p. 430.

Francke's separation from worldly things and people was short-lived. He reports that he soon became more interested in competing with fellow-students for honors and not only used his excellence in Latin and Greek as a springboard to advancement and numerous honors, but, unfortunately, "thus with great work and effort deviated even further from the true foundation and goal of the study of theology."[20] He continued to encounter the same conflicts in nearby Erfurt, where he went in 1679, at the age of sixteen, to attend university. He then went off to Kiel on the financial support of the Schabbel family foundation administered by his uncle, Anton Hinrich Gloxin. Here Francke stayed and studied with the Reform orthodox professor Christian Kortholt. During this three-year period Francke was under the close scrutiny of Kortholt, himself a former recipient of Schabbel foundation funds, who sent frequent reports of Francke's progress to Gloxin. The Schabbel foundation was created to help educate needy and deserving theology students and promote in them the values found in Pietist-type circles, requiring of them a pious lifestyle.

> Thus one must necessarily avoid conversation with women, all marriage contracts, idleness, games, feasting, public beer and wine halls, fencing arenas, dance halls, etc. as such means beguile even pious people into bad company and all manner of vice.[21]

Under Kortholt, who had studied and taught at Rostock (where Heinrich Müller had been professor of Greek, professor of theology and Rector while also serving pastor and, later, Superintendent[22]), Francke encountered Reform orthodoxy close up, and, in Kortholt's home, spent much time with the son of Christian Scriver, with Adam Herold who had recently come to Kiel from Oxford and Leyden, and with Justus Joachim Breithaupt who would later be an enthusiastic supporter of Halle Pietism.[23] Kiel, of course, was in close contact with English and Dutch cities because of the trade routes extending from Great Britain through the Netherlands and northern Germany. Reform orthodoxy had been influenced greatly by English and Dutch theologians, particularly by those stressing a personal faith and a

---

[20] *WIA*, p. 9.

[21] Quoted in Weigelt, *Studien*, p. 53.

[22] *Evangelische Volksbibliothek*, pp. 227,228.

[23] Weigelt, *Studien*, p.54.

devout life.[24] This preoccupation with a burning faith manifested
in a rigorous Christian life was characteristic of Francke as well.
Horst Weigelt writes:

> The influences of Reform orthodoxy on A. H.
> Francke's theology can be demonstrated effortlessly in
> the emphasis on a minute self-examination, an ascetic
> lifestyle and a religious-ethical sanctification.[25]

The already-sensitive Francke received at Kiel, then, further
psychological reinforcement to consider high ethical standards
and a harsh view of himself as fundamental to the Christian life.
The money he needed in order to continue his studies dried up
abruptly in 1682 and he left Kiel for Hamburg, where he studied
Hebrew under the famous Hebraist Esdra Edzardus. He then
returned to Gotha for private instruction where, so it appears, he
sorely missed the fellowship and influence of the pious circle at
Kiel.

At this point Francke apparently once again had cast off any
progress in the Christian life made while at Kiel, for he writes,
"The condition of my soul when I arrived at Hamburg was very
bad and stained through and through with love of the world."[26]
After one-and-a-half years in Gotha he "earnestly beseeched" his
uncle to give him further financial assistance: *"Te, ut Patronum
Summum, pro mea salute non rogo tantum, sed et obsecro, velis
studia mea legato Schabbeliano rursus ire adjectum."*[27]

Francke's report of his stay in Gotha reveals further components of his understanding of the Christian life: the divine-human
relationship is one of give-and-take:

> God also gave me to see that he had more and
> more withdrawn his hand from me because I had not
> made room for his mighty, fatherly hand which had so
> often lured me so strongly to conversion, but rather I
> had sunk ever deeper into love of the world.[28]

---

[24] Stoeffler writes, "It is well-known that the faculty at Rostock had
long been open to the claims of Reformed piety." *German Pietism during the
Eighteenth Century*, (Leiden, 1973), p. 5.

[25] Weigelt, *Studien*, p. 54.

[26] *WIA*, p. 14.

[27] Quoted in Weigelt, *Studien*, p. 56.

[28] *WIA*, p. 14.

It reveals, too, that a true recognition and knowledge of sin is necessary, for although Francke had observed all the religious customs of the day such as church attendance, confession, etc., "...it always remained stuck in my heart that to desire honor, wealth and the good life was no sin."[29]

We see, too, that concrete evidence of faith is important for Francke, for despite his minimizing of outward show, certain visible manifestations (or the lack thereof) indicate the presence (or lack) of true faith, "For where there are no fruits of faith...there is also no faith, but rather a mere presumption of faith, and, in fact, [there is] nothing but disbelief."[30]

And, finally, despite his life-long emphasis on education, he sees erudition as definitely of minor importance in comparison with sincere faith:

> ...in fact, I was nothing but a merely natural person who had much in his head, but was very far from the righteous being which is in Jesus Christ.[31]

In 1684 Francke left Gotha for Leipzig, a center of Lutheran orthodoxy where, after two semesters, he was awarded his master's degree in 1685. It was here that Francke's final understanding of the Christian's relationship to Scripture was formulated and where he encountered another type of mysticism—the Quietism of Miguel de Molinos.[32] Francke's turn from a purely *"wissenschaftlich"* (academic) approach to Scripture to a more

[29] *WIA*, p. 14.
[30] *WIA*, pp. 14, 15.
[31] *WIA*, p. 15.
[32] Molinos (c.1628–1696) espoused several aspects of mysticism which Francke and many other Pietists (e.g. Gottfried Arnold and Gerhard Tersteegen) did not accept such as the progression of the soul from devotion to Church, then to Christ, and finally to God alone, in which devotion the believer attained perfection through total annihilation of the will. Molinos also, in his letters, claimed "all external observances, mortifications, and even the resisting of temptation were a hindrance" to this state of perpetual union with God. *The Oxford Dictionary of the Christian Church*, (London, 1974[2]), pp. 928, 929; Molinos' *Guida Spirituale*, however, contains much that is very similar to the Pietist way of thinking. See also Herbert Stahl, *August Hermann Francke: der Einfluss Luthers und Molinos' auf ihn*, (Stuttgart, 1939); also Peschke, *Bekehrung und Reform*, pp. 13–40, esp. 30–40.

existential, affective interaction with the text arose from his participation in the *Collegium philobiblicum* which was begun in 1686 as a critical study of the Bible and subsequently, on the advice of Spener, became a group discussion of short texts with devotions or edification as the main point.[33]

> This forced a shift in emphasis from the salvation
> event to the word event. In this Spener-Halle Pietism
> helped to pave the way for today's existentialist
> interpretation of Scripture.[34]

Despite the existence of other *collegia*, this particular gathering gained quite a public reputation,

> ...because the world raised such a cry over the
> *collegia philobiblica* and *pietatis*, as they were called,
> as if they were innovations and *conventicula* from
> which one could expect nothing but disorder.[35]

This is hardly surprising, since the meetings grew very rapidly and soon had to be moved from Paul Anton's room to a university lecture hall.[36] Significant is the fact that

---

[33] Martin Schmidt, *Pietismus*, (Stuttgart, 1972), p. 64. Francke describes the *Collegium philobiblicum* in this way: "The best of all was the *Collegium Philobiblicum*, the beginnings and progress of which I considered it necessary to report in detail. M[agister]. Paulus Antonius, now Theol. Lic. and Superintendent of Rochlitz, and I once discussed that the study of the two fundamental languages, namely Greek and Hebrew, was done so little. We both lamented it so much, that finally H[err] Antonius desired that the Magisters themselves should practice them with each other, which pleased me immediately and, as we agreed upon it, without delay we talked about it to some friends among the Magisters, that they should meet with us and begin such a *collegium*." WIA, p. 17; Weigelt writes that the impulse to form this group was given by Johann Benedikt Carpzov who on 15. July 1686 preached a sermon in which he encouraged students to read Scripture with more enthusiasm and asked why, amidst the many other groups at school, there was no *Exercitium biblicum*. One week later the first *Collegium philobiblicum* was held in Paul Anton's room in the home of Professor Otto Mencke. Weigelt, *Studien*, pp. 56, 57.

[34] Weigelt, *Studien*, p. 57.

[35] WIA, p. 18.

[36] Francke writes, "Now the *Collegium* grew ever stronger and was opened to students who asked to be allowed to attend as auditors. Thus the room soon became too small for us and we found it necessary to look about

representatives of the Reform orthodox movement such as Veit Ludwig von Seckendorff and Ahasverus Fritsch were among the guest speakers at the *collegia*. Spener also attended a meeting in 1687 and thereafter became a close friend of Francke's.[37] This new, affective type of interaction with Scripture only served to intensify the sense of personal, individual responsibility which Francke had already experienced.

Another moment which was important for Francke's inner development during his time at Leipzig was his encounter with the work of the Spanish Quietist Miguel de Molinos.[38] Since his arrest in 1685, Molinos had been one of the rages of the theological world, and a disputation was to be held at Leipzig concerning the orthodoxy (or lack thereof) of his writings. A shortage of material in Latin, however, caused no small problem, and Francke, as the only *Magister* in Leipzig with an adequate knowledge of Italian,[39] was given the task of translating Molinos' *Spiritual Guide*. This translation was to become significant for several reasons: it was Francke's first published work,[40] it aroused suspicions that he was a less-than-orthodox

---

for a larger place." *WIA*, p. 19; At this point, 16. February 1687, it was taken over by Prof. Valentin Alberti and moved to a lecture hall. Weigelt, *Studien*, p. 57. Alberti and Carpzov later became two of the most bitter opponents of Pietism in Leipzig.

[37] "In both one finds a high esteem for the orientation of knowledge to practical piety, the doctrine of the connection of *fides* and *bona opera* as well as the love of conventicles [small groups]." Weigelt, *Studien*, p. 58;

"Finally, Spener's basic religious thinking exercised a formative influence on the theology of Francke. ...Still, there remains a number of differences between the views of these two men. The store of theological thought of Spener is richer and more comprehensive than Francke's, as well as being oriented toward other issues." Erhard Peschke, *Studien zur Theologie August Hermann Franckes*, Band I, (Berlin, 1964), p. 152.

Francke clearly remains throughout his life much more a person of the 17th century than of the 18th. In spite of his knowledge of several languages, he seems to have been influenced mainly by the pious writings of the Puritans, Reformed Pietists, and his immediate predecessors and contemporaries in the so-called Reform orthodox movement rather than by humanistic, Enlightenment-oriented writers, even though he was in regular correspondence with thinkers such as Leibniz. Reform orthodoxy found in Spener a kindred spirit and friend. In Francke it found a true brother and son.

[38] Weigelt, *Studien*, p. 58.
[39] *AHF*, p. 39.
[40] *AHF*, p. 39.

crypto-Molinist,[41] and it very likely strengthened his already extant tendency to see human beings in an either/or way. It is always a bit dangerous to psychologize, but we must wonder if perhaps Francke became something of Molinos' defender as a reaction to both Molinos' thought and to being attacked. We think immediately of Luther, who during the Leipzig debate in 1519 was accused of being a follower of the heretical Jan Hus. While claiming that he in fact did "repulse the charge of Bohemianism," Luther, after subsequently reading Hus' statements from the *acta* of the Council of Constance stated, "Among the articles of John Hus, I find many which are plainly Christian and evangelical, which the universal Church cannot condemn."[42] While Luther certainly embraced Hus quite a bit more firmly than Francke did Molinos, Francke's testimony reveals that he did indeed consider Molinos' work, at least in those areas in which sentiments similar to those of Arndt are found, to contain "much [which is] of profit and greatly conducive to [one's] edification..."[43]

Francke no doubt focussed on the emphasis Molinos placed on the stark contrasts of life.[44] As we have seen, Francke already felt strongly that knowledge *per se* was neither salvific nor even a valid goal of the Christian life. Thus he would find much in Molinos which makes perfect evangelical/Pietist sense, such as,

Non consistit sanctibus in formandis altis &
subtilis conceptibus scientiae & attributorum DEI, sed
in amore DEI, & in abnegatione proprias voluntatis.[45]

Basic to Arndtian, Reform orthodox, and Pietist thought is that self-denial and love of God rather than erudition and

---

[41] Francke writes, "Thus, from this time my detractors, who wanted to make their insults known, falsely charged me with having embraced Molinos' false principles, of being misled thereby, and of thereafter imparting them to others." *WIA*, p. 21.

[42] Quoted in Roland Bainton, *Here I Stand: A Life of Martin Luther*, (Nashville, MCML), pp. 115, 116.

[43] *WIA*, p. 21.

[44] "In his *Guida spirituale*, Molinos expressed even stronger than Arndt the contrast between *thought and faith*, scholarship and piety." Peschke, *Bekehrung und Reform*, p. 30.

[45] Quoted in Peschke, *Bekehrung und Reform*, p. 31; Also "A DEO vilis, adeo superba, adeo ambitiosa est propria natura, adeoque sui appetitus & proprii judicii ac opinionis plena est, ut nisi refraenaret eam tentatione nollo plane remedio a pernicie vindicari posset." Ibid. p. 35.

"reason" are the fundamentals of godliness.[46] In this line of thought, however, we see a view of reason and education which does not reject outright the intellectual life, but rather rejects the abuse and misuse of the intellect by turning it into an end in itself, a means to attain personal glory, or the ultimate standard which would thus make of it an enemy of faith and of God. This understanding of the intellect and its use is found in Arndt, Molinos, Müller, Kortholt, Spener and Francke.

There is much in Molinos which is akin to Pietist thought, and his writings no doubt served to reinforce Francke's already strong views on the either/or condition of the person, the understanding of *Anfechtung* as a God-given opportunity for personal growth in piety and godliness, the tendency towards an almost Pelagian understanding of the individual's role in his or her salvation, and the concept of a particular, divine "breakthrough" into a person's life. These ideas were already found in Arndt and, to a lesser degree, in Reform orthodoxy. H. Stahl suggests, however, that Molinos not only influenced Francke's thought, but played a role in his conversion experience as well.[47] Be that as it may, while the ideas of Molinos no doubt helped solidify Francke's thinking, they certainly added nothing startling or new. Francke seems to have taken what "felt right" to him and simply ignored the rest (e.g. the contemplation arrived at through the stripping away of one's images of God). As mentioned above, Molinos' influence may have received its strength less from the power of his ideas than from the basic agreement between his thought and that of Francke, as well as from Francke's need to defend himself—and Molinos.

---

[46] Arndt, for example, writes, "For there is a great difference *between the mind*/with which one knows Christ/*and the will*/with which one loves him... To know Christ through mere scholarship/and not have love is worthless." *Wahres Christenthum*, p. 723;

Heinrich Müller writes, "Much knowledge, little conscience....You boast of your great learning. The devil knows more than you and yet must burn eternally in hell....Love betters, knowledge puffs up....Learning without deeds is a cloud without rain, a tree without fruit." *GE*, #123, pp. 129, 130;

Ahasverus Fritsch writes, "In matters of faith/I am the arch enemy of my reason/so far as it attempts to attack my faith/and cast doubt upon the great mystery of God." *Gottlob*, p. 191.

[47] "Thus his conversion occurs in no other time than in the influence of Luther and Molinos." Stahl, *August Hermann Francke*, p. 71.

Remembering that Franckes' *Lebenslauf* was written several
years after his conversion experience, and thus anticipating some
degree of embellishment and stylization, we may assume that
Francke's youth was indeed full of tension, and that in any case
his presentation of his inner conflicts demonstrate his view of the
human condition. In these conflicts we see a struggle between
God and Satan which is fought out chiefly in individuals. The
outer and inner realms each have their own demands and pitfalls,
and one must be prepared to bring them into order and submission, or end up being meaningless or, worse, wicked.

> Now as concerns my Christianity, it was,
> particularly in the first years when I was in Leipzig,
> quite bad and lukewarm. My intentions were to become
> a distinguished and learned man, to become rich, and to
> live an easy life also was not unpleasant to me. ...I was
> concerned more to please people and put myself in their
> favor than the living God in heaven....In summary, I
> was inwardly and outwardly a man of the world and in
> wickedness had not decreased, but rather increased....
> Thus I can say that indeed for twenty-four years I was
> not much better than a fruitless tree which indeed had
> many leaves but mostly bad fruit.[48]

Another basic element of the Christian life appears in
Francke's report: persecution on account of one's faith. The true
Christian experiences the hostility of the world, this hostility at
times coming from the "worldly" wing of the church, i.e. the
Lutheran orthodox.[49] Francke confesses that during his student
days,

> I was free there of persecution because I had
> learned to appear pious with the pious and in truth to
> be wicked among the wicked, and to compromise
> myself.[50]

---

[48] *WIA*, p. 23.

[49] C. H. von Canstein, a Halle supporter at the Berlin court, writes to
Francke of some pious refugees, "Yet it is important that some miners who
were persecuted in Hessen for their fear of God have come to Canstein..." *Der
Briefwechsel Carl Hildebrand von Canstein mit August Hermann Francke*,
hsg. von Peter Schicketanz, (Berlin, 1972), p. 332. On persecution in
general, Müller writes, "It profits me much that I displease the world: its
enmity, God's friendship..." *GE*, #1, p.2.

[50] *WIA*, p. 23.

This theme of persecution occurs in the sources of Pietist thought as well. Richard Baxter, a Puritan known well to the pious in Germany, wrote in his book, *The Saint's Everlasting Rest*, "Should not we be more active for our own preservation, than our enemies are for our ruin?" Of the four enemies which he names, two are "scoffers, persecutors."[51]

In retrospect Francke perceives the presence of the gracious and patient love of God, in that

> God did not cast me away on account of the deep corruption in which I had become stuck, but rather had patience with me and helped my weakness.[52]

But it is just in this area of divine providence that the Pietists seem most theologically schizophrenic. On the one hand Francke discovers

> that one has no reason to complain about God, rather he [God] is ready to open every door where he finds a heart which is sincere and earnestly seeks his face.[53]

That is, God is perceived as reacting on the basis of a person's intentions and actions, which sounds rather like works-righteousness. This was a major source of contention between the Lutheran orthodox and the Reform orthodox/Pietists. Francke loses no time, however, in bringing solid Lutheran doctrine onto the scene.

> God always went on just before me and cleared away the clods and debris, so that I would be convinced that my conversion was not my work, but his.[54]

The question, however, is whether Francke and others in this school of thought[55] actually were convinced that *gratia*

---

51 *The Practical Works of Richard Baxter*, (Grand Rapids, 1981), p. 43.
52 *WIA*, p. 25.
53 *WIA*, p. 25.
54 *WIA*, p. 25.
55 Arndt, for example, writes, "This [the return to one's origin, which is God] cannot occur/unless a person repents with all his might/and separates his mind/will/and memory from the world/and from all fleshly things/and turns his soul with all its desires to God through the H[oly] Spirit/rests and

praeveniens was indeed at work here, or whether they simply used this type of language to satisfy their particular theological needs (they were, after all, all educated under respected, orthodox professors) while in practice actually promoting a form of Pelagianism in both justification and sanctification. Or perhaps the emotional/mystical experiences of many Pietists caused the God's initiative *vs.* human action issue to become blurred. This is apparently more a problem for interpreters of this movement than for the Pietists themselves. Müller, a shaper of Pietist thought, can write on the one hand,

> For there is no power in you. You are wretched/if God does not have mercy on you; blind/if God does not illumine you; weak/if he does not strengthen you; comfortless/if he does not comfort you; fall easily/if he does not hold you up; remain in sin/if he does not justify you; are lost eternally/if he does not seek you.[56]

That is, God simply must be all in all, and do virtually everything for the person. Yet Müller can write on the other hand,

> As you grasp God in your faith, so he is to you. If you hold all in it, he will be all to you; if you hold nothing in it, he will be nothing to you; as you believe so shall it be unto you....[57] [and] Accordingly prepare your heart as a dwelling place for God, your dearest friend. He desires to be with you if only he finds your heart prepared....First cleanse your heart of all sinful desires and worldly lusts.[58]

At the end of the 16th century William Perkins had written that,

> A serious desire to believe and endeavour to obtain God's favour is the seed of faith...God doth not despise the least spark of faith, if so be it by little and little increase and men use the means to increase the same. Man must therefore stir up his faith by

---

retires from the world through a quiet Sabbath; then God begins to work in him." *Wahres Christenthum*, pp. 738, 739.

[56] *GLF*, I, vii, pp. 73,74.
[57] *HLK*, I, iv, p. 31.
[58] *HLK*, I, xi, p. 187.

> meditation of God's word, serious prayers and other
> exercises belonging to faith.[59]

Thus we see that even though the actual works of grace, renewal, sanctification, etc. are ascribed to God, the perceptions, longings and actions of persons play a role in determining the intensity and nature of the divine-human relationship. There appears indeed to be some manner of preparation necessary if God is to be active in one's life.[60]

Francke's use of language reveals his profound acceptance of divine intervention in a person's life. Divine providence was for him simply a fact of life in which God, in God's grace, not only removes all the *"Klötzer und Plöcke"* from his path, but even guides the hearts of others for the the good of the individual. Francke reports that God used his cousin (who was now in charge of the stipend for his studies) as the means to remove him to the place where he could finally turn forever from the wicked world, and to God.

> For God arranged it that I had to leave Leipzig,
> where I was still held prisoner by this and that
> hindrance, in that [God] moved the heart of my cousin,
> D. Gloxin, so that he...told me I should be off to
> Lüneburg.[61]

As things turned out, this "God-arranged" trip to Lüneburg was life-changing indeed. Let us now turn to the watershed experience of Francke's life.

---

[59] *The Work of William Perkins*, edited by Ian Breward, (Appleford/Abingdon/Berkshire, 1970), p. 230.

[60] It is interesting that the English Calvinists reacted against Perkins, the Dutch Calvinists against William Ames, and the German Lutheran orthodox against the Pietists on the same point, albeit for different reasons. To the strict Calvinists this "preparation of the heart" ran counter to the idea of election, while to the doctrinally concerned Lutherans it smacked of works-righteousness and was not a trusting, "passive" faith.

[61] *WIA*, p. 25.

CHAPTER 2

FRANCKE'S CONVERSION EXPERIENCE

Francke's theological understanding, his practical approaches to life and ministry, social perspectives, indeed Francke himself cannot be understood apart from his rather dramatic and powerful conversion experience which occurred in Lüneburg in late 1687 during his stay with the celebrated theologian, and old friend of Francke's father, Superintendent Caspar Hermann Sandhagen,[1] who had studied at Rostock under Müller. This conversion experience was the dynamic culmination of a virtually life-long emotional, psychological and (as the Pietists would interpret it) spiritual struggle. The conflictual phenomena present throughout Francke's life all appeared, and in the extreme, in a brief and traumatic period in which in Francke worldliness contended with godliness, reason with faith, flesh with spirit, unbelief with belief, self-assertion with true *Gelassenheit.* All these were the classic struggles of Christian mysticism and of the *Urväter* of Pietism.

Despite the inspiration of his pious childhood, Francke felt that in his ultimate quest, "namely to become a true Christian,"[2] he had been a failure. He remembers his student days in Leipzig as characterized by a bad and lukewarm faith, dreams of personal glory and wealth, concern for personal popularity, and brief periods of intense, but short-lived and quite fruitless remorse.[3] He (and humanity in general) is a conflicted creature with little strength and virtually no hope of progress apart from divine intervention. Until the will is surrendered, even emotional outbursts in prayer are of no help. "I often fell to my knees and promised God some improvement. But the results proved that it

---

[1] *AHF*, pp. 43ff; Schmidt, *Pietismus*, p. 64; Caspar Hermann Sandhagen had also been subsidized as a student by the Schabbel Foundation. He was Superintendent in Lüneburg from 1672 on, and was named General Superintendent of Schleswig-Holstein in 1684. He did not assume that position until 1689, however, because of the conflict with Denmark at that time. *WIA*, p. 25, n. 141. Sandhagen's Pietist tendencies and his pastoral skills are described in glowing terms in Johann Georg Bertram, *Das Evangelische Lüneburg*, (Braunschweig, 1719), pp. 236ff.

[2] *WIA*, p. 25.

[3] *WIA*, p. 23.

was merely a fleeting passion."[4] Francke clearly was looking for the fruits of a living faith and apparently was finding very few. In spite of the enormous emphasis Pietism placed on the inner person,[5] one's outward behavior was under close scrutiny, as it reflects the person's inner condition.[6] Because of the interconnectedness of the inner and outer person, Francke, shortly after his conversion experience, wrote up a long list of Christian do's and don'ts to help the believer maintain his or her godliness.[7] The world's most common enticements against which one must ever struggle seem to be "great advancement, the esteem of the world, temporal honor, great scholarship, and easy living."[8] Such worldly alternatives to pious goals can only result in personal discontent.

> Meanwhile, I found little rest and contentment in my soul, for I knew well that I had strayed far from the good beginning in true Christianity that I had once made in childhood.[9]

Thus it was a rather agitated Francke who arrived in Lüneburg at his uncle's bidding. His understanding of life was by now rather firmly fixed and his goals in Lüneburg were primarily spiritual rather than academic. That he should embark on a course of study with spiritual growth rather than purely intellectual purposes in mind manifests yet another element of Pietist thought, namely that doctrine and scholarship must be integrated into daily life, with the Christian life taking precedence

---

[4] *WIA*, p. 23.

[5] "In short: the outer is nothing to God/if the *inner* is not there." *SFA*, III, p. 34.

[6] "In Francke's congregation one tended not to conceal, 'insofar as one had seen an open sign of unrepentance, what one thought of [the unrepentant one's] life and death'." Eberhard Winkler, "Exempla fidei, Verkündigung und Seelsorge in der Bestattungspredigt bei August Hermann Francke," in *Pietismus und Neuzeit: Jahrbuch zur Geschichte des neueren Protestantismus*, (Bielefeld, 1975), p. 23, n. 6.

[7] A prime example of this is Francke's *Lebensreglen*, a booklet on the practical, everyday disciplines of the Christian life, including a 6-page "Appendix on Christian Perfection". See Sattler, *God's Glory*, pp. 199–237.

[8] *WIA*, p. 10.

[9] *WIA*, p. 10. Emotions play a very significant role in Pietist thought. While Scripture provides the objective criteria by which one can examine oneself, one's heart and conscience provide the subjective (but nonetheless potentially accurate) input.

over academic hair-splitting and mere intellectual assent to and comprehension of the creedal verities of the faith. Nonetheless, critics who accuse Pietism of crass anti-intellectualism miss the mark, for although the conflict between faith and reason was common to Pietist thought, and dry intellectualism and academic ambition were attacked as wicked and worldly matters, scholarship *per se* was not considered evil.[10] Rather, scholarship could be used for either godly or ungodly purposes.[11] This tension between faith and reason, and the temptations often connected with academia, were part of Francke's life.

> My theology I grasped in my head and not in my heart, and it was more a dead science than a living understanding...Yea, I had no other concept of theological studies than that they consisted of one having the theology lectures and theology books firmly in one's head, and being able to carry on an erudite discussion of them.[12]

Francke was also well acquainted with the regular Christian disciplines, namely church attendance, confession, attendance at the Lord's Supper, prayer, hymn-singing and the like, yet he sensed none of the inner reality to which these outward

---

[10] The faith/subjective knowledge *versus* fact/objective knowledge conflict is common to mysticism and Pietism. cf. Stahl, *August Hermann Francke*; also Peschke, *Bekehrung und Reform,* p. 13ff; Peschke writes, "His criticism was turned not against scholarship as such, but rather against its abuse." (p. 39)

[11] In *Timotheus*, for example, Francke exhorts his students to avoid too much study of the books of men and of worldly subjects. He cautions them against reading Scripture "more for the sake of outward scholarship of the language/which in and of itself is not to be despised..."(p.22); Elsewhere he writes, "While you are yet young/and have the time and opportunity for it/learn the primary languages/even if you do not study theology/or will study no further/such will forever be a precious treasure to you..." *LR*, p. 74; Thus we see that the goals of the student determine the moral value of scholarship. It is well known that Luther called reason the "devil's whore", and not only distrusted it, but rejected it outright. It must be noted, however, that he did this only insofar as reason claimed precedence over faith. cf. *Luther's Works*, vol. 43, (Philadelphia, 1966), pp. 52–55. In other contexts, Luther appeals to reason as something valuable and helpful (*Ibid.*, vol. 45, p. 372), and calls it a thing of superior worth.

[12] *WIA*, p. 13.

manifestations of faith allegedly correspond.[13] He was plunged into deeper and deeper and ultimately decisive turmoil when he was invited to preach in Lüneburg's Johanneskirche. In his preparations to edify the congregation concerning the difference between a "true, living faith" and a "merely human and imagined faith" he became aware that he had no true, living faith of his own. At this point he postponed his preaching date and entered upon a period of deep anxiety and agitation which ended in his conversion experience and a profound change of heart. His *Wiedergeburt* (rebirth) or *Bekehrung* (conversion) was

> as significant to Francke as was the experience on the road to Damascus to St. Paul, the experience in the garden at Cassisiacum to St. Augustine, and the experience in the tower of the monastery of the Black Friars to Luther. It seemed to prescribe for him the way in which men ordinarily enter upon a really meaningful relation to God, and it constituted for him the incontrovertible ground of personal religious certainty.[14]

Francke's conversion experience made clear the gross difference between the "stinking manure pile of this world" (that is, what is by nature) and the "all too lovely" streams of living water (that is, what can be by rebirth).

Francke reveals that he relied on human reason not because it is sufficient, but "because in my heart I had experienced little of the new nature of the Spirit."[15] His anxiety and crisis of faith deepened as he failed to find comfort in, and finally stopped searching through, textbooks and Scripture. The Bible, that book through which the Spirit of God normally operates, is empty for Francke because he has failed to penetrate to the core, or kernel of it, namely the living Christ.[16] Then, in a scene in which his life flashes before his eyes, rather as in the experience of a

---

13 *WIA*, p. 13.

14 Stoeffler, *German Pietism*, p. 11. Again we see the crucial role of the affective elements of the person.

15 *WIA*, p. 26.

16 Francke's division of Scripture into shell, or husk, and kernel is typical of mysticism and Pietism, and corresponds to his fundamental understanding of the world and humanity, which he perceives to be in a state of tension between things worldly and godly, outer and inner. cf. *WIA*, pp. 232ff.

person facing imminent death, he comes to see the ultimate source of his distress and of his "worldly-minded heart," that is, unbelief. Unlike the drowning person, however, Francke is bereft of even straws at which to grasp. Reason has proven to be an enemy, the Scriptures seem to hold no power, human words are woefully inadequate. Nonetheless, Francke reports that, "I was not yet so wicked that I could cast the truth of God to the wind out of a worldly-minded heart."[17] Stahl points out that here we see in Francke the presence not of willful disobedience, but of despair: "This, 'I cannot believe' does not contain the actual, 'I will not believe.'"[18]

As Francke then surveys his life in this moment of despair, he sees everything he has thought, said, and done in his life "as sin and a great abomination before God."[19] This is, of course, in keeping with Lutheran doctrine that there are no good works apart from faith. It also emphasizes the vast gap between the worldly and the born-again person in Pietist thought. The unregenerate person (and the old Adam who clings to him or her even after rebirth) is one massive conspiracy of heart, mind, soul and body to remain both in and of the world with all its unseemly and ultimately deadly desires. Only God can bring the person from his or her state of sin; in Francke's case through the affliction of his conscience. Clearly a glimmer of faith (may we call it a "*Seelenfüncklein*"?) remains, for Francke cannot cast God aside completely. He tries to ignore his wretched state, but the "misery," "great depression," and "inner wretchedness" remain. This is, however, a good sign, for in Pietist thought the road to true repentance and thus to eternal life normally passes through personal sorrow and anxiety over one's sinful condition and damnable state. Thus Francke, looking back, ascribes his anxiety and troubled conscience to the grace of God.

Hereupon follow several days in which Francke continues to struggle with what he calls his "atheistic mind" and the doubts which it creates in his tormented heart. During his conflicts, however, by the grace of God two events occur which bring him joy, which trouble him further and which finally cast him into

---

[17] *WIA*, p. 26.
[18] Stahl, *August Hermann Francke*, p. 6.
[19] *WIA*, p. 26.

even deeper despair.[20] These events, which did not happen "by coincidence," were evidence to Francke that God interacts with people in very direct ways. In his later account of the creation and maintenance of the institutions at Halle, *Segensvolle= Fußstapfen*, he describes similar experiences in which the all-loving and all-powerful God miraculously meets not only spiritual, but material needs.[21] Indeed as we have seen, the very

---

[20] "Once, as I was eating, I asked to go with my host to a nearby Superintendent, and he agreed. Meanwhile, I took a Greek New Testament which had been by the table, to read. As I opened it, my host said, *Yea, in this we surely have a great treasure.* I looked about and asked him if he had seen to what I had opened. He said no. So I said, look at the answer, *We have the treasure in earthen vessels* etc. 2. Cor. IV. My eyes had fallen on such words just as he had spoken. I took this quite a bit to heart and I thought that this had not come about by chance. It seemed as well that a hidden comfort had sunk into my heart through this, but my atheistic mind soon used depraved reason as its tool to rip the power of the divine word from my heart again. I continued on the way next to my host, and met the Superintendent at his house, who invited us to have a seat in his room. Hardly had we taken a seat when the Superintendent began to discuss how one can know whether one has faith or not. They discussed so many things concerning this question that a believer would have been greatly strengthened by it. But I sat there, initially astonished, and wondered whether such a discussion of highest need to me could come about by accident, since no one, no one in the entire world, knew the least of my circumstance. I listened to them intently, but my heart would not be comforted; rather I was all the more convinced by it that I had no faith, because I recognized in myself precisely the opposite of the signs of faith as they were quoted from the foundation of Scripture." *WIA*, pp. 26, 27.

[21] Francke reports: "Around St. Michael's Day [in 1699], I was in the utmost need, and as I walked out into the beautiful weather/and contemplated the clear heavens/my heart was greatly strengthened in faith (this I ascribe not to my powers/but rather solely to the grace of the LORD), so that I thought to myself: *How glorious it is/when one has nothing/and can rely upon nothing/but knows the living GOD/who has made the heavens and earth/and trusts in him alone/and thereby can have peace even in want.*

Now even though I well knew/that I would have need of something that very day/my heart was so strengthened in faith/that I was cheerful and confident. I returned home/and immediately the man appeared/who was on that day/as it was a Saturday/supposed to pay the workers. He intended/to get the money from me/and go out and pay them/so he asked me if I had received anything [money]. *Has anything come?* he said: I answered: *No/but I have faith in GOD.* Hardly had I spoken the word/when a student reported to me/ who brought thirty Talers from someone/whom he would not name.

fact that he had arrived in Lüneburg for this life-transforming experience is ascribed neither to the astute, or even coincidentally fortunate, decision of Gloxin's to send Francke to stay with Sandhagen, but directly to God who moved Gloxin to this decision.[22]

Nonetheless, even the providence of God is stymied by Francke's "depraved reason," and Francke derives little comfort from these divine interventions. Despite his despair, Francke presses on in deeply emotional prayer. The subsequent dramatic change he experiences is proof for him that God indeed responds to those who persevere in affliction and pray with sighing, weeping, and total sincerity. This is a common theme For Francke and Pietists in general.[23] It is important to keep in mind that these painful afflictions are seen as gifts of God which, unlike devilish affliction which is to be resisted because it leads to faithlessness, wantonness, and death,[24] is to be accepted with total submission, joy, and the anticipation that God will end the suffering at just the right moment and bring even greater blessings and joy to the life of the believer.[25] Thus affliction is a divine aid to the nonbeliever, in that it acts as a goad and a

---

I went back into the room/and asked the man/how much he needed this time to pay the builders? He answered: *Thirty Talers.* I said: *Here they are*, and asked as well/*whether he needed more?* He said: *No*: which then greatly strengthened us both in faith/in that we recognized so evidently the wonderful hand of GOD/who gave in an instant/when there was need/and as much/as was needed." *Fußstapfen*, pp. 38, 39.

[22] *WIA*, p. 25.

[23] Francke points out that one reason people fail to receive is that "Perhaps you have not yet sought such with earnest prayer." *LR*, p. 62. and, "They/the disciples/poured out their hearts before him/and He/the Savior instructed/strengthened and comforted them. All of which is recorded/that we may learn/how we also are to interact with our Savior/in our hearts/in Spirit and in truth/and how to speak with him." *SFA*, III, p. 112.

[24] *SFA*, I, p. 513.

[25] "Should you not yet see in yourselves the complete victory/yea do not let your courage sink because of it/*do not cast your confidence away/which has a great reward*/Heb. X. 35. Begin again/if it did not go well today/ it may go better tomorrow/begin anew to serve your dear God with your whole heart and soul/only do not cast away your confidence/but rather let it remain firmly grounded in the grace of JEsus CHrist/and it will strengthen you more and more/and show you his grace and power more and more." *SFA*, III, p. 83.

reminder, and to the believer as well, in that it is also a necessary element of sanctification.[26]

Throughout his long conversion experience, Francke endures the assaults of faithless reason. He refers to it in negative terms again and again: as a poor substitute for the Holy Spirit,[27] as something which—as a substitute for faith—leads to "unrest and doubt,"[28] as a tool of an atheistic mind which corrupt reason used as a tool to rip the power of the divine word from his heart,[29] as a means of resisting spiritual counsel,[30] and as a rival to God which must be brought into subjection to faith.[31]

In the end, however, Francke's perseverance is rewarded. From deep despair and spiritual isolation he is brought to a genuine faith.

> Then, in a twinkling, all my doubts were gone; I was sure in my heart of the grace of God in Jesus Christ; I could call God not only God, but also my Father. All the sadness and unrest in my heart was taken away in a moment. On the contrary, I was suddenly so overwhelmed as with a stream of joy that I praised out of high spirits the God who had shown me such great grace. I arose again of a completely different mind than when I had knelt down. I had bent my knee in great sorrow and doubt, but arose again with inexpressible joy and great assurance.[32]

Here we see the concept basic to Pietism, that humanity is made to have a personal, joyful relationship with God which transcends the legalistic, very doctrinaire approach fostered, in the

---

26 "Should the person not be brought to an awareness of his nothingness immediately by the Word of GOD/GOD is able to help him with *outward affliction*/so that he may in fact see and experience/that he knows nothing/nor can he do anything/but rather must, like a poor, useless particle of dust, await all help from GOD." *SFA*, II, pp. 825, 826); "We shall never come to true and lasting rest if it does not happen through discipline." *CP*, p. 102.

27 *WIA*, p. 26.

28 *WIA*, p. 26.

29 *WIA*, p. 27.

30 *WIA*, p. 27.

31 *WIA*, p. 28.

32 *WIA*, p. 28.

Pietist view, by dead orthodoxy. The God of the confessions and creeds becomes "my father". The personal involvement of the living God in the life of the believer is crucial to Pietist thought, as is the believer's participation in God.[33]

In this new relationship with God, a totally new perspective is actualized in Francke. Whereas all along he had been aware of the dangers of the world, in his awakened state he is certain "that all the world with all its desires and glory could not awaken such sweetness in human hearts as was this."[34] Francke's joy is complete, in that all the lessons of childhood, all the messages of the myriad volumes of devotional literature with which he was familiar were now made real to and in him through what he perceived to be, despite his earnest pleadings, a divinely-initiated religious experience. It was the watershed experience of his life and indeed was his inauguration into the ministry, for,

> The Wednesday after this I gave the sermon which
> I had been charged to give with great joy in my heart
> and from true divine conviction...[35]

"And that is thus the time to which I can actually reckon my true conversion."[36] Now he discovers it much easier "to renounce [my] ungodly nature and worldly desires, and to live chaste, upright, and piously in this world."[37] He values even a tiny speck of faith much more than high learning alone, calling knowledge (apart from a holy life) "*dreck*" (dung).[38]

---

[33] For a discussion of this, see "Teilnahme an der göttlichen Natur" in Martin Schmidt, *Wiedergeburt und neuer Mensch*, AGP #2, (Witten, 1969), pp. 238–298.

[34] *WIA*, p. 28.

[35] *WIA*, p. 29.

[36] *WIA*, p. 29.

[37] *WIA*, p. 29.

[38] Francke writes in *DE ORDINE STUDII THEOLOGICI*, "Fundamentum boni ordinis est cura Vnius Necessarii a Christo commendata*. *Luc. X. 4f." *Methodus,* p. 241. He stressed the importance for theology students of a personal relationship with Christ, and a heart-centered, rather than a head-centered, knowledge of the Bible. He laments the second-class status of Christ and Scripture among his students. "Thus the pagan things remain in the schools, the πάρεργον or major work/and God's Word the ἔργον or minor work. Thus most are graduated/and have no idea/what to do with God's Word/much less/that they should have diligently

Finally, he avers that suffering, in the form of the hostility of worldly people and as burdens given by God in order that he "might learn to test and refine [his] faith,"[39] is standard material of the Christian life. The believer can take comfort in the fact that, although God may place ever greater burdens on the person as he or she increases in faith, "by the divine power received from him [God], the last and greatest would always be much easier to bear than the first and lightest."[40]

H.-M. Rotermund points out the basic difference between Luther's and Francke's conversion experience, a difference which reflects the thrust of Pietist concern in general:

> In his inner struggle, Luther stood between the wrathful and the gracious God. The assurance with which he was concerned was the assurance of forgiveness, an assurance which must be ever won anew out of the tension between *simul justus—simul peccator.* Francke, on the other hand, stood between certainty of God and unbelief. The certainty of the reality of God broke in upon him in a unique act and was then held fast by him without temptation.[41]

While the conversion experiences, sermons, etc., of Luther and Francke do not demonstrate a particularly different understanding of humanity, indeed they are quite in agreement, these differences in their experiences reveal Francke to be more representative of his own era (obviously) and of the Pietist view of the person in general. Luther's spiritual shift was from belief in the existence of a wrathful, demanding, and avenging God, while Francke's was more a transformation from "practical atheism" to "true faith". Here it is important to be aware of the two basic types of atheism against which Pietism fought: the inborn tendency—a result of the fall—toward unbelief, and "practical atheism" which is the lifestyle and attitude of those who, although born, baptized and confirmed into the Church, lived as if God were either uninvolved in the daily affairs of humanity or were even nonexistent.

---

acquired the whole foundation of their salvation from it." *Timotheus*, pp. 22,23.

[39] *WIA*, p. 29.

[40] *WIA*, p. 29

[41] Hans-Martin Rotermund, *Orthodoxie und Pietismus*, (Berlin, 1959), p. 14.

This concept of "practical atheism" makes possible the Pietist sermons and literature in which ostensible Christians are exhorted to repent and be converted, or, as it is frequently put, be born again. This "practical atheism" is a scourge of Christianity and must be recognized and eliminated, lest it pollute and finally overcome true Christianity. It is, so to speak, as if the church member's baptism and confirmation did not "take" until he or she underwent a period of repentance and rebirth.

Unlike the radicals, the Pietists sought to bring all people to Christ within the already-existing Lutheran Church, although they were not sparing with their criticism of it. For example, Müller aroused the wrath of many when he called the baptismal font, the pulpit, the confessional, and the altar "the four dumb idols of the Church,"[42] rejected (as did Francke, too) offers of money for hearing confessions, and wrote to Spener, "We are saving Babylon. Ah, would that it only wanted to be saved."[43].

They also sought to renew their own Lutheran Church from within, through renewed individuals. Although almost all the Pietists engaged at one time or another in diatribes against the other confessions, they nonetheless were very open to friendships and correspondence with like-minded (pietistic) Christians of other confessions. For Müller and Francke the issue was not that of forming the true Church, but of reinvigorating a worn-out, arid one through sincere and even emotional love for God and neighbor. In this program of renewal, the individual human being is of central significance. Thus it can be said that the Pietist always spoke and wrote to and for individuals, each of whom had to experience in his or her own life the judgment and grace of God, and who personally had to carry out God's will for his or her own particular life.

At this point let us do something rather uncharacteristic of Pietism. That is, let us examine systematically the individual as perceived by Müller and Francke. As we analyze the various components of the individual, we are doing something the Pietists rarely did, since they were not concerned with developing a systematic, anthropological perspective. Nonetheless, they did have a fairly explicit idea of who a person is, and they were equally explicit about what this individual must do in order to be

[42] *Evangelische Volksbibliothek*, p. 230.
[43] *AP*, p. IX.

saved and be pleasing to God. Above all, the person is in need of divine assistance, for, as we shall see, humanity is, despite a good start, by nature sinful.

CHAPTER 3

THE PERSON BY NATURE

In Müller we find statements such as,

> You are indeed only a handful of earth/[and] have
> this origin from foul, stinking material/which is
> abominable not only in itself/but also in all people.[1]
> [and] A wild beast will not harm you, unless it is
> forced to by necessity and hunger. But a person desires
> to hurt you. Thus, beware of people as of the devil.[2]

In Francke we read of

> Corruption/which is *inward*/and thus all the more
> hidden; ...the corruption/which is upon all people/
> which is in one word the poison of sin/which runs in
> the veins of the natural person/and which cannot be
> sufficiently explained.[3] [and] I know myself to be a
> poor and wretched worm/who with its original and
> actual sin/has merited God's wrath and displeasure and
> eternal damnation.[4]

Because of statements such as these, great stress frequently
has been placed on the negativity of Pietism *vis-a-vis* human
nature. We must agree that the Pietists indeed took a rather bleak
view of the human condition. This is only part of the story,
however, for they also held that humanity had not always been
so corrupt, indeed, had been created the apple of God's eye and
the crown of creation.

The first humans, Adam and Eve, were without blemish.
God had created humanity upright, "that is, in his image," as
Francke claims.[5] In Müller's *Geistlicher Dank=Altar* an engrav-
ing depicts Christ painting a picture of a man. Beneath this

---

[1] *GLF*, I, vi, p. 50.
[2] *GE*, #118, p. 123.
[3] *SFA*, II, p. 418.
[4] *WIA*, p. 367.
[5] *SFA*, II, p. 418.

picture we find the words *HAC PINXIT JHOVA*.[6] Indeed, it took an outside force, Satan, to bring about the abominable condition of human nature as it currently is, for after creation, "The devil came/and spoiled the creatures of God/that they did not remain good."[7] The assumption, then, is that if Satan had not interfered, and if Eve and Adam had not given in to temptation, creation would have remained in its positive, "good" state. Müller points out that the human body reflects God's love,[8] and he even defends the flesh: "Indeed, sin is not the flesh/but rather dwells in the flesh/but yet it has put its roots down deep in the person."[9] Thus sin, while an integral part of post-Fall humanity, nonetheless has its origins outside humanity.

That which is good in humanity, the image of God, is so deeply imbedded that it is never completely eliminated (although most of Pietist language would lead one to think otherwise), and even is an essential component of the possibility for a person to be converted and sanctified. Müller asserts that people are the "noblest creatures," nobler even than the angels, not only because human nature is united with God's nature in Christ, but because it is *created in such a way* that it can bear the marks of Christ.[10] This understanding of human nature is fundamental to, even necessary for, the Pietist view of the individual's role in his or her conversion and sanctification, and is seen in Francke's pedagogical thinking wherein he encourages teachers to "paint with living colors" the "soul's true nobility as it exists in its renewal in the image of God."[11] This technique is far more effective, so Francke, in moving children to diligence and obedience than the "satanic depiction of the glories of this world."[12]

---

[6] *DA*, p. 210.

[7] *SFA*, II, p. 418.

[8] "The doctors count in the human body three hundred and fifty-six bones and six hundred and forty-six veins large and small. And in each little vein and little bone the love of God has reflected itself." *GLF*, I, ii, p. 10.

[9] *GLF*, I, ii, p. 10.

[10] "In the Old Testament the first fruits of the cattle and fruit were consecrated to GOd, according to this custom the first fruits were considered to be the most precious. If, then, we are the first fruits of the creatures of GOd we are the noblest creatures of GOd, nobler than the holy angels, because our nature is united in CHrist with the nature of GOd, as well as because our nature is so created that it can bear the marks of Christ." *HLK*, I, i, p. 1.

[11] *PS*, p. 98.

[12] *PS*, p. 98.

Indeed the credit, glory, and initiative for the individual's conversion are ascribed to God, but there needs to be some remnant of the *imago Dei* which is yet capable of renewal and of responding to the promptings of the Holy Spirit. Francke sees this sort of divine leftover as adequate grounds for the legitimacy of God's high and holy demands upon humanity, even though the fulfillment of them "is not possible in this life for anyone, not even the born again."[13]

Important here is that God is fully justified, so to speak, in demanding of humanity what was once given to Adam and Eve. That is, the first people apparently were capable of living fully, truly blessed (*gottselig*) lives, but chose to do otherwise.[14] While the person is totally depraved in the sense of being in no way capable of keeping any divine commands,[15] there nonetheless remains that which God can prompt or awaken to faith and sanctification through the Holy Spirit via chastisement, *Anfechtungen*, love, etc. Francke speaks of "awakening" the image of God which has become dormant as a result of the Fall.[16] Müller maintains the mystical concept of the "*Seelengrunde*."[17] We find this concept as well among the Calvinist Puritans. Perkin's idea of the fall into total depravity leaves in the individual that which is still the image of God.[18]

---

[13] "...thus GOd did not forsake his right to require of us again what he once entrusted [to us]." *CP*, p. 280.

[14] This thinking is found in the Pietist lineage as early as in William Perkins, who speaks of "His free choice, both to will and perform the commandment concerning the two trees and also to neglect and violate the same, whereby we see that our first parents were indeed created perfect, but mutable..." *The Work of William Perkins*, p. 188.

[15] "My GOd/you require many and great things of me/faith/love/fear/obedience/humility/and other virtues. But I have nothing/that I can give you/I am by nature poor/blind/naked/wretched and deplorable." *Gottlob*, p. 204.

[16] "But when the image of GOd/in which he was originally created/is reawakened in him....then he is revived/and experiences/how kind and good our GOd is." *SFA*, I, pp. 379, 380.

[17] Winfried Zeller, *Theologie und Frömmigkeit*, Band 1, (Marburg, 1971), p. 108.

[18] "By this we see that sin is not a corruption of man's substance, but only of faculties. Otherwise neither could men's souls be immortal, nor Christ take upon him man's nature." *The Work of Willam Perkins*, p. 192.

Francke appeals to Scripture to show that originally humanity was a living "*Conterfait*" (likeness) of God, and that God is not at all responsible for the corruption of this divine likeness.[19] In this he also follows Arndt in extolling the high nature of pre-Fall Adam, and in placing the blame squarely upon human decision and action.[20] These thoughts are by no means unique to Pietism, but they demonstrate the Pietists' high regard for humanity insofar as it is God's creation, and insofar as the image of God remains within people. Pietist thinkers also were not hostile toward the flesh *per se*, but only as it is in its fallen, sinful condition. Much of their language concerning the flesh is quite vitriolic because the flesh is where sin is most clearly seen. Nonetheless, no matter how splendid humanity may have been at one time, humanity is now fallen, and what is now of crucial, indeed eternal significance is how the person responds when God touches his or her heart.[21]

Clearly, the preponderance of Pietist literature speaks of the wretchedness of humanity by nature, "by nature" meaning the fallen and corrupt nature which is now the universal and inescapable state of all people. The pre-Fall condition of humanity is an almost irrelevant issue. Pragmatists *par excellence*, the

---

[19] "Did, then, GOd the Lord originally create us humans in such wretchedness of sin/in which we now see the whole world lying? Far from it! It cannot go unrecognized from the Word of GOd/that GOd originally created humanity upright/namely in his image; and you have been taught before of what the *image of God* mainly consists/namely in *holiness and righteousness*. GOd the LOrd expressed himself in the mind and will of humanity/as well as other powers of the soul/wisdom/holiness and righteousness/so that humanity was a living likeness of the most high GOd; as one can examine in the I. chapt. of the 1. book of *True Christianity by the blessed Johann Arnd.*" SFA, II, p. 418. (See note 20 below)

[20] "The image of GOd in humanity is the uniformity of the human soul/mind/spirit/inner being [*Gemuth*]/will and all inner and outer powers of body and soul/with GOd and the Holy Trinity/and with all its ways/virtues/will and characteristics." *Wahres Christenthum*, p. 3; "The Fall of Adam is disobedience against GOd/through which humanity turned away from GOd to itself/and robbed GOd of honor/in that he [humanity] wanted to be GOd....This Fall occurred first in his heart/then broke out through the bite of the apple and became apparent." *Wahres Christenthum*, p. 9.

[21] The manner in which and with what degree of power or gentleness God touches the heart is of secondary importance. "But much depends indeed, be the divine stirring of the heart strong or weak, that, for his part, the person recognize the divinity of such stirring, and, accordingly, not toss it to the winds, but rather seek to use such rightly." *Rührung*, p. 22.

Pietists saw no need to dwell upon the Edenic couple except, for the most part, to illustrate the depths to which humanity has fallen.

Müller and Francke stressed the terrible result of the Fall, the extreme and fundamental change in human nature. It is both their starting point and underlying assumption in education, pastoral care, sermons, bible studies and devotional messages. Peschke writes that, "Francke's thought begins not with creation, but with sin."[22] Müller emphasizes more than Francke the goodness of creation, but by no means minimizes humanity's deep corruption. It is humanity's depraved condition with which the Pietists concern themselves, since this is also humanity's current condition. Humanity has moved from harmony into a tension which will not be resolved this side of death. Sin remains, even for the born-again, a constant source of temptation and unease.

Original sin, sin as a part of the person's very nature, is a legacy of Adam and Eve, and characterizes humanity's life apart from God. It brings wickedness and eternal death. Sin is simply a fact of life and it affects everyone, even the smallest of children.[23] It also afflicts the whole person.[24] Müller writes, "No sooner born than damned," and continues, "Oh humanity, this applies to you and me. In Adam we sinned. In Adam we are damned."[25] In contrast to the inbreathing of life by God, the serpent inbreathes the poison of original sin which permeates the whole person and poisons the entire human race.[26] Müller, too,

---

[22] Peschke, *Studien,* I, p. 18.

[23] "Now then if we, beloved in the LOrd, 1. would consider *the pagan plague of lust* [literally: venereal disease] *forbidden in the sixth commandment,* and thereby see *how this rules in the person before conversion:* so we only reasonably have to consider how this disease is not only common, but is a completely universal evil with which all the children of Adam are infected from their mothers' wombs; indeed, even children may not be excepted from it." *CP,* p. 174; Arndt points out that we need only observe a child to see what self-centered and deceitful creatures human beings are. *Wahres Christenthum,* p.11

[24] "But this original sin is a spiritual illness/and is not only a pollution of the body/but is also a pollution of the spirit/the soul, and the inner being [*Gemüth*] of the person." *SFA,* II, p. 475.

[25] *GE,* #60, p. 59; Also, "If I am born a human being, I am at the same time born a sinner." *GE,* #105, p. 107.

[26] "I am speaking of the poison of original sin/which the old serpent breathed into us all in Adam. Just as natural poison penetrates the whole

emphasizes the existence of original sin within even the apparently innocent child. It is simply a matter of time until the latent, but real, sin is actualized.

> From my mother's womb the badness which condemns hangs on to me. For just as the ways of a wolf are born into a young wolf even though it has not yet torn apart a sheep, so sinful wickedness clings to every child from conception on...[27]

The two basic categories of sin are "original" and "actual,"[28] and while they are not identical, they are inseparable. Original sin causes actual sin, while actual sin reveals the deeply corrupt nature of humanity.

Albeit that sin entered the human race via Satan's activity and the decision of the primal couple, the "heart and root" of all sin is disbelief, or unbelief. In describing the Fall, which began with "our first parents" being enticed into unbelief by Satan, Francke existentializes the event by making it into a prototypical event actualized in every individual.[29] Thus sin is the basic characteristic of humanity in general, and of each person in particular, by nature. The person is not only incapable of belief, but actually becomes an enemy of God. Francke states, "By nature we are atheists and idolaters. By nature we are all despisers of the name of GOd and his honor and glory."[30] The Pietists depicted hu

---

body/flesh and blood/marrow and bone/and leaves nothing healthy in the person/so has the hellish poison of sin run all through body and soul." *GLF*, I, xvi, p. 422.

[27] *GE*, #60, p. 59.

[28] "I know myself to be a poor and wretched worm/who with my original and actual sin has merited God's wrath and displeasure/temporal death and eternal damnation." *WIA*, p. 367.

[29] "For first the devil enticed our first parents into *unbelief*/saying: *Did God really say it*? And cast doubt upon GOd's Word. Then he enticed them into *arrogance*; that their *eyes should be opened/and they would be like God*: then he led them into *love of creatures* [what is creaturely]/and thus occurred their entire fall. The roots for it were laid in unbelief: the arrogance came next before the actual Fall/and the Fall followed upon the love of creatures/in that they turned from God to creatures. The very same thing occurs in every fall and corruption/when the heart turns from God and sinks into creature-love." *SFA*, I, p. 516.

[30] *CP*, p. 211.

manity in vivid language. According to Müller, people are less than animals in all virtues, and worse in all vices.

> But with your wickedness you surpass the unrea-
> soning animals. You are filthier than a pig/more
> poisonous than a viper/more violent than a lion or a
> bear/more cunning than a fox or serpent: and/while one
> finds a particular vice in each animal/one finds in you
> all the vices in one heap. ...While no animal is so bad/
> that it does not have some good in it/yet all the
> intentions of your heart, from youth on up, have
> always been wicked and have inclined toward evil.[31]

In the sermon "The deep corruption of humankind," in which he recounts the parable of the prodigal son, Francke compares fallen humanity with a wretched and hungry swineherd. He points out that the sinful individual who could be dining on heavenly manna is instead satisfied with pigfeed, lust, and swinish pleasures.[32] As we have seen, Francke felt himself to be a poor worm (n. 28). Ahasverus Fritsch writes that humanity is not only nothing but grass, mist, smoke, shadow and wind,[33] but is even less than a worm. Because Christ, in becoming human, humbled himself like an earthworm,

> it is only reasonable/that I, wretched, sinful
> human/I, who am by nature none other than a worm
> and maggot/(Job 25) should deem myself even less/than
> a worm/and humble myself even deeper.[34]

A problem arises in that while the born-again, and thus spiritually illumined person (such as a Pietist), is very much aware of his or her spiritual depravity, the natural person is not at all cognizant of his or her condition. On top of everything else, the "old man" suffers from spiritual blindness which makes "him" fall prey to the conventional, but non-christian, non-biblical ideas about salvation, the Christian life, and life in general.[35] Knowing nothing of the desperation of the human

---

31 *GLF*, I, vi, p. 51.

32 *SFA*, II, p. 423.

33 *Gottlob*, p. 76.

34 *Gottlob*, p. 41.

35 "For a person/who is still in blindness/knows not where he should go: now he follows the example of other people/and thinks/so many people

condition, the person is, of course, also blind to the possibility of salvation. Müller laments,

> Shameful likeness of a natural person! We are by nature unwise, blind, wrong people for apart from Christ is neither light nor knowledge, a fleshly person knows nothing of true blessedness, and nothing of the way to attain it.[36]

This means that the natural person is incapable of drawing suitable conclusions from the clear messages of God's love which abound in creation. "The creature [creation] is created for this/that it may lead us to God... But we are superficial/are like pigs/who enjoy the acorns/and have no regard for the tree."[37] This blindness, however, is a purely spiritual deficiency. In a sermon in 1698 Francke preached,

> If one considers the person *before his conversion/* he is completely blind in spiritual things/and the dark- ness has totally closed and blinded his eyes/that he can see and know nothing/of anything/that is divine/heav- enly and spiritual.[38]

The spiritually blind person, although unable to be truly wise, can nonetheless be well-educated academically, and even know Scripture thoroughly and become a teacher and doctor. To make his point, Francke uses Pharisees and Scribes as prototypes for contemporary academics who are worldly-wise and spiritually blind.[39]

This blind, directionless existence plays right into Satan's hands, for when one serves any power other than God, or seeks

---

do it/it surely is not sin: now he follows the old customs/and thinks/it has been this way so long/it surely cannot be otherwise now: now he follows the prominent, wise people/who live so and so/[and thinks] it cannot be wrong: now he follows the clergy and other educated men/as he imagines/they must surely know/what is right and wrong; they do it themselves/so it must not have too much significance: now he follows this one/now that one/and thus takes no sure step/does not know/after whom he should follow/and has no sure rule and standard in his life." *SFA*, I, pp. 493, 494.

[36] *HLK*, I, viii, p. 86.

[37] *GLF*, I, ii, p. 9.

[38] *SFA*, I, p. 479.

[39] *SFA*, I, p. 479.

anything other than God's glory and neighbor's good, one is in the service of sin. Müller writes,

> Such people are like a dead corpse/which one drags/wherever one will/they are mules of Satan/who saddles and rides them at his pleasure/such a person must dance/according to how the devil pipes for them through sinful desires.[40]

It is only because of God's protective providence, or simply the lack of opportunity to sin, that the unregenerate individual refrains from, or at least hesitates before, sinning.[41] And as long as one remains in the natural condition, "so long must he know that he is also still under the domination of this vice, even if he does always not sense in himself an urge for such [a particular sin]."[42] Not only is humanity's condition one of perversion, darkness, and enslavement to Satan, but it is a degenerative condition in which sin grows with time, even a short time. Francke uses the analogy of a seed: as one holds a seed and hardly thinks that it contains the whole tree, so one hardly thinks of the gross corruption lying hidden in a newborn child.[43]

Compounding the problem is the fact that humanity does not wish to learn of its corrupt, spiritually fatal condition.[44] Not only

----

[40] *GLF*, I, vi, p. 62; And Francke preaches, "As soon as the person has fallen into sin, he has become a prisoner, a servant and a slave of the devil..." *SFP*, p. 230.

[41] *CP*, p. 89.

[42] *CP*, p. 90.

[43] "If one has a little seed/who would think/that in such a little seed lay hidden the entire tree/with its roots/trunk/branches/twigs/leaves/blossoms and fruit/as one sees them later, with time. Thus when one sees a small, just-born child/who would think/that in it lay hidden such corruption/as is manifested with the years? One often sees in small children some signs of their *recalcitrance/impatience/*and *disobedience.* Such vices grow in them with the years/indeed, with the months and weeks; yea, one sees/that with time more and more sins and vices spring forth from the poisoned spring of the heart." *SFA*, II, p. 424.

[44] "If we would truly participate in the cleansing of [our] sin/we first must recognize rightly/of what we must be cleansed. But in this a person is very reluctant: and he will much sooner/undertake to do this and that from GOd's Word/and resolve to better himself to some degree in outward things/than actually go within himself/that he may see and earnestly consider the impurity/and the wretched condition of his soul." *SFA*, II, p. 480.

is the person unable to see, but he or she does not wish to see or
to believe.

> Indeed as long as the person continues in his
> natural blindness and fleshly [self-] assuredness/he does
> not believe it/when one tells him/that his heart is so
> evil/that it is the devil's den and hideout/that serpents
> and scorpions of all sorts of foul lusts and desires live
> in it/and the evil spirits have there their entrance and
> exit.[45]

Such is the condition of the individual by nature.

Here a few words are in order about the Pietist understanding
of the material nature of humanity. We detect what seems to be a
hellenistic influence, that is, a certain antagonism toward things
physical. This no doubt reflects the standard Lutheran understanding of the flesh at that time, and the influence of medieval
mystics such as Bernard, Tauler and Suso. Again we find
another point of tension, for while Müller can write that surely
sin is not flesh, but rather dwells in the flesh, he also writes,

> We are indeed nothing other than wretched dust,
> we have our origins in foul, stinking material which is
> abominable not only in itself, but in all people. We are
> an impure, stinking vessel full of wicked smells.[46]

In a sermon on death, Francke, too, betrays an underlying negative attitude toward the flesh. Not only do the body and soul
separate at death, but the body is seen as a curtain which gets in
the way, and which had prevented the soul from contemplating
"freely and unhindered" its Savior and Bridegroom.[47] Elsewhere
he calls the body "the least part of [one's] being."[48]

---

[45] *SFA*, I, p. 246.

[46] *HLK*, I, vi. p. 47.

[47] Francke quotes John 5:24, then continues, "With which words he
clearly testifies how already in this life one may in faith have eternal life/and
in this way can have victory over death/that/even though one may die
naturally/and must undergo the separation of body and soul/one nonetheless
need not see death as death/and be terrified by it. For through faith one has
already passed from death to life/and thus natural death is nothing other to
him than a rending of the curtain/which lay in the way/that one may not
contemplate the Savior and Bridegroom of his soul freely and unhindered."
SFA, III, p. 57.

[48] *SFP*, p. 673.

Francke clearly uses the language of Platonism when he says of the body, "Indeed, this mortal hut in which we are, is itself a cell and prison in which the immortal spirit is trapped."[49] He bemoans the fact that while even the heathen recognized their bodies as prisons, many who call themselves Christians and should know this from experience are not even aware of it.[50]

The term *flesh* is used to indicate not only the person's actual physical being, but also his or her corrupt nature, or even his or her nothingness.[51]

All this antagonism, however, in no way means that the body is unimportant. Müller points out that "The soul moves the body/the body is the soul's tool."[52] While the Pietists speak badly of the body, and tend to speak as if body and soul were separate entities, they nonetheless see the person functioning as a unity.[53] Thus what the person does with his or her inner life has an affect on the outer life, and vice versa. This means that no area of life can be neglected. Nonetheless, the starting point and primary concern of Pietism is the inner person.

---

[49] *SFP*, p. 230.

[50] *SFP*, p. 230.

[51] *SFP*, p. 257.

[52] *GLF*, I, xi, p. 195.

[53] "For body and soul together are one person/who does his works spiritually and physically at the same time." *Wahres Christenthum*, p. 272.

CHAPTER 4

THE INNER PERSON

In discussing the inner person, we encounter the real interest of the Pietists, because the inner person is the determining factor in what sort of life an individual leads, and where that person will spend eternity. The heart, soul, conscience and mind make up the inner person. The Pietists perceived the heart to be the essential center of the person, and the soul to be the essence of his or her existence, although they had a tendency to use interchangeably words such as heart, soul, spirit, *Gemüth* and the like. We will not discuss the human spirit here simply because it is subsumed under the heading of soul. Pietist language does not lend itself to systematization precisely because so many terms are used interchangeably, and because different inner components take on more than one role. The sinner can be plagued, for example, by heart or conscience, and Francke can begin a statement telling how the *heart* is comforted, and finish it with examples of how this calming of the *soul* is a source of joy.[1] With this in mind, we turn to the very core of the individual.

THE HEART

The center or core of the individual is the heart. It is the dwelling place of Satan or God, the locus of conversion experience, the starting point of regeneration (if the heart is not transformed, the will is hamstrung), the seat of emotion and the strongest friend or foe of the person. The importance of the heart is reflected in this statement by Ahasverus Fritsch:

> Gottlob was asked by one of his good friends/of which enemies did he have the most to fear? The archdeceiver/he answered. Who is this? said the other. Your own heart: answered Gottlob. You have no worse enemy/than your own deceitful heart.[2]

In Pietist thought, the term "heart" tends to be an allusion to things inward in general, to those components of the inner person with which one must reckon and contend. Pietist language is full of references to the heart, and rare is the sermon

[1] *LR*, p. 71.
[2] *Gottlob*, p. 83.

which makes no appeal for the heart's contrition, surrender, transformation, preservation (against sin and in godliness), examination, or strengthening. Johann Porst, one of Spener's successors at the Nikolaikirche in Berlin took even the occasion of the dedication of a new organ to exhort the people in the pews to examine their hearts in singing:

> Well, my dear listeners, have you all taken this opportunity to examine your hearts, how you stand before God and have sung to this point? If you have been singing merely out of habit or, rather, not in true devotion of the heart, not in spirit and in truth, and thus without the impulse and leading of the Holy Spirit, you have deceived yourselves pitifully.[3]

We must keep in mind as we examine the Pietist understanding of the heart that it is a rather flexibly used term.

We are not surprised to find that the heart, prior to its surrender to Christ in repentance and conversion, is a center of wickedness, defiance, arrogance, and even filth.[4] Because the heart is by nature impure, it would remain an abomination before God even if the person were to avoid all outward sins.[5] The heart's wickedness is found not only in its willingness to cooperate with the devil and the wicked world, but in its ability to deceive the person.[6] A perverse heart often corrupts even the

---

[3] "'Die edle und wohlgeordnete Musik der Gläubigen': Eine pietistische Orgelpredigt Johann Porsts", in W. Zeller, *Theologie und Frömmigkeit*, Band I, (Marburg: 1971), p. 180.

[4] "Among other things, it is a very impressive testimony thereto, when it says in Jer. 17, 9: *The heart is a defiant and desperate thing*; actually, *a defiant and deceitful thing*, which has many nooks in which evil can hide itself." *CP*, p. 241.

[5] "This must be clearly before the eyes of the person: and then he will see/how from his youth his heart has been a manure-pile/in which the evil spirits have had their passage/and have worked so many and all manner of sinful and evil desires/and in particular/how Satan reveals his power in his and other people's hearts through unbelief/that/even if he were free of outward sins/and thereby outwardly received the praise of other people/his heart was nonetheless an abomination in the eyes of GOd." *SFA*, II, p. 476.

[6] "They [the devil and the world] strike fire, but our heart receives the sparks of it in its desires. Yea, we have in our fleshly heart a friendly enemy, a treacherous Judas, who is in a secret pact with the devil and the world,

the heart is responsive to the conscience acting as a sort
dog which alerts the individual to the perilous condition
her heart.

> *Dear person/your conscience must be truly awak-*
> *ened in your life/or you will wake up with horror in*
> *hell. So, only truly uncover the evil ground of your*
> *heart/contemplate it earnestly/how things stand with*
> *you...*[22]

s the conscience which moves the heart to seek Christ and
e free of "such restless conscience and wretched condi-
'23 Thus the individual is prompted by the conscience to
e his or her heart to receive Christ. The field which must
owed up to receive the seed of the divine Word is, "Our
our mind/our soul [*Gemüth*]/our spirit/however we wish to
..."24

he person, laden with a troubled conscience and a broken
, can now turn to God in true repentance, and with a "true
."

> But, just as faith cannot exist without repentance/
> with faith there must first *be a true heart*. One should
> not enter in with a hypocritical/but rather with a *true*
> *heart*/which truly offers itself up and surrenders itself to
> GOd the LOrd.25

The mark of a true heart is purity or cleanliness. If the heart is
t rid of love of the world, there is no room for Jesus to
ter,26 and if it is to become Christ's dwelling place, it must be
pt clean. This is done through the regular and, above all,
ncere pouring out of one's heart before God. Here we en-
unter a sort of "Which comes first?" situation, for the person is
alled to pour out his or her heart before God and await divine

---

22 *SFA*, I, p. 846; "Are, then, your hearts so hard/that nothing can
move you? Your conscience will surely convince you." *SFA*, II, p. 40.
   23 *SFA*, p. 61.
   24 *SFA*, I, p. 437.
   25 *SFA*, I, p. 322.
   26 *SFP*, p. 23.

person's best intentions: "We often begin without an evil intent,
yea, with all intentions to the good, and yet nothing but sin
comes of it: Our evil heart does this."[7] Because of its deceptive
nature the heart can appear pure, but actually be full of filth.[8] The
person tends to look outside him- or herself for sources of sin,
and tries to put the blame on the world, when in fact the world is
already within the individual like a snake which the person
carries and nourishes in his or her heart. "It was not the world in
the apple which corrupted Eve and us all; rather it was the world
which lay in the heart, that is, the evil, forbidden desires of the
world."[9] On the one hand the heart is full of corruption and
worldliness, and on the other it is by nature empty of life, as a
house without a well is empty of water.[10] This, then, is the
abominable condition of the human heart, and it is necessary that
one recognize it, so that he or she can renounce his or her
wickedness, seek the water of life [Christ] which cleanses one of
filth and corruption, and fills one with life, and thus be saved.

In order to be moved to repentance and overcome the deception of the heart, the individual must perceive it as it actually is,
that is, he or she must see both its wickedness and the cause of
its corruption, unbelief.[11] To do this, however, a person needs

---

kisses us and yet hands over the fortress, when we do not expect it." *HLK*, I,
xxii, p. 527.
   7 *HLK*, I, xxii, p. 527.
   8 "The heart is a true slough and pool of sin/in which all manner of
destructive worms grow and creep: Some are deceived, however/that he does
not consider his heart to be so evil/because occasionally the evil desires are at
rest in him/and are as sunken away/then his thoughts appear to be devout and
holy/the desires pure and chaste/the words kind and edifying/and the works
earnest and Christian: That lasts only as long/as he does not get excited/I
would say/so long as he has no opportunity and enticement to sin/but when
this is aroused/worldly lusts arise so thickly/that one can perceive nothing
but slime and uncleanness/in all thoughts/words and works." *Gotthold*, pp.
160, 161.
   9 *HLK*, II, v, p. 695.
   10 "And see, in its old birth the human heart is like a house which has
no fountain; and one must go all about in order to fetch water and suffers
from want. But when one who has no water in his house digs for it until he
comes to a spring, then he has his fill of water." *CP*, p. 231.
   11 "As He [Jesus] here accuses his disciples of *foolishness* and
dullness/of heart/He shows them at the same time/in what such foolishness
and dullness consist; *namely/that they had not believed/all that the prophets
had spoken*." *SFA*, I, p. 760.

divine assistance. Although Scripture and the Law of God testify clearly to the heart's wickedness, one still needs direct help from God who alone can examine the depths of the human heart.[12] Only then can the heart be made pleasing to God. "If it is not first made clear to one what a treacherous heart he has by nature, it is not possible that his earnestness be acceptable and pleasing to God."[13] We see here the necessary role of the emotions in coming to the truth about oneself. It is at this moment of awareness, just prior to conversion, that one often feels a stirring of the heart. This is not imagined, nor is it a solely psychological reaction. The phrase, "divine stirring of the heart," is not simply a figure of speech describing the person's hyperactive emotions. Rather, it is an actual and unforgettable affective experience instigated by God, an event.[14] The initiative is God's, but it is up to the individual to respond appropriately. God touches different hearts in different ways and in varying degrees of intensity. Of importance, however, is whether the person carries on in faith.

> If only this [God's prompting] occurs, and thus a true divine stirring of the heart has gone on, then it does not matter at all whether the stirring is strong and very perceptible or only gentle and without particularly great sensibility. But much depends indeed, be the divine stirring of the heart strong or weak, that for his part the person recognize the divinity of such stirring, and, accordingly, not toss it to the winds but rather seek to use such rightly.[15]

---

[12] "For this reason it is reasonable that one should be convinced that his heart is by nature false, spiteful and deceitful not only by the Law of GOd, and [should not only] believe the clear sayings of Holy Scripture that he is so constituted; but as he hears from the Word of GOd, GOD alone can examine his heart rightly, and uncover for the person its hidden depths: Thus he should turn with prayer and pleading to this same one [God] who alone can help him to such a most necessary knowledge." *CP*, p. 242.

[13] *CP*, p. 242.

[14] "...namely one has felt a particular movement in his soul [*Gemüth*] through this [the reading and hearing of, or meditation on God's Word], and has received from it such an impression in his soul which one does not forget so easily, but can remember this much more than many thousand other words which one hears otherwise, or which have not gone through his heart in such a manner: This is what one calls a divine stirring of the heart." *Rührung*, p. 15.

[15] *Rührung*, p. 22.

To use this divine touch right that is, sincerely, for repentance w is superficial and, thus, is of no val about the heart's condition, the plac is in one's own heart. This must b devout, that is, heartfelt prayer. As feet into church, so one must procee of faith," on God's road into the h parable of the lost coin in Luke 15 an standing of the person of the mediev woman not with the God who seeks person seeking the image of God lost to find it, one must first sweep out and own heart by the light of the Holy Spirit

A standard element of repentance i heart.

> For there are two parts to
> Contritio and fides, *the crushing, o*
> *sorrow for sin* (in which is necessa
> recognition of sin) *and faith*.[19]

In Francke's description of a contrite hear imprecise—but biblical—manner in whic language. He points out that Scripture calls c *"a distressed spirit, a broken heart,* [*Gemüth*]..."[20] In the same sermon, Franck honor to experience in one's soul the pangs science, this being nothing but another percept of a "broken heart and a contrite spirit."[21]

---

[16] "If you repent of your sins, ask GOd that he repentance to take root in your heart, so that it be no sup which is only shallow, but rather that it may have a true heart." *SFP*, p. 1208.

[17] *SFA*, I, p. 267.

[18] *SFA*, II, pp. 139, 140.

[19] *SFP*, p. 1200.

[20] *SFP*, p. 1199.

[21] "In conclusion I am also speaking to you who alre sin and are of a broken heart and a contrite spirit over it. You has deigned to let you experience such in your souls, namely v a person's sin and the wrath of God strike his conscience." *SFF*

Here of watch of his or

It i thus b tions. prepa be pl heart/ call i

hear hear

n e k s c c

help,[27] but God finds no pleasure in words unless they come from a changed, cleansed heart.[28] Here the only solution can be that God accepts the person's imperfect motives, as we shall see in our section on the will. Seen theocentrically, all that happens is of God. Experienced anthropocentrically, there is human effort required and expended in the cleansing of one's heart.

We encounter two types of "changed heart." The one is the heart which is changed as a result of repentance and a crying out to God, *"miserere mei,"* which is necessary for the changed heart of faith.[29] The other is the changed or new heart wrought in the believer by God which is necessary for sanctification. The one is the heart made completely new by God in response to the unbeliever's plea. The other is the reborn heart of the believer which God continues to renew and make ever holier. The person's newness of heart must be made apparent, or one may assume that he or she has not been born again after all.[30] A changed heart brings about a sea change in a person.

---

27 "But always let this be your most important [thing]/that you/ according to the counsel of the just mentioned LXII. Psalm *pour out before Him* (more than before all people) *your heart* (and all that is therein/like to the last little drop of a pot)/and all that oppresses and troubles you/as best as you can/lay it before Him in simplicity/and patiently await his help." *SFA*, I, p. 758.

28 "If our heart is not in the right condition/how can the words please Him/even if they sound good outwardly? For He judges the words according to the heart." *SFA*, I, p. 755.

29 *SFA*, I, p. 1027; "Behold/it is not possible/that you could say in truth: You believe in the LOrd JESUS/if your heart is not changed." *SFA*, I, p. 1029; This desire for change must be no half-way (half-hearted?) affair: "Now those/who find/that heretofore they did not want to surrender their hearts to the LOrd JEsus/deny Him and rebel against Him/and can/so far as they remain in their recalcitrance/expect nothing other/than that such will bring death and sure destruction." *SFA*, II, p. 29.

30 "Thus GOd gives to each person/who he bears anew/a second heart. Then the world says: how has the person become so completely different? He no longer talks/as he talked before; he tends no longer to do/what he did otherwise; They marvel at this/but do not see/that the ground of his heart has been changed. But this must be truly changed in a person/otherwise he is not born again." *SFA*, II, p. 21; Here we see the problem of identifying the "truly" born-again Christian by outward appearances. A lack of behavioral change indicates that the heart has not been transformed. Even if there is a change in behavior, this change is meaningless if it is only superficial, and

> Wherever JEsus changes a heart/there rules/instead
> of the love of the world which was therein before/GOd's
> love; where before the person's heart was a murderers'
> den of evil spirits/in which much wrath and vengeful-
> ness reigned/afterwards it becomes a pleasant temple of
> GOd/in which GOd spreads his grace and mercy/and
> works gentleness/which the person desires to pour out
> in love/not only toward his friends/but even his worst
> enemies/and seeks to do good to all people. Where
> before the person's heart was a slough full of unclean
> spirits/and he harbored many vile desires/afterwards he
> received instead in his heart many godly thoughts/as it
> is according to Matth. V. 8: *Blessed are the pure of
> heart/for they shall see GOd.*[31]

This rather noble new condition, however, is not attainable in
this earthly life, for the heart is never completely free of sin. The
temple of God can yet become a public tavern full of all manner
of wickedness and vice. This reality, then, calls for the strictest
vigilance.[32] Müller compares the person's relationship with his
or her heart to that of a wise salesperson who keeps a close eye
on an untrustworthy employee, and who goes over the day's
receipts with the employee every evening.[33] Scriver introduces
an ameliorating and pastoral note to the rather rigorous and per-
fectionistic Pietist demands:

> See to it well/that you do not house and harbor
> wicked thoughts in your hearts. I am not saying/that
> you should have no wicked thoughts/for I would want
> too much/and would say and require/what is impossible
> for the human heart/after the Fall...[34]

---

the heart has not first been transformed. It seems that here the Pietists were
stuck in a vicious circle.

[31] *SFA*, II, p. 376.

[32] "The human heart should be a holy/well-guarded temple of GOd/
behold/it is like a public guest-house and tavern/where all manner of
[boisterous] fellows/nasty/vain/wicked thoughts come and go freely/and defile
the holy dwelling place of GOd. If you are wise/guard your heart with all
diligence." *Gottlob*, p. 187.

[33] *HLK*, I, xvii, p. 428.

[34] *Gotthold*, p. 885.

The heart also is seen as the seat of the person's thoughts, indeed Francke writes of the need to examine its thoughts,[35] and of course the majority of these are wicked.

The best for which the Christian may hope in this life is the *"Bevestigung"* (strengthening, or literally, fortification) of the heart. This can occur in the Christian to salvific ends or in the non-christian to fatal ends, should the unbeliever's heart be fortified in its wickedness.[36] It is one thing for a person to recognize his or her frailty and thus cry out for the strengthening of his or her heart. It is quite another matter for a child of the world to cry out for this strengthening, however, because the child of the world has no idea of what he or she is asking.[37] The Christian is in desperate need of such divine support and such a strong heart because of the "old Adam" or corruption which hangs on and seeks to regain total control of the heart. Should the believer succumb, he or she faces the danger of a harsher punishment than if he or she had never turned to God in the first place. The other reason the believer needs God's strength is the "seduction of the world" which is great in word and deed.[38] Just what, then, does this necessary element of the Christian life look like?

> So, then, this is the true strengthening of the heart, when the person receives a true assurance and joy that he may know GOd to be his dear father, and himself to be his true child: that he may regard JEsus Christ his true Savior and Redeemer, and with joy in his heart may call him his brother, who has obtained and wants to grant him eternal inheritance: that he may have the Holy Spirt dwelling in his heart, that he may be a temple and dwelling place of the same, that he may be ruled and led into all truth by him; for *they who are led by the Spirit, they are children of God.* Rom. 8, 14.[39]

---

[35] "Thus, if you would be a Christian/examine yourself well/and search your heart/whether all its thoughts can stand with the love of a pure heart/of a good conscience and of unstained faith/or may struggle against them...." *LR*, p. 60.
[36] *SFP*, p. 873.
[37] *SFP*, p. 875.
[38] *SFP*, p. 876.
[39] *SFP*, p. 880.

Particularly significant in this description are the clearly subjective criteria. Not only is the fortified Christian led by the Holy Spirit, which has moral and intellectual as well as emotional connotations, but the believer receives particular *feelings*, that is, he or she experiences certainty and joy, and *knows* him- or herself to be a child of God, to be redeemed. Müller writes, "Here below my heart is my heaven. Where God dwells with his grace, there heaven must be."[40]

The question of divine initiative and human initiative appears here, as, it seems, everywhere in Pietist anthropology. On the one hand, Francke writes, "But if one asks: *How shall I attain to it*, that I may receive this fortification of the heart? As we have already... heard, it happens *through grace*."[41] As always, Francke here uses the term grace in the strict Lutheran sense of unmerited, divinely initiated gift. One can ignore or disdain it, accept and then lose it, but it always and only comes as a gift. On the other hand, however,

> Now if it is a serious matter to us that we attain
> to the true fortification of our hearts, then the way is
> that we simply remain in the word of Christ as the
> word of truth, persevere in the earnest practice of
> prayer, converse with Jesus our only Savior daily, and
> continually meditate upon his resurrection, ascension,
> and seat at the right hand of GOd.[42]

That is, unless the Christian actually does something—in this case Bible study, prayer and meditation are the required behaviors—he or she misses the way to have his or heart strengthened. The dilemma remains (for us, if not for the Pietists): just who responds to whom?

Whoever takes the initiative, and whatever happens in the person's heart, the heart remains the core of the individual and determines every area of his or her life. "For were this source [the heart] not changed in us, all else could be of no use."[43]

---

[40] *GE*, #10, p. 10.
[41] *SFP*, p. 881.
[42] *SFP*, p. 881.
[43] *CP*, p. 248.

person's best intentions: "We often begin without an evil intent, yea, with all intentions to the good, and yet nothing but sin comes of it: Our evil heart does this."[7] Because of its deceptive nature the heart can appear pure, but actually be full of filth.[8] The person tends to look outside him- or herself for sources of sin, and tries to put the blame on the world, when in fact the world is already within the individual like a snake which the person carries and nourishes in his or her heart. "It was not the world in the apple which corrupted Eve and us all; rather it was the world which lay in the heart, that is, the evil, forbidden desires of the world."[9] On the one hand the heart is full of corruption and worldliness, and on the other it is by nature empty of life, as a house without a well is empty of water.[10] This, then, is the abominable condition of the human heart, and it is necessary that one recognize it, so that he or she can renounce his or her wickedness, seek the water of life [Christ] which cleanses one of filth and corruption, and fills one with life, and thus be saved.

In order to be moved to repentance and overcome the deception of the heart, the individual must perceive it as it actually is, that is, he or she must see both its wickedness and the cause of its corruption, unbelief.[11] To do this, however, a person needs

---

kisses us and yet hands over the fortress, when we do not expect it." *HLK*, I, xxii, p. 527.

[7] *HLK*, I, xxii, p. 527.

[8] "The heart is a true slough and pool of sin/in which all manner of destructive worms grow and creep: Some are deceived, however/that he does not consider his heart to be so evil/because occasionally the evil desires are at rest in him/and are as sunken away/then his thoughts appear to be devout and holy/the desires pure and chaste/the words kind and edifying/and the works earnest and Christian: That lasts only as long/as he does not get excited/I would say/so long as he has no opportunity and enticement to sin/but when this is aroused/worldly lusts arise so thickly/that one can perceive nothing but slime and uncleanness/in all thoughts/words and works." *Gotthold*, pp. 160, 161.

[9] *HLK*, II, v, p. 695.

[10] "And see, in its old birth the human heart is like a house which has no fountain; and one must go all about in order to fetch water and suffers from want. But when one who has no water in his house digs for it until he comes to a spring, then he has his fill of water." *CP*, p. 231.

[11] "As He [Jesus] here accuses his disciples of *foolishness* and *dullness/of heart*/He shows them at the same time/in what such foolishness and dullness consist; *namely/that they had not believed/all that the prophets had spoken.*" *SFA*, I, p. 760.

divine assistance. Although Scripture and the Law of God testify clearly to the heart's wickedness, one still needs direct help from God who alone can examine the depths of the human heart.[12] Only then can the heart be made pleasing to God. "If it is not first made clear to one what a treacherous heart he has by nature, it is not possible that his earnestness be acceptable and pleasing to God."[13] We see here the necessary role of the emotions in coming to the truth about oneself. It is at this moment of awareness, just prior to conversion, that one often feels a stirring of the heart. This is not imagined, nor is it a solely psychological reaction. The phrase, "divine stirring of the heart," is not simply a figure of speech describing the person's hyperactive emotions. Rather, it is an actual and unforgettable affective experience instigated by God, an event.[14] The initiative is God's, but it is up to the individual to respond appropriately. God touches different hearts in different ways and in varying degrees of intensity. Of importance, however, is whether the person carries on in faith.

> If only this [God's prompting] occurs, and thus a true divine stirring of the heart has gone on, then it does not matter at all whether the stirring is strong and very perceptible or only gentle and without particularly great sensibility. But much depends indeed, be the divine stirring of the heart strong or weak, that for his part the person recognize the divinity of such stirring, and, accordingly, not toss it to the winds but rather seek to use such rightly.[15]

---

12 "For this reason it is reasonable that one should be convinced that his heart is by nature false, spiteful and deceitful not only by the Law of GOd, and [should not only] believe the clear sayings of Holy Scripture that he is so constituted; but as he hears from the Word of GOd, GOD alone can examine his heart rightly, and uncover for the person its hidden depths: Thus he should turn with prayer and pleading to this same one [God] who alone can help him to such a most necessary knowledge." *CP*, p. 242.

13 *CP*, p. 242.

14 "...namely one has felt a particular movement in his soul [*Gemüth*] through this [the reading and hearing of, or meditation on God's Word], and has received from it such an impression in his soul which one does not forget so easily, but can remember this much more than many thousand other words which one hears otherwise, or which have not gone through his heart in such a manner: This is what one calls a divine stirring of the heart." *Rührung*, p. 15.

15 *Rührung*, p. 22.

To use this divine touch rightly is to repent from the heart, that is, sincerely, for repentance which is not rooted in the heart is superficial and, thus, is of no value.[16] Despite the harsh words about the heart's condition, the place to seek Christ in repentance is in one's own heart. This must be done through faithful and devout, that is, heartfelt prayer. As one may walk with physical feet into church, so one must proceed on spiritual feet, the "feet of faith," on God's road into the heart.[17] Francke takes the parable of the lost coin in Luke 15 and, reminiscent of the understanding of the person of the medieval mystics, compares the woman not with the God who seeks the lost sinner, but with a person seeking the image of God lost through the Fall. In order to find it, one must first sweep out and cleanse and search one's own heart by the light of the Holy Spirit.[18]

A standard element of repentance is a contrite, or broken, heart.

> For there are two parts to true repentance: Contritio and fides, *the crushing, or true regret and sorrow for sin* (in which is necessarily included the recognition of sin) *and faith.*[19]

In Francke's description of a contrite heart, we see the rather imprecise—but biblical—manner in which the Pietists used language. He points out that Scripture calls contrition of the heart "*a distressed spirit, a broken heart,* or *stricken soul [Gemüth]...*"[20] In the same sermon, Francke says that it is an honor to experience in one's soul the pangs of a troubled conscience, this being nothing but another perceptible manifestation of a "broken heart and a contrite spirit."[21]

---

[16] "If you repent of your sins, ask GOd that he would cause such repentance to take root in your heart, so that it be no superficial repentance which is only shallow, but rather that it may have a true grounding in your heart." *SFP*, p. 1208.

[17] *SFA*, I, p. 267.

[18] *SFA*, II, pp. 139, 140.

[19] *SFP*, p. 1200.

[20] *SFP*, p. 1199.

[21] "In conclusion I am also speaking to you who already know your sin and are of a broken heart and a contrite spirit over it. You dear ones, GOd has deigned to let you experience such in your souls, namely what it is when a person's sin and the wrath of God strike his conscience." *SFP*, p. 1214.

Here the heart is responsive to the conscience acting as a sort of watchdog which alerts the individual to the perilous condition of his or her heart.

> *Dear person/your conscience must be truly awak-*
> *ened in your life/or you will wake up with horror in*
> *hell.* So, only truly uncover the evil ground of your
> heart/contemplate it earnestly/how things stand with
> you...[22]

It is the conscience which moves the heart to seek Christ and thus be free of "such restless conscience and wretched conditions."[23] Thus the individual is prompted by the conscience to prepare his or her heart to receive Christ. The field which must be plowed up to receive the seed of the divine Word is, "Our heart/our mind/our soul [*Gemüth*]/our spirit/however we wish to call it..."[24]

The person, laden with a troubled conscience and a broken heart, can now turn to God in true repentance, and with a "true heart."

> But, just as faith cannot exist without repentance/
> with faith there must first *be a true heart.* One should
> not enter in with a hypocritical/but rather with a *true*
> *heart*/which truly offers itself up and surrenders itself to
> GOd the LOrd.[25]

The mark of a true heart is purity or cleanliness. If the heart is not rid of love of the world, there is no room for Jesus to enter,[26] and if it is to become Christ's dwelling place, it must be kept clean. This is done through the regular and, above all, sincere pouring out of one's heart before God. Here we encounter a sort of "Which comes first?" situation, for the person is called to pour out his or her heart before God and await divine

---

[22] *SFA*, I, p. 846; "Are, then, your hearts so hard/that nothing can move you? Your conscience will surely convince you." *SFA*, II, p. 40.

[23] *SFA*, p. 61.

[24] *SFA*, I, p. 437.

[25] *SFA*, I, p. 322.

[26] *SFP*, p. 23.

THE SOUL

If the heart is an intangible but nonetheless real component of the person, the soul, while equally intangible, seems a bit easier to define.

> *The soul of the person* is an immortal spirit/gifted by GOd with glorious powers/with understanding/with a will/with memory/and with other movements and desires.[44]

Again we encounter a word with several usages. It can mean the soul *per se* (as described above), the inner person in general, or (infrequently) the whole person.

As for the soul *per se*, each individual has one. We cannot say that each individual *is* one, for the person is more than simply the soul, even though it is as soul that one initially survives death. The soul is irreplaceable, and it has one chance at this life, this chance coming during the person's earthly existence, the results (or judgment) appearing at death.[45] In the rather lengthy quote below, Müller describes the soul in detail.

> First, the soul is noble through this/1. that it is created in the image of God. Moses describes the origin of the soul. *And* God *the LOrd made humanity out of the clay of the earth/and blew a living breath into his nose/and so the person became a living soul.* Gen. 2.v.7. It requires no extensive disputation/whether God made the soul outside of Adam's body and put it in by blowing or whether/by blowing the soul was created in Adam's body: We learn here/that the soul has its origin in God/and thus quite reasonably seeks its rest in God/ as the child loves its mother's breast/who has begot it. 2. That the soul is a spirit/and thus is immortal. So it is reasonable that it would busy itself with the immortal God/just as the mortal body busies itself with mortal things. 3. That God has created the soul as a mirror/in which one is able to see his image. Now, as long as the soul clings to God/you see God in it/but

---

[44] *Wahres Christenthum*, p. 270.

[45] "Indeed, many a wicked person acts so thoughtlessly/as if he indeed had 10 souls to lose/although a [soul]/once lost/is lost completely and forever." *Gotthold*, p. 564.

when you turn it to the world/you find nothing therein
but what is world and worldly. Just as one sees in a
mirror now heaven/now earth/according to how one
turns it. Ah! what a pity/that the soul/which can bear
God and heaven/must burden itself with the world and
its filth. 4. That God wishes to share [him]self with the
soul/for this reason he made it responsive by his
image/that he could have a friendship with/dwell and
work in the soul/if it were like him. Thus, the nobility
of the soul requires/that it disdain all/that is not God.
God and the world cannot dwell together in the same
heart/the more the world departs/the more God enters.
This nobility of the soul is to some degree illustrated
in nature; for the soul naturally has its roots in the
heart/and its highest powers in the head. By the heart is
signified its depths/by the head its heights. Jeremiah
speaks of the heart in the 17th chap. v.9. *Who can
fathom it?* So is it also with the soul. No earthly thing
can fill its foundation: Because it is of God/it wishes to
be filled with God. And just as the head is the highest
member on a person/so the soul must strive with its
love for things above. But many people deny this
nobility of their souls/and say of them what David says
in the 44. Ps.v.26. *Our soul is bent to the earth/our
belly clings to the ground/*like a mole always creeps on
its belly/and roots about in the earth...

Second/our soul is noble in this/that it has been
purchased so dearly through the blood of God....Surely
it must be a noble soul/for which God himself poured
out his blood/what could be more precious/to redeem
the condemned soul/than the blood of the great God:
This meditation dampens the love of the world powerfully within us/for Christ has redeemed us from the
world/and the grace of our redemption disciplines
us/that we may disdain worldly desires. Tit. 2. v.12....

Third/the nobility of our soul consists in this/that
it is consecrated by the Spirit of God. When in the Old
Testament God wished to consecrate the tabernacle/he
revealed his glory/and filled the entire dwelling. By this
it was set apart from common use to godly use.
Through faith the Spirit of God dwells in the soul/then
it is set apart from the world/and becomes the sanctuary
of God. The means of our consecration are on God's

side/baptism/the Word and the Lord's Supper/on our side/faith.[46]

This shows in depth the Pietist view of the soul. We find in the soul's origin in God one of the fundamentals of Pietist anthropology. So important is this fact, that Müller claims that there is really no need to even discuss the matter—the soul comes from God alone. Without this assumption the Pietists could not have emphasized so strongly their audience's life-long desire for reunion with God. Nor could they have selected writings of mystics such as Bernard, Tauler and the Frankfurter as models for their anthropological and devotional thought. Here, too, we find justification for the Pietist treatment of people as responsible for their behavior, despite their total depravity. The soul remembers, as it were, its origins and longs to be restored or, so to speak, rehabilitated. We see, too, that the soul, with its origins in an infinite and immortal God, is immortal, and thus operates on its own spiritual plane in which it is at home as the body is upon the earth. The immortality of the soul is even attested to by the "learned heathen."[47]

Again the either/or stance of Pietism is present. The soul is compared to wax which can bear only one impression at a time.[48] This image, common to the mystics, is used frequently to emphasize the absolute nature of the demands which God and world place upon one's soul.

---

[46] *GLF*, II, v, p. 759ff.

[47] "Some of the learned heathen came to this/that they not only confessed the immortality of the soul/but also proved it from the the fear and joy of the human conscience. For if the soul perishes/what torments the person/when he dies?: The anxiety of the conscience was to them a mighty witness/that the soul must have something painful to expect after death." *GLF*, I, xxiv, pp. 639, 640; Despite their high regard for certain pagan philosophers, the Pietists did not claim for them access to ultimate wisdom, which only a Christian can have, for the philosophers are ignorant of the means of their salvation: "Verum enim vero, vt ill: sapientiam assectati sint, ad veram tamen sapientiam, teste Paulo Rom. I & 1 Cor. I. & II. minime peruenerunt. Etenim τὸ βέβαιον λαὶ τὸ πιστὸν καὶ ὑγιὲς quo pacto consequerentur illi, qui corruptionem mentis humanae, crassiusculam saltem, persentiscerant quidem, at tum originem eius, tum medelam penitus ignorarent?" *Methodus*, pp. 105,106.

[48] See Ernst Benz, "Symbole der Unio Mystica in der Barock-Mystik", in *Symbolon: Jahrbuch für Symbolforschung*, Neue Folge, Band 1, (Köln), pp. 11–30.

The soul, like the heart, is the dwelling place of God. There is no contradiction here, as the soul comprehends both heart and mind, and all inner elements. The purpose of this indwelling is that God may exercise the divine will through the soul as the body's animating component. This is the God-intended destiny of the soul: unity with, and responsiveness to, God. As the dwelling place of God, the soul is transformed. Unlike eastern mysticism, in which the soul is functionally and essentially transformed to the point of annihilation, for Müller and Francke the soul retains its individuality while being transformed in orientation and function.[49] Most people, however, are turned, body and soul, to things earthly, and thus simply miss out on any possibility of personal transformation.

A natural consequence of the soul's divine origin is its time-lessness, that is, as God "neither slumbers nor sleeps," so is the soul ever at God's disposal, quite apart from external circumstances, such as one's sleeping body. The only qualification is that the soul be connected by faith with its source. To underscore this thought, Francke quotes a "holy teacher":

> But our souls are so created/that they can comprehend and hold much in themselves. GOd works and creates according to his nature every hour and moment/ but our soul is so made that every hour and moment it can be created and worked in/if it only holds/and turns to the beginning/from which it sprouts/just as the flowing little brook ever holds to its source/from which it springs.[50]

It is a shibboleth of Pietist thought that the soul is precious because it has been purchased by the blood of Christ.[51] This is, of course, a stylized manner of speaking about the cost of redemption. Completely in Pietist character, Müller is not content to finish his discussion of the soul's worth with this reminder of

---

[49] "What food and drink are to the body/he [Christ] is to the soul/bread of life/and a river of living water. As the outer person has his growth and strength from food and drink; so the inner person from Christ. Yet herein lies the difference: The flesh changes food into itself; but the soul is changed into Christ/indeed not the nature/but according to desires and works/that is/it is filled by him with all of the fullness of God." *GLF*, I, xi, p. 193.

[50] *SFA*, I, pp. 129, 130.

[51] "What could have been more precious to save me from sin than the blood of the great God?" *GE*, #231, p. 281.

the shed blood of Christ. He goes on to create an object lesson for the reader: the only appropriate response to the shedding of Christ's blood for one's soul is the utter rejection of all which would render this purchase null and void. Remembering and meditating upon the cost of redemption cools one's worldly passions.

The history of the human soul is the story of the whole person. The soul began in pristine purity, a natural enough result of its divine origin.

> Now just as GOd's substance and nature is good
> and holy: So also was the substance and nature of the
> soul in the beginning and originally good and holy. As
> there is nothing evil in God's nature: so also was there
> nothing evil in the human soul.[52]

Now, however, the soul is called a wilderness, or desert, "because it is empty of all virtues/bleak and desolate/[and also] full to the top with poisonous sin—worms/snakes/frogs."[53] Because of this, the soul is to be guarded carefully. The unbeliever needs to surrender his or her soul to God in Christ, and the believer must be careful not to let the soul be overtaken by ever-present sin. If the body is to be resurrected, the soul must be given over to Christ, but for the soul to function as God's throne and servant, the body must be sanctified as well.[54] In this sense the Pietists see the person both as a duality and as a unity. Francke exhorts his listeners to look after their souls above all else, since from the inner person springs the power of change and holiness (and thus of salvation).[55] "The salvation of the soul is to be put ahead of the earthly [things]/Luc. 19/20."[56] One is to care for the body in the service of the soul. Müller writes, "The maid over the mistress. Is that not a topsy-turvy thing? So behaves the one who cares more for his body than for his soul."[57] One need only look after one's soul, and God will

---

[52] *Wahres Christenthum*, p. 271; See also Müller, "You were beautiful in Adam and became ugly. God's image was Adam's adornment: as God blew the soul into Adam/into the same soul he poured light/wisdom/righteousness/and his whole likeness." *GLF*, I, xiv, p. 287.

[53] *GLF*, I, xvi, p. 405.

[54] *Wahres Christenthum*, p. 272.

[55] *SFA*, I, p. 158.

[56] *SFA*, II, p. 178, marginal note.

[57] *GE*, #248, p. 303.

provide for the physical needs. This theme, found in Matt. 6, is taken literally and axiomatically by the Pietists. "If you care for your soul, God will care for your body....Without your worry God cares for the body if you look after your soul."[58] As we shall see in our section on the outer person, this does not mean that one should abuse the body or simply ignore it. Rather, one is not to pamper it and fret over it. Negatively, one must avoid preoccupation with things physical and worldly to the neglect of the soul, and must certainly keep from outright sin.[59] Positively, the individual must also care for his or her soul through the ordinary means of salvation; especially the hearing of God's Word,[60] as well as baptism, confession, and the Lord's Supper. Careful inspection of the soul is good, even necessary, since it is the connection between God and the person. It is the soul which, made in the image of God and fallen, yet retains the spark of the *imago Dei*, and which can find its rest and peace in God alone.[61]

THE CONSCIENCE

> Your conscience is the tablet on which you find
> everything written that you have thought, said and done
> in your lifetime. This witness never leaves you, and it
> is as near to you as you yourself are! What no one sees

---

[58] *GE*, #248, p. 303; We have seen that, in Francke's opinion, the Halle *Stiftungen* existed by this concept.

[59] "To the body he gives food and drink, to the soul he gives not one bit of comfort from God's Word, he lets it starve; the body he clothes and adorns, the soul he lets lie naked and bare, indeed unclean and in blood; should the body suffer only a little pain, he seeks advice as if pale death is perched upon the lips of the sick person; if there is a little money to be made in the market, many a person fasts and skips his meal; but if the soul is to humble itself before God, to win his grace, there is no thought of fasting, then none of his sacrifice must be from the belly. Is that right?" *GE*, #246, p. 303.

[60] "Accordingly, you should be a faithful shepherd of your soul/pasture it daily with the Word of GOd/and seek to present it blameless before GOd...." *SFA*, I, p. 835; Müller writes, "A bit of bread easily satisfies the body, if the soul is first fed with God's Word." *GE*, #248, p. 303.

[61] "The reasoning soul has yet a spark of the divine image in it/that it will not be filled and possessed by anything other/than God himself. So, even if it already had everything in heaven and on earth/it could not be satisfied: And this is its nature....Thus it has a constant inclination toward God/and is not at peace/until it is united with God." *GLF*, X, x, pp. 248, 249.

is not hidden from it. Should it sleep for a while, it
will finally wake up, especially when affliction comes:
should it not speak sooner, it will surely speak in the
moment of death.[62]

Conscience is at once the name given to the emotions
springing from the condition of a person's heart and soul and
behavior, and to that part of the person which serves as judge, as
it were, over one's inner and outer life. As an intangible part of
the person, it belongs to his or her inner being, but it serves to
judge and influence the whole person. The Pietists spoke far
more of the conscience as something painful, as that which
gauged and revealed one's sin and wickedness, than as a cheery
element in a person. Müller writes of a troubled conscience:

> Conscience, conscience, oh what are you? A
> mirror, before which no sin can hide; an accuser, which
> will not be silenced; a witness, which one cannot
> refute; a tormenter, which gives rest neither day nor
> night; a fiery brand, which cannot be extinguished; a
> wound, which cannot be healed; a gnawing worm,
> which will not die; a fire that burns forever.[63]

There is a relentless quality about the conscience in that not
only are all of a person's sins recorded by it like a spy who acts
as God's bookkeeper,[64] but these reports are etched deeply into
the account book of the conscience[65] and cannot be removed
except through the daily reading of the ledger (which is possible
only for a believer[66]), accompanied by many tears and much

---

[62] *GE*, #112, pp. 113, 114.

[63] *GE*, #61, p. 59.

[64] "Do not forget another spy/which ever eavesdrops and hears/sees and
knows everything/that we do in secret by ourselves/or speak/do or think/in
private with others; I mean the watchful conscience; What is it other than
God's appointed bookkeeper/over our whole life?...Why then are you not
afraid of your conscience/which is always taking inventory/and one day may
charge you with more/than you would like?" *Gotthold*, p. 266.

[65] "In the end, this judgment [as one sows, so shall one reap] is spoken
to the godless one by his own conscience, in which all his thoughts, words,
and deeds stand written as on a tablet, and this is so deeply inscribed that it
cannot be erased by human power." *HLK*, I, xxiii, p. 556;

[66] "Just as a housefather has a daily ledger in which he records the day's
business; so the godly person his conscience. The fleshly person has it, too,
but for him it remains a sealed book. The man of God reaches daily into his

repentance.[67] The conscience not only notes one's open, or coarse, sins, it also causes one to feel shame over his or her wicked heart.

> Our conscience so convinces us, that if we should bring the thoughts of our hearts to light, and put them before everyone's eyes, we would be ashamed, and wither for shame.[68]

The conscience also plumbs the religious depths of a person, revealing his or her inclinations and condition in every part of his or her life.[69] It permits no excuses.

> Before this witness there is no excuse. Did you do it unwittingly? Ah, your conscience convinces you that you knew full well. Did you not mean ill? The truthful witness in you convicts you that you testify falsely about yourself.[70]

So that the sinner may be tormented into repentance, and that the believer may be kept from backsliding, the conscience raises the following question,

> Are your things in order? How goes it with the physical/and with the spiritual? How has one given an accounting with dear God? What will GOd say/if today he demands an accounting/and it is not correct?[71]

---

conscience [and] opens the book, should he find that he has not intended this or that honestly, as he rightly should have, he recognizes the misdeed...." *HLK*, I, xvii, p. 429.

[67] *HLK*, I, xxiii, p. 557.

[68] *HLK*, I, xvi, p. 385.

[69] "I now take your own conscience as help. For this is a rapid witness, and will immediately, as I say this, show each one in what sort of condition his soul is; whether he serves the living GOd or, instead, sin and the world; whether he walks in the darkness or in the light; whether he has begun to fear GOd and his Word or has turned from the the true fear of GOd, and loves the lust of the eyes and of the flesh and arrogant ways; whether he has a true trust in GOD or senses and feels in his own heart, when distress breaks in, that the trust he thought he had in GOD is in truth not grounded in him at all. In all of it I call upon each of your consciences." *SFP*, p. 33.

[70] *GE*, #112, p. 114.

[71] *SFA*, II, p. 345.

Scriver points out how very important the nagging of the conscience is:

> If my conscience would not say/what is wrong/
> how could I live so confidently? If the conscience could
> not gnaw and bite/how little regard I would give sin?[72]

Part of the conscience's power comes from its proleptic participation in the individual's last judgment. Every present verdict rendered by the conscience is simultaneously the verdict given at the future divine judgment.

> Now, from the conviction of your conscience and
> through the penetrating power of the Spirit of GOd,
> how many of you must recognize yourselves as such
> who until now still lived in fleshly [self-] confidence,
> and were never truly awakened from the sleep of sin and
> became sober: In this hour I hold you all, however
> many of you there may be, before the future judgment
> of GOd.[73]

This connection with the final judgment is by no means an intellectual exercise; a bad conscience is an all-enveloping experience, a true "foretaste of hell" and "an open hell" in which one is "sucked dry" as he or she is tortured with Satan on one side and the Law on the other.[74] The devil and a bad conscience are alike in that each has all one's sins recorded.[75] The sinner's conscience seems to have a life of its own, a life which seems to be immortal. Not only does it confess freely on judgment day to all the sins catalogued and brought forth by God,[76] but it goes on

---

[72] *Gotthold*, p. 367.

[73] *SFP*, p. 34.

[74] "Imagine a poor sinner/as he stands before the judgment of God. Inwardly his own conscience is testifying about him/and his thoughts accuse one another: for the conscience is a seat of dead works/in which they turn into gnawing worms. This pain is like no other: it is a foretaste of hell/ stretches the person on the devil's rack/sucks him dry/that he withers like grass/and forgets to eat his bread/as his days vanish like smoke/and his bones burn like fire...thus, the bad conscience is like an open hell/troubles and afflicts even in the midst of peace. From without, Satan stands to the right of the poor sinner/the law to his left. Here the misery really gets going." *GLF*, I, xvi, pp. 394, 395.

[75] *GLF*, I, xvi, p. 395.

[76] *SFA*, I, pp. 1032, 1033.

in hell to torment the damned person for his or her failure to love his or her neighbor, for despising the Word of God, etc. "Indeed, they will not have the least rest even in hell/the conscience will torment them most horribly..."[77] Should a person die as a Christian, the gnawing conscience dies with him or her; if he or she dies as an unbeliever, they live on together forever in hell.[78] Thus it behooves a person to be sure that his or her conscience does not sleep, for a conscience which is lulled by worldly habits into sleeping through today's sins will awaken on judgment day with terrible consequences.[79]

The person has two choices in the face of a bad conscience: one can either try to run from or, at best, ignore it, or one can examine it and purify it by pouring it out before God. The person who attempts to avoid or ease his or her troubled conscience through worldly pursuits is compared to a man sick with anxiety: he tosses and turns in his bed, and rolls about seeking a more comfortable position, but how can inner turmoil be calmed by outward activity? Or such a person is like a stag which is shot, and dashes about wildly, yet in spite of his exertions the bullet remains in his flesh. "So experience often testifies/that the wounded conscience may dash about from one place to the other/and yet always keep the dangerous wound."[80] Even if a person is able to quiet his or her conscience, it will not remain so for long.[81]

---

[77] *SFA*, II, p. 57.

[78] "The aroused conscience gives us a foretaste of the torment of hell/ that we may be all the more diligently concerned/to escape it. Better/that the worm of the conscience gnaw at us here/where it must die/when we die/than that it gnaw at us there/where it will never die/because we will never die." *Gotthold*, pp. 367, 368.

[79] "For it may be that some among you have a *conscientiam dormientem*, a sleeping conscience, and do not wish to be awakened yet by my present call from this, your slumber. Therefore I take the living GOD himself as my helper, who is mighty to awaken all your hearts from such a sleep of self-assuredness, and to illumine your eyes with the light of life." *SFP*, p. 34.

[80] *Gotthold*, pp. 188, 189.

[81] "And whether you want to cover over the accusations of your heart/ under the desires of the world or under bad company/and not think of them/it reawakens nonetheless/the bad conscience always comes/like a barking dog/ and howls again/and gnaws at you/like a gnawing worm." *SFA*, II, p. 23.

The wiser choice, then, is to follow the example of the mystics, and examine oneself daily.

> Tauler says in one place: For myself, I am not afraid to say, whoever does not turn to the ground of his soul and his conscience with all his strength at least once a day does not yet live as a pious Christian should live...Heart, I make a covenant with you this day: I will never go to bed unless I have considered how you are looking.[82]

If the conscience is not examined and cleansed each day, it will become filthy and accustomed to sin.[83] The integrity of the inner life is shown by Müller's advice concerning how to stay beyond reproach: "If you would remain blameless until the judgment day, pour out your heart before God every day in the daily examination of your conscience."[84]

There are certain rewards for a good conscience even in this life, for the earnest Christian can cast off the slander of the devil, and find comfort and joy because of his or her clear conscience. "Phooey on the poor devil who must arm himself with lies!....My joy's only comfort and rock stands fast, that I have an innocent and peaceful conscience."[85] This anthropocentric and subjective foundation of one's comfort and joy did not go unnoticed among the opponents of Pietism. Nonetheless, the light of heaven shines through a pure heart, and a good conscience brings the sweetest joy.[86] As the bad conscience receives no small amount of its threat and power through its connection with judgment day and hell, so the clear conscience grants proleptic participation in paradise.

> The joy of the conscience is a paradise of the soul. If the conscience is peaceful, one senses the presence of the Holy Spirit and of divine comfort.[87]

---

[82] *GE*, #22, p. 23.

[83] "A careful mother wipes the dust from her furniture often, otherwise it will cover it; so a careful Christian cleanses his conscience daily, otherwise sin continues to hang on it, and becomes a habit." *HLK*, I, x, p. 167.

[84] HLK, I, xxii, p. 542.

[85] *GE*, #181, pp. 210, 211.

[86] *HLK*, I, xiii, p. 256.

[87] *HLK*, I, xiii, p. 256.

THE MIND AND REASON

The mind is another component of the inner person, and plays a major role in one's earthly pilgrimage. It is usually referred to in connection with the heart and soul, and then generally with evil desires for honor in the world, money and temporal pleasures. We have seen in Francke's case how he hoped to make his agile mind his vehicle to worldly esteem and advancement. The mind is referred to as mind *per se*, and in the categories of "thoughts," "knowledge," "understanding," and "reason." Thoughts are determined by the condition of a person's heart, and the capacity of the mind to contemplate the things of God is enhanced or diminished to the degree to which his or her mind is preoccupied with heavenly or carnal things.

We find that the mind is referred to as a sort of inclination. It is in this sense that the individual is exhorted to "put on the mind of Christ," for having the mind of Christ changes one's orientation from constant longing for things worldly to seeking the glory of God and the good of one's neighbor.[88] The unconverted mind, like the unconverted heart, busies itself solely with temporal things.[89] Francke says,

> this is the goal of the coming of his Son in the flesh/that he may give us *a new mind*/a completely different mind/than we have by nature/that is, the *spiritual mind*/which he himself/the Son of GOd shares with us through his Spirit...[90]

Emphasizing in a sermon that not only teachers and preachers, but all Christians, should have the mind of Christ, Francke stresses the need to be like Christ in every way.[91] In order to

---

[88] "It is precisely the mind of CHrist which we must put on/that we may not desire to be in the world for our honor/comfort and profit's sake; but rather that our whole mind/our whole heart/our hopes and dreams be to serve our neighbor/and thus to live in this world to glorify our heavenly Father. Now, flesh and blood cannot reveal this to us/nor give us power for it; but we must receive this from GOD our heavenly Father through the Holy Spirit." *SFA*, I, p. 466; By contrast, the person with the mind of a pagan seeks to gain advantages over his or her neighbors, and get their possessions. *SFA*, II, p. 783. See also SFA, II, p. 594.

[89] *SFA*, I, pp. 826, 827; *SFA*, I, p. 445.

[90] *SFA*, II, p. 593.

[91] *SFA*, II, p. 597.

have the mind of Christ, one must submit to Christ and be born again. As with all other areas of life, God's demand on the mind is total. The power of God grasps "the person's whole mind," and removes it, giving him or her a different, "spiritual" mind.[92]

While little is said about the mind *per se*, much is made of one's thought, since thinking is an inescapable part of human life.[93] Müller points out that a person's thoughts seem to come in all sorts of ways and have a great influence on one's inner life. This is especially true of wicked thoughts, some of which one gathers up on purpose, some of which seem to just drop in, as it were, and need to be guarded against, and some of which are deliberately put into the heart by the devil.[94] Some thoughts are wicked, not because of their inherent evil, but because they are untimely or, as Scriver says of them, "disorderly." There are otherwise perfectly good thoughts which simply come at the wrong time, such as a sermon idea to a preacher in the midst of prayer, or the needs of home to a householder at worship.[95] Sometimes a person is plagued by too many thoughts or by thoughts which wander.

> Wavering/useless or fickle thoughts drag you about from one corner to the other/so put most of your thoughts in order/that you may not be tormented by your thoughts. A servant does not squander his LOrd's gifts in his presence/provided he has the least fear of him/and [yet] you would employ the powers of this mind on vain, empty things. Much good is swallowed up, as it were, by empty thoughts/and extinguished/like a fire is extinguished by water.[96]

Not surprisingly, the old Adam clings to the mind and causes the believer to think, and be plagued by, evil thoughts.[97] Scriver

---

[92] *SFA*, II, p. 598.

[93] "Gotthold found one of his family sitting in deep thought/and asked him: What was he meditating/thinking so about? He answered: Nothing. Gotthold went on; It is impossible/that a person could think nothing." *Gotthold*, p. 833.

[94] *GLF*, I, xii, pp. 283, 289.

[95] *Gotthold*, pp. 60, 61.

[96] *LR*, p. 97.

[97] But we must not take it to mean/that in a born-again Christian/of whom we say/that he loves GOd with his whole heart/now no thoughts /no desires/no outward works are any longer against GOd: rather...even after

points out that it would be useless for him to proscribe thinking
wicked thoughts, since this would be impossible. He exhorts his
readers to be careful, however, that they do not harbor or cling to
these thoughts.[98] This theme is taken up by Francke and Müller
as well. Müller writes,

> Whoever burdens himself with sinful thoughts/
> piles wood on the fire/and feeds the snake/which he has
> in his breast. With people it goes: Thoughts are free:
> but with God it goes: *What are you thinking that is so*
> *wicked in your heart?* And as Paul says to the Hebrews
> in the 4. chap. *God judges one's thoughts.* So, whoever
> entertains for long thoughts of money and the
> world/entertains the accursed idol...[99]

Thus we see that a person's thoughts, and how he or she
handles them, are of great importance, because "the heart is as
the thoughts are..."[100] They are, "the soul's wings/with which
they either soar to heaven/or into hell..."[101] Scriver goes on to
stress that, as we have seen, the first step to actual sin is to have
wicked thoughts, and that these wicked thoughts constitute the
real connection between original and actual sin. He, too, ascribes
some wicked thoughts to the inspiration of Satan.[102] Francke

---

rebirth we have original sin in us/*which always clings to us*/Hebr. XII. v. 1.
Because the old man is still in us/... so it is that even one/who truly has
love for GOd and neighbor/is tempted by sinful thoughts..." *SFA*, II, p. 639.

[98] *Gotthold*, p. 885.

[99] *GLF*, I, xvi, p.398; Francke also warns against holding on to: "Indeed,
you will hold on to no thoughts/which you could not speak out without fear/
for you may hide them from others/but not from GOd/for he understands
your thoughts from afar/therefore hate and turn away from all indecent
thoughts/as soon as you become aware of them/and even see them at a
distance/as long as you remain and tarry in such thoughts/GOd must lament
that you have departed from him and left him alone." *LR*, pp, 38,39; And,
using very similar language, "You must also test your thoughts/say not:
Thoughts are free/who can tax one's thoughts. A child can stamp out a spark
easier/than a hundred men can put out a great fire. Lusts arise from thoughts/
and these also grow through one's thoughts/*but lust/when it has conceived/
bears sin/but when it has finished/bears death.* Jac. I. 15. So, test your
thoughts/or your soul is in eternal danger." *LR*, pp. 59, 60.

[100] *Gotthold*, p. 884.

[101] *Gotthold*, p. 884.

[102] *Gotthold*, p. 886.

regrets that people tend to ignore as best they can any good thoughts which may spur them to holier lives.

> No doubt, now and then a good thought comes to you/which accuses you and says; *You should take your Christianity more seriously/you should not do this and that*; but you let it go by immediately/and let it take no root in your hearts/that it may also gain strength...[103]

One must learn rather to let go of wicked thoughts, and to hold fast to the edifying ones.

Thoughts of God should fill the heart and mind at all times, if possible. Francke writes that if one's vocation requires sufficient concentration that one cannot keep God in mind, one must think about God again at the first opportunity.[104] One is to work at keeping God in his or her thoughts. While allowing for the apparently spontaneous or devil-inspired appearance of thoughts in the mind, the Pietists nonetheless viewed the mind as subject to a person's volition. This makes comprehensible Francke's concern to break the person's will, as we will read later, and his exhortations to wrestle the mind into submission so that it, like the will, may be completely surrendered to God.

Another dimension of the mind is reason. Contrary to some popular opinion, even among the well-educated, the Pietists did not criticize reason without qualification. Reason has its proper place in the scheme of things. While it cannot bring about the vital change of heart, one should nonetheless "Let reason have its work in the outward life, where it belongs, and where it is useful."[105] The great stress placed on education by Pietist pedagogues indicates quite a high regard for the intellect. The Pietists did not despise reason *per se*.[106] Francke even calls *Wissenschaft* a gift of God, whereas ignorance works to Satan's advantage.[107] Problems arise only, and especially, where reason

---

[103] *SFA*, II, p. 773.
[104] *LR*, pp. 103, 104.
[105] *SFA*, p. 743.
[106] *LP*, V, p. 292.
[107] "So scholarship [*Wissenschaft*] is also a gift of GOd. For this is no gift, that one be ignorant; rather to have scholarship and use it rightly is a precious gift of GOd; and the devil has a dreadful contrivance, that he keeps people in ignorance." *LP*, VII, p. 376.

attempts more than that of which it is capable.[108] Indeed, God deals with people as "reasoning creatures." God desires

> to interact with us, not as lifeless clods or stones, but as with reasoning creatures who should find themselves in the order which he has prescribed for them in his Holy Word.[109]

In the spiritual arena, however, reason and its dangerous tendency to subordinate all else to its judgment must be abandoned because, for one thing, it simply cannot get the job done. True Christianity, that is, saving faith and holiness, is knowledge, revelation *and* action. Reason can only take one so far, then falls short.[110] For another, it can actually disrupt the salvific involvement of the Holy Spirit in a person's life. Knowledge of one's abominable condition is necessary if one is to be saved, as is the knowledge of the way to salvation. One reason Christ came was that he might be a light which illumined the Gentiles (Luke 2:32). Francke explains this verse as follows:

> Through the first, where he is described to us as light to illumine the Gentiles, we first, accordingly, reject all natural power, wisdom and understanding as in no way capable and adequate, that through them we may learn to know and understand our deep need and

---

[108] See E. Peschke, "August Hermann Francke und die Bibel", in *Pietismus und Bibel*, hrsg. von Kurt Aland, (Witten, 1970), pp. 579ff; While this article deals primarily with Francke's understanding of Scripture, the Pietist view of the proper role and limitations of human reason is made clear. We must remember, too, that Francke had Christian Wolff expelled from the faculty at Halle for teaching that unaided human reason could attain to moral truth. In this, Wolff had claimed for reason territory which, in Pietist thought, belonged solely to the divinely illumined mind. See also F. deBoor, "Erfahrung gegen Vernunft", in *Der Pietismus in Gestalt und Wirkungen*, hrsg. von H. Bornkamm, u. a., (Bielefeld, 1975), pp. 120–138.

[109] *EP*, p. 891.

[110] "So must one here below be converted, become like a child, yea, abandon all the old maxims from school and university, if one would be a true servant of JEsus Christ. One must consider the mystery of the cross the right wisdom, seek the true wisdom of the ancients, follow in the footsteps of the faith of Abraham, yea in the footsteps of JEsus Christ and his holy Apostles, willingly bear Christ's disgrace, take his yoke upon oneself, and follow after him, or one remains only standing before the door and does not see what are the right matters in the study of theology." *LP*, V, p. 269.

corruption, and how we may be helped out of them. For no human wisdom teaches us what sin is, and how we may be free of sin and be reconciled with GOd, that we attain to peace with him again and become his children and heirs. This we must learn to understand by the illumination of Christ and his Spirit.[111]

As we have seen, reason has its proper place in the outer world. In the inner, however, it must surrender itself to Christ, and be judged as foolishness.[112] After all, "You boast of your great scholarship. The devil knows more than you, and yet must burn forever in hell."[113] Another problem with reason is that it, unlike the Word of God, is not reliable in the long run. It is simply too frail and provisional to be trusted.[114] And it is especially unhelpful, even harmful, in the midst of affliction since, unlike the believing heart and mind which trust in the promises of God, reason, limited by its narrow perception, can see no escape or rescue, and thus causes one to simply give up and fall into deadly despair.[115]

Reason is not the only good thing about the mind which can become bad. Unless it is used rightly, knowledge, too, can become spiritually fatal for a person. Both Francke and Müller quote I Cor. 8: 1, "Knowledge puffs up," as a warning against over-valuing the mind and the accumulation of data.[116] Here we encounter a chapter from Francke's personal history. His fear that students tend to pursue biblical studies for the "wrong reasons" reflects both the Pietist view of theological studies and his own experience as a student.[117] Francke and Müller are also

---

[111] *SFP*, pp. 386, 387.

[112] "All human reason, understanding, wisdom and power must prostrate itself before CHrist and be judged by him as foolishness and darkness." *SFP*, p. 387.

[113] *GE*, #123, p. 130.

[114] "Ah, why are you proud of yourself on account of your scholarship? A minor illness can weaken your head, break your mind, ruin your memory." *GE*, #123, p. 130.

[115] *SFA*, II, p. 834.

[116] *SFA*, II, p. 796; *GE*, #123, p. 130.

[117] "Or if one takes up Holy Scripture only to the end/that one be well-educated in Scripture [like a scribe]/and achieve much knowledge/one tends to conceal beneath it self-love/ambition/and all manner of other pharisaical vices. And today this is the goal of many scholars/*which then would be masters of Scripture/and know not what they say/nor what they*

one in warning against "Much knowledge, little conscience. [Viel Wissens, wenig Gewissens.]"[118] This is yet another arena in which the Pietists draw directly from the mystics, albeit with modifications. Natural human reason is not only incapable of comprehending the deepest things of life, and of attaining to the truth, especially the Word of God, but it is actually a hindrance.[119] Human reason and "high science" (to which Francke refers as a "scientia speculativa"[120]) are too skeptical and too full of speculation and raw, unapplied information to accept the clear and simple message of Scripture. "Here lies the guilt/that the eyes of their understanding were not simple."[121] Müller writes, "No knowledge is the highest knowledge,"[122] for the more one fills his or her head with facts, figures, etc., the less one knows of oneself and the source of one's, and all, being. Thus the person must empty him- or herself of this extraneous material in order to increase his or her consciousness of the inner, essential being. In the Pietists, as in the mystics, this emptying is intended to facilitate greater unity with God. Information *per se* is not bad.

---

affirm/1. Tim. 7. Yea, this is the perverse manner of humanity throughout/that in Holy Scripture it busies itself more with useless questions/or great mysteries/than with first laying the right foundation in repentance and faith." *WWD*, II, p. 2.

[118] "Of what use is much knowledge, when there is no conscience with it." *GE*, #123, p. 129; Francke exhorts theology students, "Should it be/that one or the other recognizes the need/to take H. Scripture ahead of all other books/it still tends to happen even at best/that one seeks knowledge/but not a good conscience. And what wonder? There are indeed theologians who have no reservations/about writing openly in the world/that they were not appointed/to make students pious/but rather only to make them well-educated. Now if even the teachers do not have the goal/to make things better through their teaching/how shall their hearers turn their souls to such ends?" *Timotheus*, pp. 29, 30.

[119] The unregenerate mind simply cannot grasp spiritual truth. It must be illumined by God: "Ad ea enim, qvae sunt Spiritus Dei, plane non pertingit homo naturalis, &, ut Christus ait, Spiritum veritatis mundus non potest accipere. Spiritualia affirmante Paulo, non nisi spiritualiter dijudicari possunt. e.g. Si vel maxime homo naturalis fusissime disserat de sensu literali praecepti qvinti, atque ea dicat, qvae in se verissima sunt, & ab intentione spiritualiter ea, qvae dicit." *Manuductio*, pp. 68f.

[120] "What does one do otherwise/than that one makes theology into a Scientia speculativa?" *Timotheus*, p. 30.

[121] *SFA*, I, p. 484.

[122] *GE*, #123, p. 130.

Rather, information which cannot (or will not) be applied to the Christian life—inner or outer—is a waste, and thus is wicked.

For the Pietists, the unifying experience of being born again and subsequent experiences of divine-human connectedness are predicated upon, and are integral to, faith in Jesus Christ alone. The Christ of experience and knowledge is the Christ of Scripture. Despite its straightforwardness and simplicity, Holy Scripture is incomprehensible to the unillumined mind clogged with meaningless data, intent upon imposing its own interpretation upon God's Word, and controlled by worldly ways of thinking. Just to desire to know the crucified Christ and him alone is sufficient, "even though I were to know nothing else."[123] To know Christ is to know that nothing good exists except by the grace of God, and nothing of eternal significance is accessible to the heart and mind except *via* divine illumination. Thus Scripture must be approached with all the tools of good scholarship, but also and primarily in faith, and with humility, relying upon God for wisdom and understanding. Otherwise, the living kernel of Scripture, Jesus Christ, remains a perceived object, not a living, experienced personal Savior.[124] Francke prescribes prayer before, during and after reading Scripture.[125] This keeps God foremost, and the human mind second. Prayer is necessary, for blind reason, out of its element, actually argues with the ways and the Word of God. "Blind reason always has some objection as long as it is not restrained by God's power."[126]

Finally, reliance on one's own reason is dangerous because it first leads itself into error, then can endanger the faith and salvation of others.

> Yea, many a person often thinks he may understand all mysteries, and can discern the hidden ways of the dear God, and walk therein; when he in fact has nothing in the ground of [his] heart but only a phantasm, possesses a shadow—and blinding work, and an outward image that he himself has made.

---

[123] *GE*, #123, p. 130.

[124] "The view that the faithful grasp the inner spiritual kernel [while] the unfaithful, on the other hand, grasp only the outer sensual husk, belongs to the basic religious perception of spiritualistic thinkers." E. Peschke, "AHF und die Bibel", p. 70.

[125] *EU*, Section 3ff.

[126] *LP*, VI, pp. 5, 6.

Now should this also be the case among many of us, it would indeed be the most shameful deception of all. Such people are also the most fit to do the greatest harm of all, and to cause the most confusion. For the greater the appearance; the greater the deception of others will be.[127]

The smarter the person, the greater the danger of falling into this deception of self and others. Scriver quotes Luther (below), then goes on to emphasize the need for careful supervision of clever souls. Note that Luther is not simply condemning human reason, nor is he describing the dangers of *arrogant* reason. Rather, he is warning of the special dangers inherent in the "very clever reason."

Believe me/*among all the dangers on earth there is no more dangerous thing than a very clever reason/ particularly when it siezes upon spiritual things/that concern the soul and God.*[a] And where a dull person needs a master/to instruct his simplicity/a clever one needs ten/to keep his reason in check/so that it does not/like a high-spirited horse/throw him.[a] Luther. Tom. 1 Jenens. fol. 92.[128]

Thus we see that the mind is a crucial element of the person. Unlike the ungodly and those seduced by mere human reason, the believer knows that wisdom and insight and good thoughts are gracious gifts from above.[129] One's ultimate destiny is determined by his or her resistance or surrender of heart, mind and soul to God. Best of all is a disciplined, sanctified mind.

---

[127] *LP*, VI, p. 132.

[128] *Gotthold*, p. 46.

[129] "They know that of themselves they can have no good thoughts; and if they have such, they praise God for them as for a gift of grace, because, as corrupt creatures, nothing good could come from them, rather everything must be put in them solely by the grace and gift of God." *SFP*, p. 421.

CHAPTER 5

WILL

While it can be said that the heart is the chief target of almost all Pietist preaching and teaching because the inner person influences the outer person's behavior, and ultimately determines where one spends eternity, a person's will reveals who he or she is, on whose side he or she struggles in the cosmic battle for human souls, and to whom he or she gives allegiance, as the will encompasses one's whole being: "The person's will is the whole person, wherever you surrender your will, there you have surrendered yourself completely."[1] As we shall see, the will seems to consist primarily of desires, tendencies, and obedience and/or resistance to those desires and tendencies. Godly obedience occurs inwardly in submission or *Gelassenheit*, and outwardly through works which conform to God's will and to the holy desires which the reconstituted heart experiences. Wicked or ungodly obedience follows the temptations and suggestions of Satan and the world and the evil desires of the unregenerate heart.

The will is the tool which, if one is born again and so desires, one can use to resist Satan and surrender to God. Indeed, a person's sanctified will can reduce the devil to a wheedler who is incapable of even ruffling a hair on one's head.[2] The will receives its impulses from the heart, is inextricably bound up with the heart, and must, like every part of the person, be made new through the radical surgery of faith and divine regeneration and growth in holiness. Here again we must differentiate between will and the heart, mind and soul in order to examine it.

As with every element of the person, the will begins corrupt, this corruption being manifested in the "*Eigenwille*" [self-will] which

> loves and seeks partly what brings it glory, partly
> what is useful to it, partly what titillates it, thus we
> compare it with a mother bearing three deformed

---

[1] *HLK*, II, ii, p. 645.

[2] "Your will is greater than all the power of Satan, so the devil must stand next to you as a wheedler and beg you to sin. He cannot ruffle a hair on your head if he does not have your will." *HLK*, II, ii, p. 645.

children in her arms,called self-glory, self-profit and
self-desire, or lust.[3]

Along with disbelief, an evil heart, and the rest of the corrupt
human nature, the wicked will is counted as the root of all evil,
and even as a hindrance to the coming of the Kingdom of God. It
binds itself with the evil of the devil and the world against God
and God's kingdom.[4] Disunity between persons as well as
between humanity and God is the result of the stubborn, selfish
will which gives way to no one else, and yet is itself arrogant,
capricious and unstable. The vices of arrogance, avarice, ambition and lust are but other names for specific manifestations of
the person's self-centered willfulness.[5] As a heart which is not
contrite is one's worst enemy, so also does a corrupt will lead to
death and damnation. "In your kingdom I am nothing, nor of any
use in heaven, if I do not have your will."[6] That is, so long as
one remains corrupted in his or her will, there is no hope of
salvation. The unregenerate will is the exact opposite of the will
which is submissive to God, "For whoever has his own will is
surely against God's will. God's will and [our] self-will are
against each other like fire and water..."[7] It leads to death.

> By nature a person loves what he wants, this is
> called self-will. As a will surrendered to God is the seed
> of all virtue, yea a person's heaven, so the self-will is
> the fountain of all sin, a person's poison, demise,
> corruption, hell. Those Israelites wanted to eat meat in
> the wilderness, their will was done, and they devoured

[3] *HLK*, II, ii, p. 645.

[4] "Ah! here [God's will] reminds us how, through self-will, as the root
of all evil, GOd is dishonored, his name profaned, and the coming of his
kingdom hindered, and how in this one binds one's own will with the evil
will of the devil and the world against GOD and his kingdom." *CP*, p. 463;
Also, "Nothing is more dear than self-will, which one can abandon only with
great difficulty, and is yet the greatest of all evils, yea, the root of all evil in
us." *GE*, #155, p. 169.

[5] "Whence comes disunity? That everything must go according to your
will, and you will give way to no one. Whence comes restlessness of the
soul? That you want this today, that tomorrow, something else the day after
tomorrow. If your will seeks what is expensive, pompous, it is arrogance; if
it cannot be satisfied, it is greed; if it wishes to be seen, it is ambition; if it
wants to live luxuriously and well, it is sensuality." *HLK*, II, ii, p. 645.

[6] *CP*, p. 464.

[7] *GE*, #155, pp. 169, 170.

death. You learn here that one's will is his death. This
means this will conceives sin, and sin gives birth to
death.[8]

In this light, it is simply madness to refuse to submit to God,
submission being only appropriate in any case. One gladly,
however, lets his or her own will reign in his or her life, even
though one knows it is leading him or her to hell.[9]

Breaking the corrupt natural will and inclining it to godly
submission, pious desires and holy behavior was of such
paramount significance that Francke instituted procedures in the
education of children specifically intended to accomplish these
goals. From the very beginning, parents and teachers, who must
be born-again believers, must participate in the child's education.[10] Education and upbringing must be concerned with two
things: understanding and will, the will being (albeit only
slightly) the more important of the two. While emphasizing the
need to "break" the child's corrupt and stubborn will, Francke
stresses as well that the will must not be forced to submit to God.

True care of the inner being is a matter of will and
understanding. There is nothing good to be hoped for
where one is concerned with only one of the two. In
most cases it is important that the natural self-will be
broken. Thus this is most to be observed. Whoever
teaches youth, that they might be more educated sees to
the care of the mind, which is good but is not sufficient. For he forgets the best, namely, to bring the will
to obedience, and for this reason will discover in the
end that he has worked without true fruit. On the other

---

[8] *HLK*, II, ii, p. 645.

[9] "It is fitting/that you submit yourself to the divine rule in deepest
humility with a completely submissive heart....You would gladly be ruled
according to your own will/even though you know/that shame/harm/death
and hell hang on your self-will." *GLF*, I, v, p. 441.

[10] "Yet it is not to be denied that all the good rules which the author
gives will be of no use if the parents do not first attend to their own true
conversion and improvement before they undertake the improvement of
something in the teaching of their children, or if such people as are thoroughly converted to God are not appointed to the task of teaching. The work
of education is beyond all the powers of the natural person. It must be guided
by the Spirit of God, where he dwells and reigns in the heart, there alone will
the proper foundation be laid." *PS*, p. 93.

hand, the mind must grasp wholesome doctrine if the
will is to follow without coercion.[11]

To this end, both parents and teachers alike must live exemplary
lives and break the child's will, not through bitter words or harsh
treatment (as the word "break" would seem to signify), but
through wise and conscientious guidance. In the home, for
example, parents are warned against many of the usual customs
of the day: threatening to give a child's food to the family pet will
only make the child envious and grudging; praising a child for
his or her lovely clothes can only impart a spirit of arrogance,
and causes the child to despise old clothes and constantly want
new ones; instructing a child to hit or kick something if he or she
falls only teaches the child to soothe him- or herself through
vengefulness; giving a piggy bank to a child along with exhortations to not spend any money shows the child how to hide greed
under the cloak of thrift, under which all greed is hidden. The
child is also endangered spiritually by parents who overestimate
the value of money, and who model behavior which is meant to
bring glory to themselves.[12]

Francke emphasizes as well that three virtues in particular are
to be "implanted" in children as early in life as possible: "love of
truth, obedience, and diligence." In this way, children will be led
early on to a "thorough and steadfast goodness." Also to this
end, children must be taught to avoid with equal earnestness the
opposite vices, namely "lying, self-will, and idleness."[13]

Obedience is the key or the behavior which conquers the
person's natural, corrupt will.

---

[11] *PS*, p. 99; Also, "The care of the inner being is to be oriented to
mind and will alike, but mainly to the will." *PS*, p. 99, marginal note; This
way of thinking applies to knowledge in general. "In general one looks/
when speaking thereof [truth]/only to that/which is in the human mind: but
Scripture leads us further/and names the real $\dot{\alpha}\lambda\nu\dot{\eta}\theta\epsilon\iota\alpha\nu$ or truth/which is
nothing other/than the righteous being in CHrist/for which an illumined
mind as well as a sanctified *will* is required in a person." *SFA*, I, p. 599.

[12] Sattler, *God's Glory*, p. 53, from *PS*, pp. 112, 113.

[13] "Next is to be noticed that there are in particular three virtues which
one must seek to implant in children who are yet at such a tender age, that
they might otherwise be led into a thorough and steadfast blessedness,
namely: love of truth, obedience and diligence. Then that the opposite vices
are to be avoided with just as great an earnestness, namely, lying, self-will
and idleness." *PS*, p. 113.

> Through earnest obedience, the domination of
> self-will and self-assertion can be put down and the
> heart can be made more and more lowly and humble,
> and instructed in sincere moderation and kindliness.[14]

It is the inculcation of a sense of obedience, or at the very least
the desire to be obedient, which will ultimately save the child
from damnation through increasing the ease with which his or
her self-will may at last be broken and surrendered to God. The
keys to this are discipline, consistency (especially between
parents and teachers), egalitarianism, avoidance of a system of
rewards for good deeds, and education concerning the difference
between mere politeness and true godly obedience and submission.[15] Thus the object of the education of children is not only
the acquisition of knowledge and wisdom, but is also the breaking of the sinful, selfish will of the child, and the creation in the
youngster of an inclination to true godliness. This is to be done
through lectures, books, personal example, discipline, corporal
punishment (as a last resort), careful observation and, of greatest
importance, love and kindness.[16] This emphasis on the

---

[14] *PS*, pp. 113, 114.

[15] "Obedience is the actual virtue which is commended to children in
Holy Scripture with extra promise. To this is necessary, however *a*) that one
does not permit the children to do this and that according to their own
pleasure and opinion, but rather makes them first get the advice of their
parents and overseers....then later it requires less effort to break their wills in
important things. *β*) That one make them be obedient not only in the hour
when they are taught and afterward let them do as they like again...*γ*) That
one not treat the children as aristocrats or great lords,as, to the contrary, one
is not to permit the servants to act other than modestly toward the children.
On both sides it is harmful if the middle way is not taken....*δ*) That when
they are to behave, one not use flattery and promises to entice and lure them
to do so, e.g. Do this and I will give you some sugar.... *ε*) That one teach
them what a great difference there is between outward obedience (as to please
others) and true obedience of the heart (as before God)." *PS*, pp. 115, 116.

[16] The rather painful- and ominous-sounding phrase, "to break the
will", does not necessarily indicate the need for harsh measures. "In spite of
Francke's apparently narrow approach to the child's education and upbringing
in terms of avoiding certain books, dancing, some theater, and so on, he
strongly emphasizes the love and joy of the Christian life that is necessary in
the Christian educational process.

In his 'Short and Simple Instruction' Francke tells us that one
should seek to bring Christianity to the child with joy and love. Otherwise
the child might adopt the appearance of pious ways, but will never fix the

subjugation of the human will, and one's subsequent obedience as basic to the Christian life is consistent with the Pietist

---

true power in his or her heart if forced. The child should not be led to consider Christianity a game, but should be made to see that one can be quite earnest about a matter yet bear it with joy and love. To facilitate this it is profitable:

> 1) That one not give the children books which are quite too long, but rather as short as possible, for they do not lose the joy as easily when they soon come to an end and receive something new. 2) That one teach them Christian doctrine in the German language and have them learn it from German books, for otherwise they easily receive an unpleasantness in Christianity and pay attention not to the doctrine [but rather] to being able to repeat the words, albeit with-out understanding. 3) That one may not overload them too much. A teacher must herein be like a wise sower which does not sow one seed upon the other and suffocate the lower with the upper. ...Some think their children and pupils are well-versed in Christianity if they can read, learn, and repeat much by rote, yet...not show the least fruit. 4) That the teacher should not be sullen, angry, vexatious, and impatient with the children in instruction and other teaching, but rather should be loving and kind. In summary, should faith and love and thus the true being which is in Jesus be awakened in such tender hearts, they must surely be introduced and led on through the sweetness of the Gospel and not the bitterness of the law.[a]

Corporal punishment, however, is acceptable under certain circumstances, if necessary, as long as the child is made aware that it is a means of last resort. And should either parent or teacher paddle a child for a particular offence both should know of it so that the child knows he will receive no further punishment from the other. Punishment must fit the offence, the parent or teacher must be must be careful not to overdo it. Francke warns that the child's health may be endangered if one, 'for example, gives a dose of the rod or otherwise strikes them on the head or in the face.' Shortly after punishment takes place the teacher must see to it that reconciliation occurs so that there are no lingering hard feelings and the child's spirit does not sink. The teacher must also be sensitive to the fact that children have different personalities and temperaments. Thus some may benefit from corporal punishment or a sharp word while others will only be hurt by it and instead require more encouragement and kindness. Untimely praise and untimely punishment, then, can both be harmful. 'But should a possibility be found to put away the rod completely and nonetheless preserve the end of good discipline, God is to be praised.'[b]" Sattler, *God's Glory*, pp. 54, 55.

[a] *PS*, pp. 122, 123.
[b] *PS*, p. 126.

understanding of the nature of life and reality in general—that is, as a sphere which necessarily encompasses action as well as thought and emotion.

If the will cannot be broken in childhood, then it must be broken in adulthood.

> ...if you feel that your self-will and God's will, self-love and God's love, the seat of the Spirit and the members, are struggling within you, recall immediately that the lesser must give way to the greater, the servant to the master. In such a way you will break with yourself and increase in the Spirit so that GOd alone may reign in you.[17]

Scriver prescribes incidents from everyday life as arenas in which the will can, and must, be broken anew each day. Here a sort of grim determination and unflinching perseverance are both preparation for greater things and outwardly manifested testimonies that one is in fact submitted to God.[18] This is not a once-for-all event, for the Christian must beware that the natural will which, like sin, ever clings to a person, does not regain the upper hand. Francke even warns one, "Guard against unnecessary laughter," although he immediately adds that, "Not all laughter is forbidden."[19] This prohibition is not simply a reflection of the Pietist's negative attitude toward frivolity, but is also a demand for self-control, that is, for the subjugation of the corrupt will's tendency to participate in the world's wicked predilections.

---

[17] *HLK*, II, ii, pp. 649, 650.

[18] "A Christian must always be on guard/and be diligent even in small things/to break his will/to keep his corrupt nature down/and to follow in the footsteps of the gentle LORD JEsus. For example: Some food is set before me/which is is not salted enough/or with which something else is wrong: Here I should not explode with scolding and cursing/like ignited gunpowder/ but rather must either gently remind my family of their mistakes/or be completely silent about it/and take the opportunity to learn/to put up with even greater offenses: I go into the streets/a dog barks at me/and runs after me/I walk by without becoming angry and upset/and practice/taking revenge on backbiters and slanderers/by ignoring them/and the like. LOrd JEsus! you of gentle heart/take my teaching and instruction with love/and help me/that I may witness in all situations/that you live/reign and dwell in me." *Gotthold*, pp. 1040, 1041.

[19] *LR*, p. 21.

The will, that is, that complex made up of desires, tendencies, etc. which we described earlier must give way to faith or unbelief, to God or Satan. Thus unless one submits willingly or, as it were, breaks his or her own will, it must be broken for him or her. One gets the distinct impression that this is not a particularly enjoyable experience. "It must bend or break."[20] In interpersonal relationships the will determines whether there is cooperation or disunity, friendship or enmity. "Will and will-not make up all the friendship and enmity in the world....Everything depends on the will. If my will and your will are one will, we are the best of friends."[21] As we have seen, however, the divine-human friendship, the agreement of wills, is based first upon the breaking and renewal of the natural will,[22] the true breaking of the will. Outward appearances of friendliness and love are no good unless they are the results of a truly broken will, for despite occasional good appearances, the natural will is never good, and the unbroken, unsubmissive will is, all appearances to the contrary, not at all free.[23]

What is free, however, is one's choice to submit obediently to the will of God. Indeed, divine pressure *per se* plays no part in a person's conscious, willful decisions.

> It is contrary to the nature and manner of the kingdom of GOd that someone would be coerced: for it is a kingdom of love. So it is that even our Savior says, Matth. 16. *Whoever wants to follow me*; and in Lucas 9. *Whoever wants to follow me.* He does not say

---

[20] *GE*, #55, p. 55.

[21] *GE*, #136, p. 147.

[22] "...should God's will be done, your own will must be done away with." *GE*, #155, p. 170.

[23] "...for your will is never good, however good it may appear....If your will is good, God's will is better still, and if God hinders your good will, he does it only that it may become better; it will be better then, when it is conformed to the divine [will], until you are submitted completely, free, [and,] have no will, other than to await God's will. Indeed, says the child of the world, that is a coerced and not a free will, why then has God given me a free will? My dear, you trap yourself; if God has given you a free will, why do you want to make it into your own [self-] will and not let it remain free? When you do with it what you will it is no longer free, but rather yours... A free will is one which is not your own will, but rather looks alone to God's will through which it also remains free, clinging to nothing but God." *GE*, #155, pp. 179, 171.

> You should and must follow me. If it was no more
> than Coactio [compulsion] and outward coercion, our
> Savior would not be served by it and it would not help
> a person, it would also not be the kingdom of GOd.[24]

In the sense that the decision of faith is an act and reflection of the will, one's will is free concerning salvation. Although the Pietists ultimately traced their conversions back, as we have seen in Francke's account of his conversion experience, to the promptings and the gracious accommodations of the Holy Spirit, from the human side of faith this decision is perceived as a personal response to the simple offer of grace and glory presented by and in Christ.[25] There is no more coercion involved here than in the case of a somewhat hungry person seeing a tasty cake in a bakery window and subsequently choosing to go in and get it, although the aroma from the bakery, the window display, etc. may indeed exercise some influence.

This concept of the freedom of the will, however, does not preclude all divine involvement in a person's life, for one ever remains subject to attack by Satan, and to resurgent impulses of the old Adam, and thus he or she needs help. We must remember here that for the Pietist, faith was far more than intellectual assent to creedal statements and clerical authority, but was seen as total submission to God in Christ; faith was an involvement in the life of God in the world, manifested in a life of obedience. Insofar as personal behavior is an element of faith (and thus of salvation), one stands in need of help in right living if he or she is to successfully resist and overcome these demonic assaults. God, therefore, occasionally intervenes in one's life to "hinder" the will so that it will not bring to fruition the evil plans it intends. This intervention is not, however, coercion, but "persuasion" in the sense that God creates circumstances favorable for the doing of good, and unfavorable for the doing of evil. Upon seeing the ease with which certain good things can be accomplished, and the possible profit arising from them or, conversely, upon seeing

---

[24] *SFP*, p. 896.

[25] "Christ does not need us. He is already blessed and nothing can be added to his blessedness. He will gladly make you participants in this because he loves you. But know, it is no slavish coercion; Christ wants a willing heart. He inclines his heart to everyone, he offers his grace and his treasures; not that he may coerce a person and force such upon him against his will, but rather as the person desires; he leaves it up to him." *SFP*, p. 732.

the difficulty of carrying out certain wicked schemes and desires, and the potential pain, embarrassment or danger resulting from them, one is "persuaded" by these circumstances to pursue the good and/or avoid the evil.[26]

This divine interference is necessary because the will remains tainted by sin, and can (and does) fall repeatedly as a result. It is obvious that "The natural person feels in his desires a hostility toward God."[27] Müller assures the reader that the Christian, too, is not exempt from this hostility. "Often the flesh resists even in the saints, and does not want what and how GOd wants."[28] The goal of the Christian, albeit unattainable in this life, is to be obedient and submissive to God in every way in every situation. Thus while the unbeliever reacts angrily to, and rejects, God's involvement in his or her life, the Christian accepts whatever God sends. This submission is not, however, a fatalistic, despairing resignation, but is a hopeful, even joyful acceptance of the manifest will of God in the life of the individual, whether it brings pain or gladness. The believer knows that it is a part of the salvation process and is under the control of a loving God who does all things for the good of the children of God.

Active obedience is the key to spiritual progress as well as to the provision of temporal needs. In fact, the act of obedience must precede the reception of grace, healing, or whatever God has in store for a person at the moment.

> But obedience/which the children of GOd show
> their heavenly Father in his leading/brings about even
> this/that they can enjoy in their hearts a great calm/an
> ineffable rest and divine peace.[29]

Note that in the quote above it is obedience which will bring about the enjoyment of peace, calm, etc., not the other way around. In the starkly either/or worldview of the Pietists, it naturally follows that,

> To the contrary, whoever refuses to follow in
> faith/in love/in the denial of the earthly/in a sincere
> humility/patience and obedience/and/what GOd the

---

[26] *GLF*, I, v, p. 38.

[27] *HLK*, I, xxv, p. 605.

[28] *HLK*, I, xxv, p. 605.

[29] *SLF*, I, p. 202.

> LOrd ordains unto him/but rather will sooner go his
> own way according to reason/and the urge of his flesh
> and blood/he has nothing but strife/nothing but unrest
> and pain/and can never have peace in his heart and
> conscience...[30]

Pietist obedience is active rather than passive in the sense that the believer is to obey God's will in anticipation of divine power, rather than wait to receive God's help before proceeding in faith.[31] While one is on the path of obedience, however, the Spirit of God is ready to help in the struggle of faith and love. Should it occur that the believer feels him- or herself tempted by sinful tendencies, he or she has recourse to God in prayer.[32] The opposite of obedience to God is, of course, willful commission of, and submission to, sin. Deliberate sin is as dangerous as if one's natural will had never been broken in the first place.

> Now to the contrary/if he would have given in to
> his will/and still willingly indulged in such sins/by
> which he was tempted/he would have indeed torn
> himself loose from God and renounced [God].[33]

Thus we see that the one who does not persevere in obedience stands in danger of losing his or her salvation. The danger of this apparent (and frequent) inclination to works-righteousness is mitigated somewhat by the ever-present references to the absolute necessity of the grace and presence of Christ for salvation and sanctification.[34] From the practical, human point of view, one

---

[30] *SFA*, I, p. 202.

[31] "If a person hears the Word of GOd and believes it, he must immediately seek to become single-mindedly obedient to it, and not think he need not do anything until he feels the power for it in himself, or notices a particular drive in himself, and until he is placed in this or that situation: but rather from then, when he believed, on, the work of faith must be begun with single-mindedness; so GOD comes forth, and grants the person all the power he needs..." *SFA*, p. 335; *SFA*, II, pp. 486f.

[32] "But to this belongs a special power of the Spirit of GOd/which one must seek in prayer if the person desires to remain firm in GOd with his will/and thus strengthen himself/so that even though he may be overtaken now and then by the sinful characteristics/which he still has within/he is still turned away from them in his will and in the bottom of his heart/and battles and struggles bravely against them." *SFA*, I, p. 633.

[33] *SFA*, I, p. 633.

[34] "This does not mean that the person should help himself through his

must press on to salvation with fierce determination. From the theoretical, theological perspective obedience is but a manifestation or fruit of the saving faith present in the person. One must obey with no thought of him- or herself, or of what could lie ahead. The believer is to keep his or her eyes on God alone. Scriver compares the person to people rowing a boat:

> Now then we should/like these people/turn our backs on what lies ahead/and in good trust in GOd/who stands at the helm/and mightily guides the little ship on to/where it is useful and blessed for us/only work diligently/and be untroubled about the rest...*Let us row and work and pray/but let GOd steer/bless/and reign.*[35]

The obedience of the upright is characterized by at least three things: 1) willingness and simplicity, that is, there is no thought of the task, but rather of the one who gives it; 2) immediacy and bravery, that is, there is no hesitation to leave everything behind and to follow Christ, even into death; and 3) humility, that is, there is no thought of pleasing oneself or of ascribing anything good to oneself, but rather to the grace of God alone.[36]

As in other aspects of life, the response of the unregenerate to the will of God is quite different from that of the believer. An attitude common to unbelievers is that the commandments of God cannot be kept at all, so, of course, why bother to try? It also does not occur to them to ask God for help. If they do happen to do something good, they do it out of the wrong motives, for example, to escape the fires of hell (rather than to please God). They believe that their occasional good deeds, together with a fairly close observance of religious customs such as church attendance, regular confession, taking the Lord's Supper and the like are proof that they must indeed be Christians. Yet, were they to speak honestly, they would have to confess that they find no joy in their "obedience," and that they respond to God's Word more from a sense of compulsion and fear than from a willing

---

own works, but rather he is pointed completely to JEsus Christ. JEsus alone can save him, otherwise he will not be eternally saved. We only show the nature of faith, which includes this (which we see in Mary [in Luke 1]), that it makes the person the servant of the LOrd, makes him obedient to him...."
SFP, p. 588.
[35] *SFA*, I, pp. 202, 203.
[36] *HLK*, I, xvii, p. 427.

ness to obey. The true child of God obeys gladly and is eager to please God.[37]

Intentions are important in God's eyes. Should the wicked person leave one of God's commands undone, it is defiance and disobedience, laziness, presumption, wantonness and similar wickedness.

> But on the other hand, if something is neglected by a faithful child of GOd/I cannot say because of it/that the command of the Father was not kept; for it is his sincere will to do it better; he is also sincerely sorry/that it has angered his dear Father/and offended [him]/he strives thereafter/henceforth to keep the divine commandments better.[38]

Here we see why the Pietists so emphasized self-examination. Not only are evil intentions dangerous to the spiritual well-being of the believer, they are offensive and anger-provoking to God. On top of this, of course, is the simple fact that good intentions may compensate for a believer's accidental oversights only if these good intentions are *sincere*. Mere wishful thinking or empty promises, however well-intended or strongly felt, will never bring one to the sanctification which leads into salvation. The works must match the words, otherwise it is a case of self-deception and subsequent damnation. Such oversights, then, are hardly errors, rather they are simply wicked decisions and actions glossed over with "good intentions." Genuine mistakes, however, present no real problem for the faithful. In fact, the loving-kindness and patience of God far exceed human patience. Thus, if a human father is able to endure the repeated errors of his children, God can certainly do so as well.[39] There is a big difference, however, between repeated mistakes and a life made up of an unbroken string of bad deeds and unfulfilled obligations and promises. Perseverance in broken commitments is

---

[37] *SFA*, I, p. 615.

[38] *SFA*, I, p. 615.

[39] "How many times do our children not do it right? how often do they follow the wickedness of their hearts/and give up/their wills to the sin/which is inborn in them? But I have never yet seen/a father disinherit his child for that/or throw [the child] in the Elbe/rather he chastises and admonishes it in a fatherly way/and hopes for improvement with increasing years: Now if we who are wicked can do that/how could GOD not do much more?" *Gotthold*, p. 728.

unacceptable to the Lord, and proves out the old maxim, "The road to hell is paved with good intentions."[40]

There is also a passive obedience normally called *Gelassenheit*. Francke laments that not only is it an unknown commodity among those calling themselves Christians, but the concept is often received with surprise when preached or taught, even though it is only reasonable that every Christian should know what *Gelassenheit* is from personal experience.[41] While *Gelassenheit* may be translated as resignation or submission, it by no means carries the forlorn, hopeless connotations often associated with such words. Rather, it consists of faith, obedience, peace and calmness of spirit and soul [Gemüth],[42] humility and hope, trust in God's leading and promises, the denial of earthly things, and patience, particularly in affliction.[43] In one sense, it is simply existing and allowing whatever befalls one to occur, accepting it as God's will. Müller quotes,

> May your will/Lord/also be my will/
> To you will I surrender/
> What pleases you/in me fulfill.
> I will not resist.[44]

Scriver's Gotthold provides us with an excellent example of *Gelassenheit*:

> Gotthold had kept a songbird in a cage for a long
> time/it had become so accustomed to its prison/that it
> not only sang happily and beautifully in it/but even did
> not wish to fly out/when the door stood open: Ah/he

---

[40] "But now if you tell yourselves that you have the desire, but have not done the work, behold your judgment: Not all who say to me LOrd, LOrd, will enter the kingdom of heaven; but rather *those who do the will* of my Father in heaven. The road to hell is paved with such will and desires, that one has nothing but good wishes and intentions, and always speaks of them, how one would gladly live piously if one only could, and approve everything, but meanwhile never go to work nor show a true earnestness: thereby one deceives himself into hell." *SFP*, p. 1270.

[41] *SFA*, I, p. 197.

[42] *Gemüth* here means the whole inner person.

[43] *SFA*, I, pp. 189, 199.

[44] "Es sey dein Will/Herr/auch mein Will/
>   Dir wil ich mich ergeben/
> Was dir gefällt/an mir erfüll.
>   Ich wil nicht widerstreben." *GLF*, I, v. p. 44.

thought/seeing such/in his heart/if I could only learn
fully/from this little bird peace with my condition/and
submission [*Gelassenheit*] in GOD's will! Ah if I could
just become accustomed to the ways of my GOd/and
believe from the heart/that he cannot intend me evil!
This little bird is indeed penned in/yet because it has its
feed/it is content/hops/sings/and does not desire to
change its conditions: To be sure, GOD often surrounds
me with all manner of affliction and constrictions/yet
he has never let me want for comfort and help/why then
am I not happy? Why do I not sing and thank my GOD
with joyful heart/even in distress?[45]

This understanding of how one should be reflects a very
profound trust in the goodness and sovereignty of God, a
sovereignty which extends to every detail of human existence. It
reflects as well the belief that God is intimately involved in the
lives of individuals in a loving way. The influence of the mystics
and Quietists is apparent. The *Gelassenheit* for which the Pietists
call presupposes not only this sovereignty and love of God, but
requires an equally profound faith on the part of the person as
well, for the faithless person could hardly say, "I will gladly be
like a little clump of wax in your hand that forms itself, like a
young shoot which is bent and twisted according to your will."[46]
This clearly mystically oriented reference to the self as wax to be
molded according to God's will is common in Pietist preaching
and devotional writings, for the Pietists saw melting or molding,
or affliction and suffering, as just one—very important—element
in God's interaction with people. In affliction, a person only
wastes time trying to comprehend the causes of his or her
suffering through the use of human reason. The only appropriate, adequate response to suffering is to apply one's will, to look
to God, and to humbly hunker down, as it were, and ride out the
storm.[47] Human reason leads a person in the wrong direction,
asks all the wrong questions, and, in the end, comes up with all
the wrong conclusions.

---

[45] *Gotthold*, p. 786.

[46] *GE*, #55, p. 55.

[47] "Close your eyes, as it were, to corrupt reason/and do not always
look to your suffering/and to your distress/in which you find yourselves/but
rather turn your eyes to the overwhelming grace of GOd/which is offered to
you in Christ/and from which alone you/without any regard for your own
worthiness and merit should be accepted and saved. Submit yourselves to the
LOrd as his sacrifice..." *SFA*, III, p. 105.

> Your reason says: Why then does he [God] need/
> to interact with me in such and such a way? If he
> wants/to help me/then why does he delay his help?
> What help is it to him/that I should complain to him
> of one problem after the other/pour out my heart before
> him so often/and tell him all my concerns?[48]

The Christian knows better, however, and presses on in humility and acceptance of his or her current situation. At times it appears that the believer has given up completely, that fear and distress have gained the upper hand. Amidst weeping and wailing, however, there yet remains deep in the believer an inner *Gelassenheit* which awaits the moment of release which God is sure to bring, and the true believer would not trade his or her God-given suffering for all the pleasures and joys of the world.[49]

---

[48] *SFA*, I, p. 473.

[49] "Now the submission is indeed hidden/but it is yet a true submission/known and apparent to the LOrd/who at just the right time[a] lets such clouds pass by/that the bright sun of grace must stream forth." *SFA*, I, p. 199; *SFA*, I, p. 331.

> [a] The concept of timely help in affliction is common to almost all Christian mystics. Whether the affliction is the result of direct intervention *via* God's self-withdrawal, or of indirect intervention through the manipulation of environmental factors, God uses these moments of intense and/or prolonged *Anfechtung* for the strengthening of the faith of the sufferer and those around him or her. Among the immediate influences on Pietist thought in this area we find this element strongly represented in Arndt and Molinos as well as in the English devotional writings so popular on the continent in the 17th century. "We may not assume that affliction is sent to us by coincidence. The time of our suffering, rather, is appointed by God...He has measured each for his cross and even knows the moment in which it will change....Therefore God has decided in his omnipotence that the moment of affliction shall last until he has fulfilled his will." [And, very significantly, as seen from the human perspective] "There is no example of God ever having abandoned a person in such *Anfechtungen*[i] ....As in Arndt, we also come across the concept of time in Molinos, in the sections on *Anfechtungen*...God will surely help when it pleases him, so that one can resist *Anfechtungen*, and precisely then when one is the least aware of it." E. Peschke, *Bekehr-ung und Reform*, pp. 36ff. What God has left undone for forty years God suddenly does in order to show that God's almighty hand frees people from all frailty.[ii]
>
> > [i] "Thus one has no example/that GOd had ever

This, at least, is one time when a person may be glad that God's sight penetrates to one's very heart.

We see that obedience and *Gelassenheit* are in a process of growth, a development connected with the progression of love and faith.[50]

> Now, just as love has its grades and stages/so also *obedience*...But the more the person increases and grows in love/the more he will also grow in obedience toward GOd and his commandments.[51]

Faith and obedience stand arm in arm.

> Indeed, the more perfect faith is/the more he stands in *Gelassenheit*/the more he surrenders himself to the will of GOd/and offers himself up to him/trusts in him/that he will make things better at the right time.[52]

As an increase in love and faith creates greater obedience and submission to God, so also does greater submission bring one closer to full citizenship in the kingdom of God. Bit by bit one enters deeper, as it were, into the realm and reign of God, and

---

> abandoned a person in such distress/and great *Anfechtungen*; but rather [has] a witness that when GOd has well purified and melted a saint in the oven of suffering/deliverance surely results from it. And this is a great comfort/when the hour of testing is over/and the person has passed the test/deliverance will surely come." *Wahres Christenthum*, I, liii, p. 18, quoted in Peschke, *Bekehrung und Reform*, n. 107.
>
> ii)"Et quanquam saepius cadas, & videas tuam pusillanimitatem, cura ut bono sis animo, nec dolore afficiaris; quoniam DEUS interdum id, quod quadriginta non fecit annis, facit, uno instanti, singulari quodam mysterio, ut vivamus demissi & humiliati & cognoscamus esse opus potentis manus ejus quod nos liberet a defectibus." M. Molinos, *Manuductio spiritualis*, II, p. 132, quoted in Peschke, *Bekehrung und Reform*, n. 165.

[50] For an overview of Francke's concept of growth, see Peschke, *Studien zur Theologie*, I, pp. 104ff.

[51] *SFA*, I, p. 990

[52] *SFA*, I, pp. 331, 332.

withdraws further from the service of Satan, the world and one's own flesh and blood.[53]

The divine claim on the person's will is absolute. "He [God] will give direction alone, or not at all."[54] It is a human tendency, however, to hold back "this and that," even though God desires the whole person and wishes to make him or her "*gantz selig*." "I ask you, give him your whole heart and your whole soul [*Gemüth*], give him body and soul as his own."[55] If and when this submission is complete, it has, so to speak, a leveling effect in which one does not see all things with equal indifference, but rather accepts all things as from God with pleasure. And why not? God has never done the person ill.

> By God's grace, I will be a simpler, more free person, clinging to no thing but purely and simply to the will of God, neither desiring good nor fearing evil, giving honor and insult, wealth and want, life and death the same esteem, satisfied alone in this, that it be God's will. Whatever he wishes to do with me, poor worm, shall all be pleasing to me. Yea, he has never done me ill. Praised be his name! Amen.[56]

The Pietist treatment of the will shows again the very non-systematic, rather ambiguous approach which characterizes this movement. On the one hand, one must obey in order to receive. On the other hand, one's very obedience is a manifestation that he or she has already received. On the one hand, the person's will must be free in order for him or her to be capable of making genuine decisions. On the other hand, God manipulates circumstances to influence, without actually coercing, one to decide in accordance with God's desire. What is very clear and unequivocal in any case, is that God demands obedience, first in the breaking or surrendering of the natural will, and subsequently in

---

[53] "Now where this subordination is of the right sort/it shows a person more and more as a member of the kingdom; indeed, the more the will of a person is like the will of GOd/the more the person may be called a true member of the kingdom of our GOd: For the kingdom of GOd dawns in a person's heart in such measure/as the person's will is submissive to the will of GOd/and the less he may also be known/as one who serves Satan/the world/and his own flesh." *SFA*, I, p. 627.

[54] *GE*, #44, p. 43.

[55] *SFP*, p. 23.

[56] *GE*, #155, p. 171.

the person's total conformity to the will of God—inwardly in *Gelassenheit* and faith, and outwardly in concrete manifestations of love for God and neighbor. This conformity of one's will to God's will is the goal of Christianity.[57] On the ultimate level, it boils down to one basic truth: "His will is my salvation, my will is my destruction."[58]

---

[57] *SFA*, I, p. 627.
[58] *GE*, #44, p. 44.

CHAPTER 6

AFFLICTION

"The best blessing is in affliction [*Kreuz*]."[1] It is virtually impossible to understand the Pietist view of the person without understanding the concept of affliction. We can hardly overestimate the significance of this element of the Christian life which appears in Pietist devotional material again and again. Affliction is one of the three inescapable and essential lessons in Christ's school of faith, that is, "the *Word, prayer* and the *cross*."[2] It is absolutely necessary to the Christian life: "Where we will not immerse ourselves in the cross of CHrist/our whole Christianity/ and our going to confession and the Lord's Supper/is in vain."[3] Christian suffering, however, is not to be confused with the suffering to which any human being is subject, and there certainly had been enough of that in Germany in the 17th century.[4] Not only had war not ceased with the treaty of Westphalia/Osnabrück in 1648, but the quality of life was crude for decades thereafter. Beyreuther reports that in Lübeck, Francke's birthplace, the streets were in disrepair, there were no street lights until 1704, all but the upper classes fetched water from common wells, and "Even bathrooms were almost unknown."[5] Of course the number of widows and orphans was extremely high as a result of the ongoing wars, occasional epidemics, and generally hard living conditions. Francke himself blames crime and general moral disarray on the sad conditions among the poor:

> Now because I found such coarse and horrid igno-
> rance among the poor people/that I almost did not
> know/where I should begin/to bring them a firm foun-
> dation of their Christianity/I was troubled from that

---

[1] *GE*, #66, p. 65. *Kreuz* can be translated as "cross" or as "affliction".

[2] *SFP*, p. 1641.

[3] *SFA*, I, p. 485; Müller calls affliction a sign of a true Christian. "Proving good is the proof. Are you proven in the oven of suffering?...A Christian is known in affliction." *GE*, #76, pp. 74, 75.

[4] See Walther Hubatsch, *Deutschland zwischen dem Dreißigjährigen Krieg und der Französischen Revolution*, (Frankfurt/Main, 1973), p. 11; Hajo Holborn, *A History of Modern Germany: The Reformation*, (New York, 1976). pp. 358, 359.

[5] *AHF*, pp. 9, 10.

time on/how they might be helped more vigor-
ously/considering well/that very great damage to
Christians and the community in general may arise
from/so many people/going about like cattle/without
any knowledge of GOd and godly things/but particu-
larly/[because] so many children/because of the poverty
of their parents/neither are made to attend school/nor
enjoy any good upbringing/but rather grow up in the
most shameful ignorance and in all manner of wicked-
ness/that with the years they are good for nothing/and
so take to theft/robbery and other evil deeds.[6]

The Pietists accepted suffering as a basic element of life.
Here we are concerned, however, with affliction as it relates to
the divine impulse to save and sanctify, and how one is to
understand and respond to it. As with the Pietist usage of the
language of the inner person—using words such as heart, soul,
spirit, etc. interchangeably—so it is with the language of affliction: suffering, affliction, misery, the cross, and *Anfechtung* are
used interchangeably. Especially in this area we encounter the
problem of prescription *vs.* description. That is, to what degree,
in attempting to talk about the essence and meaning of suffering,
do the Pietists at the same time legislate its existence and form?
Indeed, Müller tells his readers that it is in the actual seeking after
affliction that the Christian life far exceeds the natural life.

So far does a truly Christian life exceed the
natural life.
1. Disdains itself.
2. Loves and thirsts after not honor/but rather
after disdain.
3. Rebukes all that/which does not wish to be
scorned with CHrist according to his life.
4. Will even gladly be scorned and persecuted for
such scorn and rebuke's sake.
5. Does not consider itself worthy to suffer such
persecution.[7]

Do we not see in these words the desire for suffering simply for
suffering's sake, and even a hint of triumphalism in affliction and
persecution? We also detect an attempt to make suffering comprehensible.

---

[6] *Fußstapfen*, p. 3.
[7] *GLF*, II, ii, p. 717.

The Pietists understand affliction in the light of Christ; that is, only a born-again believer can know and understand what it actually is.

> Beloved friends in Christ Jesus our most worthy
> Savior/the world knows as little/what right and true
> suffering are/as what right and true comfort are.[8]

The world's error lies in the fact that it sees well-deserved punishment of sin as Christian affliction [*Christen=Creutz*], when in fact this suffering is simply the same as that of "all Jews, pagans and Turks." Francke claims that many ills may have been avoided had the sinners "walked in the ways of the Lord" and "armed their minds with the patience of our Lord Jesus Christ."[9] The suffering of non-believers is not necessarily and always, however, punishment for sin. It is also a divine tool for awakening the unregenerate to their condition of depravity and wretchedness. That is, it is a device by which God attempts to bring non-believers to Godself,[10] as well as to draw back believers if they have strayed. The point of some suffering is that those who are far off may be brought to a genuine acceptance of God's Word, to Jesus Christ himself, to true and prayer repentance, to a solid foundation for faith and patience and steadfastness.[11] In summary, affliction is the thread that runs

---

[8] *SFA*, II, p. 276.

[9] *SFA*, II, p. 277.

[10] *SFA*, II, p. 733.

[11] Using the royal official, or *Königische*, in John 4:47–54, Francke provides the logic behind divinely-sent affliction:

"And so it is/if one goes forth without affliction/and is immersed in lust of the eyes/lust of the flesh and arrogant living/or squanders his life in luxury/there no verse goes to his heart/even were it full of comfort/ rather one reads and hears it superficially/and lets the power go/but where the heart is softened and made tender through suffering/and is weaned, as it were, from the breasts of love of the world/Is. XXVIII, 9. Ah! how there shall all comfort come into play/which is given to the sorrow-bearer/the wretched/the poor/the least/the weary and heavy-laden?[a]

Second affliction *drives* [one] to *CHrist* himself/that one not only hears the Word/but is lured/pulled and driven/by the Word to CHrist.[b]

Third affliction also drives [one] *to an earnest prayer*/as we see in the royal official/that as soon as he came to JEsus/he asked him/that he would come down/and help his son. Yet there is an even *better reason*/ that the person seeks to attain to a true and living faith. So long as

through the whole story of one's pilgrimage from darkness into light, from sin to salvation, and even through the life of a believer.

---

people neither experience trouble/nor feel any need/they indeed pray/ but out of habit/without devotion/sincere desire/childlike confidence/fervor/ perseverance; But in and under the cross [affliction]/be it inward or outward/a person begins to learn the art of truly praying.[c]

Fourth affliction drives [the one] *under Anfechtung or trial to the good*/as we see in the royal official/with whose request JEsus did not immediately comply/but rather chastised him/and appeared to know about him/as he said: *If you do not see signs and wonders/you do not believe*....Now there faith is not yet grounded deeply enough/and GOd looks upon such with compassionate love/so he helps the person/not immediately according to his childish desire/but rather leaves him struggling a little/so that he may dig even deeper beneath the trial/and may lay a sure foundation for his faith/indeed the Savior puts his hand to the task, as it were/and helps the person to dig/so that it may be a divine foundation/upon which faith is put.[d]

And so *fifth* we also see here/that distress also works *patience and steadfastness*/Rom. v. 3. for the royal official was neither backsliding nor surprised in such trial/did not say: If you will not help me/I will go to other doctors/and see/how I can be helped; rather remained steadfast/ asked and pleaded: *LOrd/come/before my child dies.* Even though he was still in great weakness/he insisted/that CHrist come with him."[e] *SFA*, II, pp. 734ff.

[a] Müller makes the same points: "Would that lost son not have been eternally damned/if GOd had not let him fall into such hunger? He afflicts and chastises you not out of anger/but out of sincere mercy/that you might not be damned with the godless world." *GLF*, I, xx, p. 523.

[b] "But now dear affliction [the dear cross] is a translator/which expounds God's Word to you/the best preacher/no preacher can explain it better..." *GLF*, I, xx, p. 530. There is a difference here, in that Francke stresses movement from hearing the outward Word to meeting Christ himself, while Müller emphasizes moving from hearing to transformation. In both cases, however, the end effect is the same, and in both the movement is brought about by affliction.

[c] "In affliction you sigh for God/the sighs touch God's heart/that he may comfort and refresh you. As many sighs as you send to heaven/so much comfort God sends down...Affliction is a mother and wetnurse of prayer." *GLF*, I, xx, pp. 531, 532.

[d] "Fear [as result of affliction] gives feet." *GE*, #253, p. 310; These feet, then, are to be used to run to Christ.

[e] "In the oven of affliction/the love of God tests/trains and preserves your faith/hope/love and patience." *GLF*, I, xx, p. 533.

And this is thus the *foundation of faith*/namely/
that one is drawn outwardly or inwardly through *affliction*/know his soul's sickness/hear/and receive the Word
of GOd with desire and love/and go on thorough to
CHrist/petition him/and persevere in asking/and not
become tired/but look steadfastly to Christ/in all trials/
until one receives help.[12]

Francke asserts that the whole Bible confirms that there is a
never-ending series of burdens encountered throughout the
Christian life. Barely is one hardship overcome when another is
laid upon the struggling believer. Blessed is the one who sees
this, does not conjure up an image of an easier Christian pilgrimage, and is ready to shoulder his or her cross.[13]

As we shall see in our section on the Pietist view of death,
affliction does not necessarily end at death, at least as the concerns the unbeliever. In life, however, both pagan and believer
experience suffering. The Christian can anticipate even greater
affliction, since to the normal human suffering (which the believer also experiences) are added extra burdens which are simply
essential elements of the Christian life. Müller uses images which
emphasize the internal, inextricable, even organic connectedness
of faith and suffering.

Just as the heavens are rarely without clouds/the
sea without waves/roses without thorns/so a Christian
without affliction... As the shadow is on the body/the

---

[12] *SFA*, II, pp. 737, 738.

[13] "This is confirmed and sealed in all of holy Scripture as a certain and
undeceptive truth, that there is no other way to wisdom than through daily
taking up the cross, through many trials, through much trouble, weariness
and difficulty. If a person thinks that one affliction is overcome, another is
right there, and waits to be laid upon his shoulder. Good for him who makes
no other image of Christianity, nor imagines anything else in the imitation
of Christ, but rather in progress on the path of true wisdom bends his
shoulders beneath the cross, and is willing and ready to take this upon
himself." *SFP*, p. 790; Müller's words are quite similar, "Thus a Christian is
rarely without affliction/if one does not come/the other does." *GLF*, I, xx, p.
517.

> glow on light/the shine on the sun; so faith/confession
> and suffering adhere to each other.[14]

Francke virtually dares one to be born again, live the Christian life seriously, and see whether the world does not begin to persecute the new believer.[15] Taking examples from antiquity, he cites the cases of Socrates who had to drink poison for rejecting polytheism, and Pythagoras who was burned for his virtuous life, and he adds, *"veritas odium parit."*[16] For Müller there simply is no question, "I am a Christian; Christian and cross-bearer is one man; Christ in the heart, the cross on the back."[17] We might say that for the Pietists human existence and suffering are almost synonymous, and that the Christian life and added affliction constitute the norm.

The inevitability of natural affliction is difficult enough for humanity, but the equally inevitable onslaught, and life-long presence, of further suffering for the Christian is not only beyond the comprehension of the worldly person, but it causes the Christian to appear to be the most foolish and wretched of people.[18] In fact, this readiness to suffer and the necessity of taking up one's cross are significant reasons why so many people reject Christianity; the world wishes to be whisked into heaven in glory, and is not ready to accept the persecution (of the world) that is a daily part of the Christian life. Indeed, the worldly person is scandalized by the foolishness of Christ's teachings on this subject.[19] As in most things, the child of the

---

[14] *GLF*, I, xx, p. 517.

[15] "Experience will teach you this/turn earnestly to CHrist/and see what the world will do with you/whether it does not do to you precisely/what it did to CHrist and his apostles/and whether you will remain without persecution: do not play the hypocrite with it/when it does evil/for example, speak useless words/but chastise it/as the Scripture commands Eph. III, ll. and see/what it says to that." *SFA*, I, pp. 967, 968.

[16] *SFA*, I, pp. 974, 975.

[17] *GE*, #97, p. 97.

[18] "For to the eyes of human reason it seems/as if no-one is more wretched than those/who serve Christ JEsus in true faith/and follow in his footsteps/because no-one is surrounded with more suffering/*Anfechtung* and trouble than precisely those/who follow their LOrd and Savior/CHrist JEsus/most faithfully and serve him." *SFA*, III, p. 275.

[19] "It also says one must take up his cross *daily*. But the world wants nothing to do with this/this does not please it/that it would be hated/mocked and rejected in its Christianity/rather it wishes to be taken by the

world and the child of God have completely different perspectives on, and understandings of, the source(s), roles and meanings of affliction in one's life.

As well as divinely-appointed suffering due to sin, one encounters a sort of natural pain which simply comes with being alive in this world. As the person is a microcosm of a macrocosm characterized by wickedness and suffering, it is only logical that he or she would suffer. This common anguish is not to be considered as Christian affliction. We see that in certain circumstances even "normal" suffering can be used by God for punishment or chastisement, but this remains nonetheless something other than Christian affliction.

> Albeit that just this outward suffering may be a hallowed affliction to the Christian/yet not in the measure/and in such actual designation/as suffering for truth's and righteousness' sake.[20]

Here, too, we discover that not all *Creutz* is *Anfechtung* (while all *Anfechtung* is affliction) insofar as *Anfechtung* has to do with specific incidents of divine intervention in a painful or difficult

---

hand and lifted into heaven with nothing but praise. So then it becomes angry over such affliction/it ridicules it/and what otherwise it is told of the teaching of JEsus CHrist/it considers foolishness/if one is supposed to follow it." *SFA*, I, pp. 957, 958; In this sermon, *das Ärgerniß des Creutzes* ("The Scandal of the Cross"), given in 1699, Francke points out that to those who are still ignorant and unrepentant (these traits go hand-in-hand) and would find God's Word loathsome even if there was no affliction involved, the cross gives even greater reason to hold back. Because so many of the "high and mighty" mock and scorn Christians, unbelievers minimize or discount entirely the integrity of the Christian faith. "And this is has been the scandal in all times/on account of which the fewest have accepted the word of truth. For it goes: *The world would gladly be saved/if only it were not for the heavy pain/which all Christians suffer.*" *SFA*, I, p. 957.

[20] *SFA*, II, p. 733; Francke bases this opinion on the grounds that the fact that Christ suffers with the believer makes Christian affliction of any affliction experienced by a Christian. The natural pain of which we spoke earlier and of which Müller says, "I am a person; a person is a small version of the whole world; in him, as in the center of a circle, all suffering comes together...if I would be a person, I must suffer." *GE*, #97, p. 97, such as poverty, illness and the like, must not be called Christian affliction when it affects a nonbeliever, "For affliction [*das Creutz*] receives its name from JEsus/the crucified [*dem gecreutzigten*] one." *SFA*, III, p. 279.

way—such as the experience of *Deus absconditus*—for the ultimate edification and strengthening of the born-again believer.[21] The Pietists, in any case, were concerned less with the discussion of the common forms of suffering such as poverty, crime, illness, homelessness, etc. as with the alleviation of them. They did busy themselves, however with discussing spiritual affliction.

The Christian responds to affliction in two basic ways: 1) by resisting common suffering in the world and 2) by patiently enduring the sufferings inflicted by a hostile world and Satan on account of his faith, while embracing any pain perceived as sent by God for the believer's correction and/or growth in holiness. This type of suffering is generally directed at individuals, although occasionally groups or even, as with the Turkish siege of Vienna in 1683, nations or cultures are afflicted by God because of, for example, the

> shameful contempt for the precious Word of GOd/the exceedingly great [self-] assurance of Christians/and the grievous discord of Christian rulers/who constantly bite at/devour and consume one another...[22]

We shall examine in a later chapter the Christian's response to suffering in the world. Here we are concerned with his or her response to personal experience of anguish, be it inflicted by

---

[21] "For one cannot name it actual *Anfechtung*/when one must feel his sin and GOd's wrath over it in the struggle of repentance: rather he must continue earnestly in this struggle/that he may recognize his sin and wretchedness...But *Anfechtung* will be used properly of those/who already have known grace and must experience it again/as for holy reasons the Savior has concealed himself in their hearts/so that he may awaken them all the more to rise up from all dullness/encourage them to prayer and supplication/ and reveal gloriously in them all spiritual powers." *SFA*, II, p. 514.

[22] *Gottlob*, p. 97; We find an isolated yet interesting statement in Müller: while it seems that everywhere one is exhorted to embrace affliction and accept persecution as a routine component of the Christian life, Müller mentions a sort of "escape clause": "Should he [your enemy] persecute your person/and that for which you are responsible/you should seek protection from the authorities/they stand in God's stead as avengers against evil. If the authorities will not help, you should consider/that you are called to suffer with Christ. Even if your enemy takes your life/you should not be moved to curse or hate him/but rather look to Paul's rule: *Bless, and curse not*. Rom. 12. v. 14." *GLF*, II, vii, p. 808.

world or devil in the form of hostility, or by God in the form of chastisement and/or withdrawal. These are the most common forms of affliction, but others are, for example, the emotional bruising of having one's testimony rejected[23] or "the most bitter affliction," the ever-present tendency of the believer's own flesh and blood to go their own way in utter disregard of Christ: "It must cause you pain/that you do not love your Savior completely/as you rightly should..."[24]

We have already seen that the world regards as foolish the adoption of a way of life in which suffering is implicit. In even greater contrast to the child of the world, the child of God is not only patient and hopeful in times of trial, he or she is actually grateful for them, and receives them joyfully. Müller points out that the very nature of divine intervention is good reason to consider it a fortunate event. "Now because your greatest suffering is God's greatest love/continue on/certain/that even your affliction will be nothing but joy to you."[25] Francke compares the great suffering of Jesus with the mere inconveniences of life which the world considers to be gross injustices:

> Consider this/you who wish to have honor and esteem in the world: If one evil or insulting word is spoken of you/you will take offence/you will be troubled by it/yea even weep/and talk much of it/that things go so badly with you/that you suffer so much/and must endure so much offence in the world.[26]

By contrast, the Christian sees personal suffering as a gracious gift of God, and is to prepare for it as best as he or she can, as

---

[23] "And it is indeed a *true and tender suffering*/whatever form it may be felt/by any Christian in general/who exhorts this or that person to the good/ but particularly his relatives/parents/sisters and brothers/children and household/and yet must see/that they will not accept such/but rather cast it to the winds. Surely to many much outward persecution will not be so painful and grievous/as this is to him/that the Word/which he speaks in innocence and in love/in order to win the other's soul thereby/is disdained/slandered/and, as it were, trampled under foot." *SFA*, III, p. 279.

[24] *SFA*, II, p. 451.

[25] *GLF*, I, xx, p. 525; And, "Therefore [because affliction makes us pleasing to God] the love of God does not seek our destruction in affliction/but rather our sanctification." *GLF*, I, xx, p. 518.

[26] *SFA*, I, p. 486.

one prepares to receive a guest sent by one's master.[27] We shall encounter this attitude again in our section on death. Müller calls affliction a game of God in which one does to wish to participate because he or she does not understand the game. It is, however, a game which is ultimately for the person's good, and from which he or she will reap a great harvest.[28]

This sort of "gain through pain" idea, this *quid pro quo* understanding of the divine-human relationship is common in Pietism in the discussion of suffering, death, and sacrifice (as in generosity to the poor). The spiritual pay-off for suffering willingly can come in the hereafter[29] or in the present, in that God loves God's afflicted children more, "as father and mother love the sick children more than the healthy ones."[30] The patient sufferer receives greater grace and blessing,[31] and the affliction

---

[27] "When a goodhearted man is shown/that his master is sending him a guest/he prepares for it/that he may not only receive him/the one his master has sent/willingly/but also entertain him to the best of his ability. Now you have often heard/God will send you affliction/and will not fail to appear/yea [will] come unexpectedly/yet you are so dull/that you will not receive this dear guest/who has paid so dearly for his shelter/with quiet patience and zealous prayer." *GLF*, I, xx, pp. 518, 519.

[28] "Now it never goes better with a Christian/than under the cross. O! how good the cross is for many a person/who would otherwise lose his soul's salvation. Ah! if many a person knew what happiness lay hidden in affliction/and could heap it upon himself with alms/he would gladly lose all his possessions. Moreover/such affliction is only a kindly mother's game of God/as is to be seen in Job/from whom God took all his goods/and afterwards gave them all back in heaps. GOd is only playing with us. We poor children often do not understand the game/and begin to cry." *GLF*, I, x, pp. 837, 838.

[29] Francke uses the example of the humiliated and exalted Christ as an example: "Then learn from this to know the *Mystery* and *Blessing of the Cross*/and know/that the more you are brought low and humbled here/the more gloriously you shall be raised up on that day with Christ your head." *SFA*, I, p. 944; "But Holy Scripture testifies in general and throughout/that those/which have suffered much before others here/and have borne and endured such out of love for Christ/shall also there *be glorified before others*..." *SFA*, III, p. 197; Müller also writes, "First you must bear the cloak of myrrh/if hereafter you wish to go clad in white silk." *GLF*, I, xx, p. 519.

[30] *GLF*, I, xx, p. 522; *GE*, #185, p. 216.

[31] "The more patient you are under the yoke of affliction/the more grace and blessing dear GOd will grant you." *SFA*, I, p. 145.

will finally be transformed into pure joy.[32] So great is the blessing occasioned by affliction properly endured (that is, in patience, hope and faith) that Müller writes,

> Ah, if you only knew! what glory lies hidden in
> affliction/you would be on your knees day and night/
> and not cease to cry out/until GOd lays affliction upon
> you.[33]

Note that here the affliction is requested of God and is not initiated or instigated by the believer, although the instigation of affliction was ever a danger in an atmosphere in which persecution was perceived as a sort of spiritual badge of honor and proof of one's faith.

Affliction is not only inescapable and a source of joy and blessing, it is also necessary for salvation.

> Ah, note well/you, my beloved/what is still high
> and unhumbled/cannot withstand the great GOd: every-
> thing here below must be humbled/be laid in the dust/
> and in the ashes before our GOd.[34]

Francke restates this rather more directly, "There is no other way to the Kingdom of GOD/than the way of the cross."[35] The way of the cross includes both abuse from the world and God's chastising affliction which saves the person from damnation by its application: "If he does not chastise us here as father, he will chastise us there as judge."[36] Francke is careful to emphasize that

---

32 "But God's love does not only seek your salvation in affliction/but it upholds and protects you in it as well/sweetens it with its comfort/helps [you] overcome/brings [you] to the desired end/and turns [life] into pure joy." *GLF*, I, xx, p. 537.

33 *GLF*, I, xix, p. 516; Müller also writes, "Those who sow with tears, must reap with joy; as many seeds of tears, so many sheaves of joy." *GE*, #187, p. 218.

34 *SFA*, I, p. 485.

35 *SFA*, I, p. 855; And, "The fewest of all people wish to go the way of the cross and suffering/of a little trouble and effort/and yet there is no other way to salvation." *SFA*, I, p. 841.

36 *GE*, #127, p. 137; Francke says, "Indeed in truth affliction is an honor for the children of GOd. It is no evil, but for their best. For through it they shall be preserved from sin, that they may not be eternally condemned." *CP*, pp. 138, 139; This very significant theological premise of Pietism

salvation is not dependent upon human suffering. Affliction is not a means to an end. "No one may think: Aye/because it is a matter of suffering/on with it/I will suffer then/so that I may earn eternal salvation with it."[37] Again we see the concern about works-righteousness that, it appears, cannot be separated from Pietist spiritual activism.

To suffer and to endure the suffering correctly is in the most basic sense the true imitation of Christ. Ultimately, all Christian suffering is inextricably linked with the suffering of the Savior. The transformation of affliction into joy occurs because of the suffering of Christ.

> Only this is to be noted well here/that the love of God may sweeten your affliction through the suffering of Christ. Just as bitter ocean water becomes sweet/ when it is run through good sweet earth and its veins: So your cross-water will be sweet and good/when it flows through the blood-dripping veins and wounds of Christ. The dear Savior took the first drink from the stream for this reason/that he may/with his lips dripping with honey/make it sweet.[38]

As God perseveres with the person in his or her moments of need and affliction, so is the Christian to remain with Christ in his *Anfechtung*. By undergoing affliction in a Christian manner, the believer manifests his or her solidarity with the suffering Lord Jesus, and thereby can receive the wine of joy in the Father's kingdom.[39] Why should the Christian expect or desire anything other than affliction? Through his own life, suffering and crucifixion, Jesus proclaimed the fate of those who would follow him.[40] Indeed, when the believer experiences the pain

---

provides the foundations for the practice of discipline in the congregation. "A father who does not discipline his child does not love it: where there is no rod, there is no piety, where no piety, there is no salvation." *GE*, #295, pp. 377, 378.

[37] *SFA*, III, p. 198.

[38] *GLF*, I, xx, p. 539.

[39] "From this [Luke 22: 28–30] we may well recognize/that we must persevere well with the LOrd JEsus in his *Anfechtungen*/that is/in affliction and suffering/if we wish to drink anew the wine of joy in his father's kingdom." *SFA*, I, p. 316.

[40] "Do not let it alienate you so much when the world despises and laughs at you: Consider/who it is/who proclaims his suffering here! Is it not

caused by God's apparent withdrawal, it is often the result of God's desire to help him or her identify better with the suffering of Christ.

> So God does...partly/that you may know/what a
> mighty kingdom is the kingdom of sin and death/and in
> some measure learn to understand the bitterness of the
> suffering of Christ/as he hung without comfort on the
> cross...[41]

The believer's suffering is also a sign that he or she is drawing ever closer to Jesus. Here the personal, mystical experiential character of Pietism comes to the fore. The Christian participates in Jesus' pain through his or her own pain.[42] Thus Christian suffering takes on transhistorical, transspatial dimensions. "The Jews crucified him in his person, the world still crucifies him in his members."[43] The believer, then, is nearest to the heart of Christ and the kingdom of God when he or she is in the midst of suffering for Christ's sake. This real presence of God is connected with the fact that the suffering occurs *ex providentia Dei* in the first place, and that God dwells in the believer.[44]

Drawing on another element of mysticism, the Pietists assure, or reassure, the believer that in God's omniscience, God knows just how much suffering one can endure, and for just how long one can endure it. It is basically a matter of simple trust—does the Christian believe that God will bring the affliction to an end before he or she is overwhelmed by it? The worldly person sees no way out, but the Pietists stress the trust-worthy

---

JEsus CHrist/the LOrd of glory/the only-begotten Son of God? But how did it go with him in the world?" *SFA*, I, p. 485; Francke goes on to describe the scorn, physical abuse, etc. that Jesus experienced. Müller asks, "You are indeed no better than Jesus; why then do you seek to have a better lot on earth than he had?" *GE*, #127, p. 136.

[41] *GLF*, I, xxi, p. 566.

[42] "My affliction [*Kreutz*] assures me that I am as near to God as Jesus. How could I be nearer? The nearer in God your heart is to Jesus, the more [you get] the pain of Jesus." *GE*, #102, p. 104.

[43] *GE*, #127, p. 135.

[44] "The love of God does not just hang such *Anfechtung* over the pious/but is also with them in the midst of the *Anfechtung*/the greater the need/the nearer GOd. ...How could he not be with us in anguish/when he lives in us?" *GLF*, I, xix, p. 503.

wisdom of God.[45] In this we see the familiar concept of "*Gottes Stündlein*" which was integral to the thinking of the mystics and Quietists, and is thus also found in the writings of Arndt and Molinos.[46] God will not allow the believer to suffer any longer or more than he or she can endure. "I will not shame my God, that I should say, it is unendurable, it cannot not be borne any longer."[47] This fact in itself encourages the Christian to hold out, the wisdom of which can be seen in Francke's own experience.

> But I must even herein praise the great faithful-
> ness and wisdom of God, which did not allow that a
> weak child should die through food that is much too
> strong or a fragile plant through a rushing wind that is
> all too strong, but rather he knows best when and in
> what measure he should place things upon his children
> and thereby test and purify their faith. Thus I lacked
> nothing in the testing, but only a little and then little
> by little a larger measure of suffering so that, according
> to the divine power received from him, the last and
> greatest would always be much easier for me to bear
> than the first and the least.[48]

The Pietists viewed illness as a form of affliction, and applied to it all the standards and formulae used in discussing inner turmoil. In this sense, they agreed with Scripture and, to a degree, modern psychology that the condiiton of the inner person determines to a great degree the condition of the outer or physical self.[49] Francke preaches that sin is often the cause of illness,

---

[45] "But you say God delays much too long with his help? Many a weaksighted heart may well say: Ah how can the merciful, friendly fatherly heart stand my suffering so long?....Just as a wise father/who gives work to his household/knows well/at what time they can be done with the work. So also God knows the hour certainly/in which your anguish shall end." *GLF*, I, xix, p. 507.

[46] "God has his certain moments/to trouble as well as to make glad/and the moment of anguish must first be fulfilled/before the moment of help arrives. But this is God's moment/when his glory can most be extended." *GLF*, I, xix, p. 506; See also Peschke, *Bekehrung und Reform*, pp. 24–30, 35–37.

[47] *GE*, #97, p. 97.

[48] *WIA*, p. 29.

[49] This does not reveal an ignorance of physical causes of illness. Rather, it affirms that there is more to human sickness than *only* physical causes.

using as his example the story in Matt. 9 of the healing of the paralytic, in which Jesus looks beyond the mere "outward sickness" and finds that sin is the cause of the paralytic's pitiable condition.[50] Müller aptly describes the stressful effects of anxiety on a person's physical condition as a withering and a weakening from within.[51] People, however, tend to overlook this reality:

> Certainly people tend in all things to fall more on
> natural causes/than upon the basic origin; and if they
> get sick/they do not think/that they have sinned against
> God/and that *sin is the cause of illness*.[52]

Although there may well be outward causes for illness, one must always look to God to discover the final source and reason for one's ailments. For Müller and Francke, every sort of human illness, be it of body or soul, ultimately rests in the hands of God.[53] This does not mean that every sick person is under the wrath of God. Indeed, Müller had been sickly from childhood on, and Francke had experienced illness in his later years. Sickness can arise as simply a natural hazard, from sin, or from God's desire to teach and heal. In any case, the Pietists stressed not God's wrath, but that illness is an occasion for self-examination.[54]

---

[50] *SFA*, II, p. 670.

[51] "So it does not remain only a matter of the anguish of the soul in *Anfechtungen*/rather it also comes to the withering of the body. For the body is devoured by inner anguish as by fire/appears troubled and miserable/wilts like a flower/withers like grass/grows feeble and sick....Anxiety eats at the body like a deadly poison/soaks into the innermost marrow in the bone/ breaks all one's powers/that we age like clothing/and wear out like a woolen cloth." *GLF*, I, xix, pp. 498, 499.

[52] *SFA*, II, p. 677.

[53] "As physical illness comes from GOd/so also sickness of the soul/ the body has its sickness/pains/hunger/thirst/frost/weakness/the soul suffers all this spiritually/when the devil and sin torment it/and let it feel no comfort." *GLF*, I, xix, p. 501.

[54] "We can find this and that external cause for our illness/a doctor can give this and that discourse about it; but it depends solely on GOD/who holds in his hand/when we shall be ill/and when we shall be well again. But this does not mean/that those/who are sick/necessarily are under GOd's wrath: Rather that we should examine ourselves/because all sickness/comes on account of sin/whether our sickness is a punishment or a fatherly chastisement of GOd/under which no one would consider himself innocent before the pure eyes of GOd." *SFA*, II, p. 678.

Sickness can be of great benefit to a person since even more than the loss of possessions or the respect of others, the loss of health causes one to look within and turn to God.[55]

> But the more difficult the evil is/the greater advantage lies therein/when GOd puts affliction upon us/and as it attains its goal in us. For the *mystery of the cross*/in which all wisdom lies hidden/is revealed even in sickness; as through it a true redemption/a genuine dying occurs in us/and our coarse and wild heart will be broken.[56]

One errs when he or she tries to strike a bargain with God and postpone his or her repentance and conversion until after God has removed the illness. Rather than see that the time of sickness is the time for repentance, people tend to promise God that once they have recovered they will lead a serious Christian life. Francke suggests that unless an inner change occurs first, the worldly person is often even worse after his or her recovery: "As it is indeed aptly said of them in the old German proverb; *as the sick one got better/the worse he was.*"[57]

Francke points out that while one may anticipate strength and patience from God in illness, in this era one is normally healed in non-miraculous ways. He emphasizes the spiritual aspects of illness and the ways in which one should attempt to remember and honor God, rather than anticipate miracles. God is to be seen

---

[55] *SFA*, II, pp. 678, 679.

[56] *SFA*, II, p. 679; cf. *SFP*, pp. 1385, 1386.

[57] "da der Kranck genaß/je ärger er was." *SFA*, II, p. 672; Francke writes on the same page, "Then may we also learn this well/how perversely people generally tend to behave in their wretchedness/that they first desire/ how they may be saved from their outward distress/and think; if they were just rid of this or that trouble/then they would surely be converted and serve GOd better: Thus [they] save their conversion until then/and think/before this it would be impossible/that they could be better....Thus they err greatly/who say: Ah if I only were taken out of my great poverty/out of my difficult illness/out of this or that danger or persecution/if I could just come to a peaceful condition! O how I would serve and fear my GOd then! But now it is impossible for me/because my heart is always so heavy/that I cannot come to that. Behold/dear people/this is a completely false opinion that your flesh and blood have put in your head." Thus we see that physical illness is among those afflictions common to humanity which, like almost any aspect of life, can hinder or promote one's salvation.

as working primarily through doctors and medicine. Miraculous healings are not ruled out, however. While Christ surely bore our sins on the cross to heal our spiritual disease,

> ...physical illness should not be ruled out, as if Christ bore our spiritual sicknesses alone, and showed himself to be our physician only in this and not in the physical.[58]

The numerous examples of divine healing in the Old and New Testaments are proof that God heals physical illnesses miraculously. God will still do so, if it is to God's glory and for the good of the Church.[59]

Whatever the manner of affliction one experiences, he or she is to endure it in submission and obedience to God, secure in the knowledge that God will not let the burden become too great or last too long. Even if the affliction should end in death, the Christian may be sure that all will end well if he or she just has faith. "I will not ask God that I may be without affliction, but that I may bear my cross patiently."[60]

---

[58] *SFP*, p. 1451; Francke uses Matt. 8: 15, the healing of Peter's mother-in-law, as an example.

[59] *SFP*, p. 1546.

[60] *GE*, #127, p. 137.

CHAPTER 7

THE OUTER PERSON

The outer person, that is, the individual one sees in society caring for neighbor, working, looking after worldly possessions, etc., reflects and, to a degree, influences the condition of the inner person. Again we have made an artificial division, for as the inner person is more an amalgam or solution than a construction, so the outer and inner person constitute an integrated whole. Nonetheless, because the Pietists made this distinction, and because one's life in the world is immediately more apparent than his or her spiritual or inner condition,[1] we treat the outer person in this section.

We will encounter some repetition here, as love of neighbor, one's vocation, and attitudes toward money and time tend to overlap. Because this study concerns the individual, we will not deal here with the Pietist hope of reforming society and, eventually, the world through the impact of pious, born-again individuals at all levels of society. Thus rather than discuss the duties, concerns, etc. of the various social classes,[2] we concentrate here on the responsibilities common to any and all individuals.

---

[1] Müller points out that, "The inner person is visible and known only in the outer practice." *GLF*, II, vii, p. 802.

[2] "Even though Pietism contributed much to the leveling of class differences through its reforming tendencies, it nonetheless remained basically with the old Lutheran doctrine of the three classes [*Stände*], the division of society into a ruling class, a teaching [or educated] class, and a house or subsistence [working] class." Carl Hinrichs, "Der hallische Pietismus als politisch-soziale Reformbewegung des 18. Jahrhunderts", in *Zur neueren Pietismusforschung*, hrsg. von Martin Greschat, (Darmstadt, 1977), p. 247; For Pietism as a social movement see also Carl Hinrichs, *Preußentum und Pietismus: Der Pietismus in Brandenburg-Preußen als religios-soziale Bewegung*, (Göttingen, 1971); Koppel S. Pinson, *Pietism as a Factor in the Rise of German Nationalism*, (New York, 1968[2]); Klaus Deppermann, *Der hallesche Pietismus und der preußische Staat unter Friedrich III.(I)* (Göttingen, 1961).

Müller writes of the "three main classes", the "*Wehr=, Lehr=. und Nährstand*" and sees the *Lehrstand* as the linchpin or crux of society, in that "The preaching office connects the rulers with the subjects, in that it holds both their duties before them." *GE*, #269, p. 339.

In the introduction to our study we indicated that the Pietists' audience was made up of "christianized" people. This explains how Müller and Francke can in the same sermon, even in the same paragraph, make ethical demands on their audiences as if everyone was in fact a zealous believer, then go on as if most were mere nominal Christians, if Christians at all. Let us turn first to how one is to care for him- or herself.

THE BODY

We have seen in our section on human nature that the Pietists did not have a particularly high regard for the body, either as "flesh" or as such. This certainly does not mean, however, that one is to abuse or neglect his or her body. Since the person is made up of both spiritual and material elements, his or her body also comes under close scrutiny, and must be made subject to the will of God. While the body may indeed be a "jail and prison," it is nonetheless to be well tended. As the tool of the soul it has certain functional value, and thus needs to be cared for properly, in order that one may glorify God and serve his or her neighbor at maximum efficiency levels. To this end the person has certain responsibilities to his or her (and the neighbor's) physical self: to feed and clothe the body and make sure that he or she gets enough rest.

The basic thought is that, while the soul is infinitely and ultimately more important than the body, there must be a balanced self-care lest both body and soul be endangered.

> Because GOd has also given you a body/see to it/that you keep it, too, according to GOd's order. If you find/that you give more care to your body/than to your soul/you have already departed widely from GOd's order. But then should you not render the necessary service to your body at all/that would also be contrary to divine order.[3]

Francke hastens to add that this latter concern, that the body is not cared for, is hardly a matter for worry, since "thousands" forget their souls, while he has not met one single person who has forgotten to look after his or her body. As with all else, the Pietist concern for the well-being of the whole person has an eye turned toward God:

---

[3] *LR*, p. 89.

> A true Christian hallows GOd the LOrd body and
> soul/and gives all his members to the service of
> righteousness/that they may be holy. Rom. VI.19.
> Therefore he keeps his whole being/body and soul in
> fitting order/that one may assist the other/to honor and
> praise GOD. I. Cor. VI. 20.[4]

Müller, ill from childhood on, saw his occasional recoveries as a
divine commissioning to a holy task:

> ...it pleased the lover of life/to wrest me from the
> jaws of death/perhaps/so that one or another soul might
> be converted through me.[5]

Thus we see that the body is important and has a place and
purpose in the order of things. This idea of maintaining oneself
well in order to fulfill God's will (glorify God, serve neighbor,
grow in holiness) is a recurring theme in the Pietist discussion of
the body.

Both Müller and Francke favor moderation in eating and
drinking. They concur that the body should not be deprived.
Indeed, it should be well cared for, yet one should also be careful
to not overfeed oneself lest the body become unable to resist
lust.[6] Moderation is one means of restraining laziness and lusts
of the flesh, and of preserving the proper desires. "So eat/that
hunger remains constantly/otherwise the desire for prayer and
work vanishes."[7] Francke warns against troubling oneself

---

[4] *LR*, p. 90.

[5] *DA, Vorrede.*

[6] "So too if one may share too little out of a sincere, good opinion/he
needs only a kindly petition according to the example of Timothy/whom a
loving Paul advised no longer to drink water/but rather to use a little wine. I.
Tim. V.23." *LR*, p. 89; "Eating and drinking is not forbidden/the nature
must be preserved/strengthened and refreshed/otherwise it could not serve the
spirit in its work. But when you stuff yourself/treat your belly with
delicacies and too much/this is eating like an animal [*Fressen*]/swilling down
your drink [*Saufen*]/and is forbidden/and thus hinders the nature in
worshipping God more/than it helps/thus Christ calls it a *burden of the
heart*/like a load keeps the wanderer/from going on/and like a bird cannot fly
to the skies/if a piece of metal hangs from its foot." *GLF*, I, iii, pp. 20,21.

[7] *GLF*, I, iii, p. 23; "When one feeds one's flesh elegantly and too
much/it is inclined to all vices/thus Paul writes in his Epistle to the Romans
in the 13. Ch. v. 14. We should make provision for the body/*but not to*

unnecessarily about food, since eating too much not only diminishes the desire for prayer and work, but also tends to make one lose sleep,[8] and since worrying about it also prevents one from being rested and restful. This is especially foolish for a Christian who should know that his or her loving God will look after these things.[9] In good Pietist fashion, Müller offers some rules concerning food:

> 1. Eat and drink at certain times: work before eating, for whoever does not work should not eat.

> 2. Do not seek delicacies, rather be content with simple food.

> 3. Do not throw away anything which God has given you, but do not become accustomed to too much.

> 4. Do not love excess, but see that you maintain your body with little.[10]

The best advice for a Christian, however, is this:

> Consider always/there are two guests sitting at table with you/body and soul/what you give too much of to the one/will be taken from the other. So eat/that you may be ready at all times to hear with joy the trumpet of the archangel.[11]

How one clothes oneself is likewise a matter demanding moderation.[12] Müller and Francke both remind one in almost identical words, "that clothing was given us as a mark of sin/that it is the noose/which we wear/as a sign/that we have merited death."[13] Francke laments that people are willing to pay much for ribbons, lace, silk and the like, but will not give even a little to the poor, as if having less clothing somehow diminishes one's

---

fulfill its lusts." GLF, I, iii, p. 20.

[8] *LR*, p. 109.

[9] *LR* p. 35, p. 110.

[10] *GLF*, I, iii, p. 23.

[11] *GLF*, I, iii, p. 23.

[12] *GLF*, I, iii, p. 23.

[13] *SFA*, II, p. 48; Müller writes, "few wish to recognize/that clothing is a sign of their sin/as the noose is a sign of one's thievery." *GLF*, I, iii, p. 23.

splendor.[14] Let there be no doubt that God looks upon one's drawers full of splendid clothing, and compares them with one's wretched heart.[15] One's preoccupation with clothing is vanity, thus dishonoring God, and is extravagant, thus harming one's neighbor by wasting money that would be better given to the poor. Beyond this, however, the Pietists prescribe simplicity in clothing because the body simply is not worth all that much attention and ornamentation. Müller reminds his readers that

> it is enough/that we must lift and carry this
> carcass/clean and wash it: indeed we need not hang it
> with velvet and silk/in the end it must become food for
> the worms/and decay in the earth.[16]

The importance of the soul as compared to that of the body is particularly evident here.

The same rule of moderation applies concerning rest. Because rest, like food, is necessary for the well-being and healthy functioning of the body, one is reminded that the body is to be cared for in this area, too. There are nine basic rules.

> 1. One must not rest more than work lest he or she become a sluggard.

> 2. One should sleep as much as one's constitution requires (some people need more sleep than others), but he or she should experiment to discover just how much sleep he or she needs, being careful not to pamper his or her body, thus getting it accustomed to more rest than it needs.

> 3. One should not rest too much and thereby be unavailable to people in need.

> 4. One should make sure he or she gets a good rest by being moderate in food and drink.

> 5. One should keep his or her mind on God, thereby preventing the 'useless worries and sudden notions' that disturb sleep.

---

[14] *SFA*, II, p. 48.
[15] *SFA*, II, p. 49.
[16] *GLF*, I, iii, p. 24.

6. One should not only rest from his or her vocation on Sundays, but should refrain from idleness, strolling, entertaining and 'other fleshly amusements'.

7. One should rest so that one may be more cheerful and fit to serve God. He or she should not refrain from physical effort only to exhaust his or her mind with intellectual games.

8. The only true rest is found by taking up the yoke of Christ (that is, by becoming a born-again believer in the Pietist mold).

9. Resting on the Sabbath is based on God's own rest. (Heb. 4:9–13)[17]

Clearly expressed again is the tension inherent in Pietist anthropology: spirituality *vs.* and within corporeality. Francke's institutions give a good example of these competing demands. On the one hand he justified the large size of the rooms and the high ceilings in the Halle orphanage by citing the need for a healthy atmosphere for growing children. On the other, he was reprimanded by the orphanage physician for not allowing the children enough time to play. On the one hand the body must be tamed and managed wisely, since it is subject to lust and idleness. On the other, it must be nourished and cared for, since it is the medium for the soul's response to God in this world.

LOVE OF NEIGHBOR

Any discussion of Pietist humanity which omits love for neighbor or "neighbor's good" is from the start inadequate. Loving one's neighbor is the prescribed way of living in society, and is predicated upon the love of God manifested in Christ, and on the equality of all persons in God's sight.

As with the inner life, the Pietists begin with God and faith, and move from there to human responsibility: "The love of neighbor depends upon the love of God. For the neighbor is God's image and child. Thus he must be loved in God/and for God's sake."[18] The love which originates in God and is poured out in Jesus Christ onto humanity is then channeled through the

17 *LR*, pp. 108–114.
18 *GLF*, II, vi, p. 778; cp. *GE*, #182, p. 212.

believer to his or her neighbor. The medium of increased love is increased faith, since faith is the door through which the revelation of Christ's love enters one's heart.[19] In this case the life of the sincere believer is described/prescribed, and is contrasted by both Müller and Francke with the unregenerate person's standard understanding of life, which each finds lamentable: "Each one for himself, God for us all."[20] Müller goes on,

> The best is, that one goes to church, takes the sacraments, lives honorably, is for himself, does not burden himself with others, is neither borrower nor lender, gives in miserly fashion. That is today's Christianity. May it be lamented to God![21]

Not so the Christian. Because the Christian has the mind of Christ, he or she lives gladly in community and cannot avoid serving neighbor in unselfish love.[22]

The believer will not be selective in love. That is, he or she will not limit acts of charity to his or her own family or social set or only to fellow Christians. This is based on Scripture, and is the fulfillment of the law of love.[23] This divinely-inspired love

---

[19] "But a growth must also show itself in love toward one's neighbor/ which then again/as mentioned/arises from the growth of faith. Namely/the more the tender and ardent mother's love/which our LOrd JEsus CHrist has toward us/becomes more evident in our heart/and the more one drinks from his breast of love this milk and this honey through the fiery and ardent desire of love/the more and the richer flow the streams of it to your neighbor/the more sincerely will he be disposed toward it/and the more he shows this in deed." *SFA*, I, p. 169; "So is being charitable a natural result of faith, like the fruit of a tree." *HLK*, II, xiii, p. 752.

[20] *GE*, #182, p. 212; cp. *SFA*, I, p. 850.

[21] *GE*, #182, p. 212.

[22] As long as one uses his or her neighbor for his or her own gain, "so long is the mind of CHrist not yet there: for this is the true mind of JEsus CHrist/that the person desires to serve his neighbor out of pure love without his own pleasure and profit." *SFA*, II, p. 616; By contrast, "Self-interest is the mind of the tax collector [publican]." *SFA*, II, p. 615, marginal note; And, when one has the mind of Christ, "Then you will no longer see/how you may get hold of your neighbor's possesions/and use them for your own profit and advantage. For this is the pagan and hypocritical mind: but rather you must obtain such a mind from GOd/that you may live in the world only to serve your neighbor." *SFA*, II, p. 783; cp. *SFA*, II, p. 60.

[23] "In the New Testament the understanding which the Jews made for

far exceeds earthly, governmental laws as well. Whereas worldly laws provide only for protection against evil, and neither require good works nor punish people for ignoring their neighbor's need, Christian love makes believers into willing servants of those who otherwise have no legal claims upon them.[24] Love of neighbor even transcends the legal demands of the Old Testament, indeed, it fulfills them.[25] Francke bemoans the inhuman attitude of most people, particularly that of the authorities, toward the poor: "One cares indeed/*that one may be rid of the poor*/but not/*how the poor may be rid of their wretchedness* and may be helped out of their poverty."[26] This is a way of seeing which dehumanizes the poor. Quite the opposite, Christian love sees through the eyes of Christ, that is, knows all persons to be equal and to be "neighbors." There can be no disregard of the poor on account of a greater regard for, or hope for favor from, the high and the mighty. "The workshop of our love is our neighbor. You should love *your neighbor*/not the rich/mighty/educated/saintly/ but rather your neighbor."[27] Nor should the love come to an end when one's "neighbor" loses his or her position, or can no longer be of assistance.

---

themselves did not apply, namely that by neighbor they readily understood the Jews, who were of their race and religion. Christ pointed to a better way in the story of the Samaritan, when someone asked him: *Who is my neighbor?* Luc. 10,19. And so Paul also said ὁ γὰρ ἀγαπῶν τὸν ἕτερον, whoever loves the other, be he friend or foe, he has fulfilled the law." *LP*, VII, p. 358; Müller likewise quotes Romans 13:8, "Consider further/how in the love of neighbor the love of God is contained as well/so then deem it the most noble virtue: *Whoever loves the neighbor/he has fulfilled the law.*" *GLF*, II, vi, p. 787.

[24] *GLF*, II, vi, p. 779.

[25] "Law must cease to be law, where love is concerned; although it does not cease, rather it is fulfilled most powerfully in love.

As if on a Sunday when you wanted to go to church, a sorrowful person would come who needed your comfort, advice, help, you need not look to Moses' commandment: *You shall keep the Sabbath holy. Exod. 20,8.* No; love is a free empress over this commandment, subjects it to herself, that it must give way to her this time. And how could you better celebrate the Sabbath, than if you were to comfort the sorrowful, meet with the troubled? There is no greater *wrong* than when one exercises love according to the law, and not the law according to love." *HLK*, II, ix, p. 714.

[26] *SFA*, II, p. 46.

[27] *GLF*, II, vi, p. 781.

This universality of love is based on the fact that the law of love applies to all; thus the wealthy must confess that the lowest of beggars is nothing less than a neighbor, and that they are to love not only with their money, but also in other ways such as direct service. Müller cites as an example the noblewoman whose bones were venerated for several centuries in the *Elisabethkirche* in Marburg: "How wonderful it would be/if we would see/how kings and princes/queens and princesses served the poor beggars and lepers/as we read of S[aint] Elisabet?"[28] This universality is also based on the great breadth of faith: as true faith encompasses every point of doctrine, so true love, accordingly, embraces every human being. Indeed, failure to love is as much a heresy and threat to the Church as is false doctrine.[29] Godly love for others is based on the presence of Christ in the suffering neighbor. Both Müller and Francke frequently cite Matt. 25:35ff. Francke also recalls the legend of St. Martin of Tours to illustrate that any good deed is done to Christ himself.[30] This means a focussing or particularizing of loving-kindness, lest in the desire to do great and mighty deeds for the glory of God, one totally misses the God who is nearby in the suffering neighbor.[31] In a splendid and profound insight into human interconnectedness, Müller begins by grounding the essence of love in the creative act of God, in the essence of nature or "Mother Earth," and in the

---

[28] *GLF*, II, vi, p. 781.

[29] Francke quotes Armand von Bourbon, *von denen Pflichten und Schuldigkeiten hoher Standes=Personen gegen GOtt/dem Nächsten und ihm selbsten/mit unumbstößlichen Grunden fürgestellet*, (Mäyntz, 1670), "His love toward neighbor should not be smaller than/but rather be just as large as his faith. Love should be just as common as faith. Love is surely not truly Christian/if it is not equally universal and general like faith. Faith should encompass and embrace all points of doctrine/without any exceptions: And love of neighbor should contain and include each and every person without the exception of any person/for heresy is no more contrary to the true church/in its attack upon truth/than the separation/the division/the splintering and the hate/in that through this eternity and unity are assailed." *SFA*, II, pp. 71, 72.

[30] *SFA*, II, p. 54.

[31] "Thus GOD will also make a fool of the world/which seeks to serve him only in great and glorious things. But then he gets himself wrapped up in one's neighbor's misery/affliction and distress/desires/that you would seek him in hunger and distress/in unhappiness and disgrace...Ah how many a person deceives himself/thinks he would serve GOd in great things! and meanwhile lets him go by here below on earth in his neighbor." *GLF*, II, vi, p. 787.

common origin of all people in Adam and Eve, and concludes with the reconstitution of human unity in and as the body of Christ.

> Beyond all this we are created for love. Nature has armed other creatures/the lion with claws/the ox with horns/the snake with poison, etc. But she has not equipped the human being in such a way/for he should be an image of love. Therefore nature also did not bring all her goods in one heap in one country/but scattered them in all lands/to the one country this treasure/to the other that/also laid a road from one land to the other through the midst of the sea/that one might associate/do business/interact/develop love and friendship/ with the other. Therefore God caused us all to grow forth from one tree/namely from Adam. Eve was not made from the earth/but from Adam/that we all may be drawn through one nature into one love. Yet in Adam the earth is mother of us all/the earth/which is of no use to us/which we trample underfoot/and yet gives us everything/bears/blesses and gives us fruit. Behold/dear people/thus your origin leads you to love. Consider your own body/how there is such an intimate friendship between body and soul: How ardently one member loves the other: How one serves the other: *There is no schism in the body*/says Paul I. Cor.12/26. *but rather the members have the same care one for the other. And if one member suffers/so all the members with it: And if one member is honored/so all the members rejoice with it.* Whoever hates his neighbor/hates Christ's member and his own fellow member.[32]

The universality of the law of love requires that every objection to charity be met and repudiated. The common response of the unregenerate person to human need is to make no response at all, but, of course, for "good" reasons. Francke rejects the excuse,

> that perhaps the people plunged themselves into poverty through wantonly wasting their possessions; Nor may we excuse ourselves/[by saying] that it may be used for evil.[33]

---

[32] *GLF*, II, vi, pp. 790, 791.
[33] *SFA*, II, p. 45.

Again, the nature of God provides the rationale for human charity: God causes the rain to fall and the sun to shine on the just and the unjust alike. Were God to wait until there were no more gluttons or drunkards, for example, the sun would never shine. But God does not withdraw blessings because people abuse God's kindnesses.[34] Müller presents and responds to several common objections to charity:

> *Obj.* How do I know Christ is in this needy person? Perhaps he is actually wicked.

> *Res.* You need not worry. Whatever you give in Christ's name is given to Christ. He looks upon your heart.

> *Obj.* My neighbor is ungrateful. I find this wearisome.

> *Res.* True, kindness is a chain about our necks. Yet do not be kind in order to be thanked. Virtue is its own reward. To be generous for gratitude's sake is to sell your kindness.

> *Obj.* Continual giving will reduce my possessions.

> *Res.* The more you give, the more you get. To give to the poor is to loan to the Lord who pays back richly. "The more blood one lets/the greater is one's health."

> *Obj.* How will my children live if I give everything away?

> *Res.* Foolish person, let God care for your children. That is the best way to care for them.

> *Obj.* Why does God not look after the poor himself?

> *Res.* God wants you to stand in his stead, and receive some of the honor. You have received in abun

---

[34] *SFA*, II, p. 45.

dance, not for yourself, but to make up the wants of your neighbor.

Obj. Experience teaches that those who give a lot suffer and become poor.

Res. That is the interest [on the loan]. The poor pray that all may be well with you, and a Christian is never better than when in affliction.[35]

Indeed, poor people are truly great treasures, "For even though you may see a stench before you/your LOrd JEsus is hidden therein..."[36] Francke points out that although the wealthy may think they are important, in Luke 6:19ff. the rich man is not even mentioned by name. On the other hand, the poor, rejected and ignored by society are precious and well known to God.[37] However important the poor may be, though, it is just not wise to give money away with no thought whatsoever for the consequences. Deception and wickedness are, after all, parts of reality, and the Christian needs to be careful that his or her alms are not wasted while the pious poor suffer needlessly as a result.[38] Again, however, this concern is not a valid excuse for avoiding one's responsibility to one's neighbor. Just because believers capable of giving still need food, clothing, and shelter for themselves, they should not fall into the all-too-common trap of making vices into virtues, by such common practices as calling pride cleanliness and greed thrift.[39]

As one is to love the poor, however ungrateful and wicked they might be, so one is to love his or her outright enemies as well. "There is no purer love than the love of one's enemy/love for one's friend comes by nature."[40] The best example is the

---

35 *GLF*, II, x, pp. 833–837.

36 *GLF*, II, x, p. 833.

37 "On the contrary/as unimportant as the poor may be in this world/of so much worth are they to dear GOd. Who knows of this or that poor person/who is here and there/or perhaps sits in his hut in great poverty? GOd knows." *SFA*, II, p. 44.

38 "One cannot deny/that on account of the terrible deception and wickedness a Christian caution must be used/that one not only sow/but also watch/how one sows and uses his seeds/so that the ungrateful do not take away everything/and the pious must do without." *SFA*, II, p. 46.

39 *SFA*, II, pp. 50, 51.

40 *GLF*, II, vii, p. 804; Francke concurs, "I know and have experienced

crucified Christ who from the cross prayed for forgiveness for those who crucified and tormented him.[41] The believer is to take the hatred of his or her enemy, and give it back in the form of love.

> Whoever hates [his or her] enemy/denies Christ. The LOrd says/body and soul can go to hell. The enemy can attack us in three ways/with the heart/ through hate; with the tongue/through curses and insults/and then with evil deeds. We should repay in three ways/the heart should love/the mouth bless and pray/the hand do well. Thus Christ goes before us.[42]

Müller takes this issue and asks two concrete, knotty questions: whether a believer should give up his or her life for the neighbor, and whether a Christian should let him- or herself be killed rather than kill a drunk who attacks him or her. With the qualification that one should not deliberately place oneself in such a situation, Müller answers the first question with a resounding yes, since the Christian is assured of salvation, while the other may need more time in this world to repent. Likewise is the believer to sacrifice him- or herself rather than deprive an attacker of the chance to receive eternal life. Müller makes clear that this does not mean, for example, that a father should allow a thief to murder his family, but he does stress that it is better to die than to kill.[43]

As well as gifts of money, gifts of kindness and mercy are called for. Both Müller and Francke stress the commonality of human nature and experience as a reason to love one's neighbor. Müller reminds people that they are not so far from their neighbor's fate: "What your neighbor is/you can become."[44] Francke reminds the believer that he or she was once in the same condition as the fallen neighbor.[45] Fritsch notes that we are all poor,

---

that nature cannot give me such [love for one's enemies]." *SFP*, p. 655.

[41] *SFP*, p. 652ff.

[42] *GLF*, II, vii, p. 803.

[43] *TE*, in Appendix to *DA*, p. 533ff.

[44] *GLF*, II, x, p. 840.

[45] "He will, when he becomes aware of his neighbor's error, be humbled anew in remembering his own wickedness which he learned to know when he asked GOD for the illumination of the Holy Spirit and the examination of his heart. Thus he will readily have compassion when he sees even the greatest wickedness in others." *CP*, p. 250; Müller writes, "Indeed

wretched worms who should plague each other less, and care for each other more.[46] Without mitigating the importance of money and goods, the Pietists called for more. Not everyone has enough money that he or she can give alms. In this case, one should speak words of comfort to those in need, give sound advice, and ask others to help and pray for the needy.[47] Love extends into every interpersonal situation: "Now as we will learn/how we should show love to our neighbor in *giving*: so we will also learn *to forgive* from the example of GOd..."[48] Müller warns against judging one's neighbor,[49] and Francke encourages the Christian to try to think the best of his or her neighbor.

> So long as it is possible, one should excuse his neighbor's failings: he will not have meant it so badly, he will not have had bad intentions, those are just rumors about him, etc.[50]

This does not mean, however, that one should attempt to deny reality.

> One should make the best of everything, so long as it can be made the best of. But things which displease GOd, and which have been brought to light, these should not be covered over.[51]

---

one's neighbor's weaknesses are a mirror of your own wretchedness." *HLK*, II, x, p. 722.

[46] "We are all with one another poor/wretched earth- sin- and affliction-worms: Ah! why do we wish to plague and trouble each other so? Should we not rather have compassion with each other? Care for one another/and help alleviate affliction and misery!" *Gottlob*, p. 189.

[47] *SFA*, II, p. 43; Also, "One should make one's neighbor's need his own need and take it before the LOrd." *SFA*, I, p. 294, marginal note; Müller writes, "Many do not have the means/to give their neighbor much/but draw within themselves his suffering/and weep with those who weep. A sincere tear of grief is more valid before God than a whole chest full of gold/which is not given from the heart." *GLF*, II, x, p. 830; This is not meant, of course, to discourage the giving of money (as much Pietist writing demonstrates), rather it is to stress the importance of giving from a heart of love.

[48] *SFA*, II, p. 784.

[49] *GLF*, II, vii, p. 784.

[50] *CP*, p. 252.

[51] *CP*, p. 252; The Christian definitely has a responsibility to God and neighbor to chastise evildoers. Francke interprets Matt. 5:13, "Therefore

As we have seen earlier, reproof and correction are also acts of love, since this is caring for the soul. Müller devotes several pages to the issue of "brotherly chastisement and other matters," wherein he claims that no true Christian can stand by in silence while his or her neighbor wallows in damning sin. While the believer needs to be careful that he or she does not embitter those he or she chastises, still the neighbor must "be punished...as often...as he sins, and one cannot remain silent, particularly when one sees it daily."[52] To this end the Christian must attempt the difficult task of separating the sin from the sinner. The believer must hate the sin, "but we must separate the wickedness from the person. The evil is the devil's/one must hate that/the creature is God's/one must love her."[53] As crucial as the distribution of alms, kind words and comfort may be, caring for the neighbor's soul is indispensable.[54] This element of spiritual concern is basic to all Christian charity.

Müller and Francke are not sparing in concrete suggestions as to how one's neighbor, particularly the poor neighbor, should be cared for.[55] Nor do they hold back on giving reasons why a person should help his or her neighbor. Again the *quid pro quo* thinking of the Pietist appears. In a series of marginal notes, Francke lists the punishments for failure to show mercy:

> Mercilessness will be punished: 1. with the pain
> of hell. 2. with the deprivation of salvation. 3. With
> the deprivation of all hope of being set free. 4. With an
> anxious conscience about the mentioned offense and on

---

consider this well/you who are present here! there are some/who call themselves Christians/and have the reputation/that they have turned to GOd; but when it comes to this/that they should chastise someone/so that they need not bear the guilt on his account; there is no one home; so it says accordingly/*Where is your mouth?* Now where is your Christianity?" *SFA*, II, p. 622.

[52] *TSB*, II, p. 1ff.

[53] *GLF*, II, vi, p. 793.

[54] "We must know even further/that we should help the poor nor only physically/but because most people are *spiritually poor* and are provided for badly in their souls/[we] should consider/helping them get better in their souls as well." *SFA*, II, p. 55.

[55] *SFA*, II, p. 47ff; cp. *GLF*, II, vii, x, pp. 844, 845.

> account of disdaining the Word of GOd[56] ...Merci-
> lessness toward one's neighbor is a bestial vice.[57]

On the other hand, "Mercy toward the poor will be rewarded: 1. with heavenly comfort and joy/ 2. with the renewal of the image of GOd."[58] Müller says much the same thing: "It is also profitable to us/if we are not vengeful. For as we are with our enemies/so God treats us in return."[59] and, "The more you love your brother/the more you draw God's love toward you...The more good you do your neighbor/the more good you have to hope of God."[60] While this sort of reasoning pervades Pietist thought, it is not the primary argument for holy living, be it withstanding affliction, praising God, or caring for one's neighbor. Müller uses it as a last resort[61], and Francke uses it particularly with people who are not yet burning with Pietist zeal and love.[62]

If the tit-for-tat approach is too vague, or the promise of reward insufficiently inspiring, the blunt threat of an eternity in hell may convince the nominal or backsliding believer that charity is an essential element of the Christian life and faith. Müller warns loveless souls,

> You tear your soul from GOd/for God is love and
> whoever does not remain in love/he does not remain in
> God. You suffer a shipwreck of faith. For faith is active
> through love. You plunge yourselves into ruin. For

---

[56] *SFA*, II, p. 56ff.

[57] *SFA*, II, p. 59.

[58] *SFA*, II, PP. 58, 59.

[59] *GLF*, II, viii, p. 817.

[60] *GLF*, II, vi, p. 797; Also, "The more you give, the more you receive." *GE*, #56, p. 56.

[61] "Should this [one's common humanity with neighbor] not move you/then consider the profit. Your benevolence profits you more than the needy person. To whom is the seed of greatest profit/the soil or the sower?" *GLF*, II, x, p. 843; cp. *SFA*, I, p. 849.

[62] Francke, for example, tells the authorities that, by their generosity, rulers: 1) are truly fathers of their lands, 2) bear God's image, 3) set an example for their subjects, 4) awaken the love of their subjects, 5) restrain evil and disorder, 6) set an example for others in authority, and 7) receive the benefits of the prayers of the poor whom they aid, these prayers being the true ramparts and walls around their lands. *SFA*, II, p. 30.

this judgment stands firm/whoever does not love his brother remains in death.[63]

Francke, too, stresses that lovelessness brings eternal death. Indeed, everything that is said of God's overwhelming love will become, if not acted upon, a source of even more severe judgment and condemnation.[64] Good works simply round out faith and make up one side of a coin, as it were, which without either faith or good works, is of no value at all.[65] Francke makes a rather snide reply to hardhearted scoffers:

> But go ahead/and scoff as much as you will/if you neither can nor want to help it/On judgment day we will speak with each other again. [here Francke quotes Matt. 25: 41-43]....then we will see/whether you will scoff at that.[66]

In the midst of sharing love in all manner of ways with friend and foe alike, the believer is reminded of Gal. 6:10, that charity indeed begins at home, and that "Common love applies to all/ brotherly love only to Christians."[67] Believers are also reminded, in a burst of good Lutheran emphasis on *sola gratia*, that despite the fact that failure to love will result in damnation, good works have nothing to do with their salvation.

> We must not think/that we earn eternal salvation thereby/GOd wishes to grant it to us out of grace. CHrist has won salvation for us. And he also wants us to enjoy the fruits of the gift of grace/as here the seed of good works is sown.[68]

Here again we see that the line blurs between God's initiating role and the person's role in salvation.

---

[63] *GLF*, II, vi, p. 796.

[64] *SFA*, II, P. 780.

[65] Francke quotes Eph. 2: 8 and 10, then goes on, "Thus one does not abolish the other; rather as the bird is created to fly: so are the faithful created for the *imitation of JEsus*/namely in the work of conversion/where Christ puts his spirit in us/that we should imitate him in good works and in his life. Now for whoever does not remain in the state of good works/the grace which he formerly received/is of no help." *SFA*, II, p.782.

[66] *SFA*, II, p. 61.

[67] *GLF*, II, x, p. 840.

[68] *SFA*, II, p. 66.

The call for the Christian to love his or her neighbor is not simultaneously a call for fellowship with that neighbor; a gift of money or kind and encouraging words are hardly signs of fellowship. Rather, separation from evil people and wicked company is a basic element of the Pietist's life in the world.[69] The world is first and foremost a desert in which the believer, as Christ did, encounters temptation.[70] It is characterized by fickleness and greed. "Indeed, for they love not me, but only what is mine; their love blossoms with my fortune, withers with my fortune..."[71] Among the children of this world we find two basic types:

> For there is a marked difference among the children of this world. There are such/to whom the truth has not yet been so clearly testified/and thus wander in sins and vices/in which they surely cannot inherit the kingdom of GOd/but who certainly would consider a better [life]/if the peril of their souls was made known to them. And there are also such/to whom the truth has been testified/and yet live in sin against their conscience in spite of it/and besides that resist the truth and keep others from it.[72]

What, then, is a believer to do? The Christian is, on the one hand, to love these "*Weltkinder*," bringing the first sort described above to the truth in gentleness and patience. At the same time, he or she must be very careful not to fall into the ways of the second sort. "So then, the Christian must neither outwardly nor inwardly/so far as it concerns sinful things/have fellowship with the world."[73] It is clear that the believer lives in tension. One cannot deny the danger inherent in frequent contact with wicked people. Müller writes, "You dare not think/you can remain quite pious/even though you have contact with the godless. No, rather consider/how difficult it is to swim against the flood."[74] Francke

---

[69] Here we are interested in what the individual's relationship with the world is to be. For an analysis of *Absonderung*, see Hartmut Lehmann, "'Absonderung' und 'Gemeinschaft' im frühen Pietismus", in *Pietismus und Neuzeit*, hrsg. von Martin Brecht, u.a., (Göttingen, 1979), pp. 54–82.

[70] *SFP*, p. 494.

[71] *GE*, #98, p. 98.

[72] *SFA*, III, p. 240.

[73] *SFA*, III, p. 235.

[74] *GLF*, I, xxii, p. 592; Also, "The best advice is that we avoid wicked company....Whoever would warm himself by the fire of the wicked [as did

says much the same, and adds, "Then flesh and blood stir. Because the person is still weak, he is easily moved to hypocrisy..."[75] Nevertheless, the believer obviously cannot escape contact with worldly people, nor should he or she attempt to do so. Indeed, the Christian is called to precisely such contact, for it is the believer's responsibility to be light in a dark world.[76] One should not delude oneself, however, concerning either one's own motives or the harsh realities of the situation which one enters.

> Many adorn themselves with this cloak/that they say/they go to worldly people/that they may make them pious and spiritual. But these should know/that the world with its temptations and charms can lead a Christian to stray from true Christianity much more powerfully and easily/than a Christian may draw the child of the world from the world to Christianity. For in this the world has a great advantage/that Christians still have in them a good bit of the worldly mind/but the world has nothing at all of the Spirit of God.[77]

Both Müller and Francke advise the Christian that everyday contact with "children of the world," both unavoidable and necessary, is an arena for self-discipline and watchfulness, lest God's honor be sullied, neighbor offended and misled, or one's own Christianity weakened or distorted.[78] Again we encounter the "Pietist trinity," as it were, in which God's glory, neighbor's

---

Peter] must deny Christ with them." *GE*, #189, p. 221.

[75] *SFP*, p. 877

[76] *SFA*, III, p. 235.

[77] *GLF*, I, xxii, p. 593.

[78] The first thirty rules in *LR* treat this particular subject, and are readily found in German in *WIA*, pp. 354–355 or in my *God's Glory, Neighbor's Good*, pp. 199–206. Müller writes, in similar language, "Indeed, as concerns common society and company/which you cannot escape in everyday life/this is not forbidden/only you should be careful. Should it happen/that you fall in with a [bad] crowd/or must necessarily be with them/ so stay firmly within the ground of your soul/and see to it/that through outward conversation/nothing falls in/whereby God will be robbed of his honor/and you of your inner peace....When you come home [from company]/pour out your heart/examine it closely/[to see] whether anything worldly remains stuck in it/then purify it anew through faith/sweep out the filth/sigh and plead/that God would change and convert the worldly-hearted." *GLF*, I, xxii, pp. 594, 595.

good, and one's own holiness are inextricably linked.[79] Francke's rather direct message in a sermon on dancing serves as a good example. He bases his entire argument on I Cor. 10:31, "Whether ye eat, or drink, or whatsoever ye do, do all to the glory of God," and on the rule that one should deny worldly lusts.[80] He sees no way, apart from a "spiritual dance" like David's, that dancing, because of the atmosphere in which it normally occurs, can bring glory to God.[81] Thus youths are confronted with particularly dangerous opportunities to participate in all manner of sinful behavior, and Christians, especially those who are weak in faith, run the risk of falling, or at least of backsliding.[82] Halle Pietism made very clear to its children and adherents that they stood "over against" the world. Martin Schmidt writes,

> Francke, more than Spener, gave Pietism a sharp profile: rigorous discipline, a work ethic, thrift, and earnestness were its characteristics. Humor and play, waste of time and money were banished. But he also gave the movement self-consciousness and pride. One knew what it meant to belong to Halle.[83]

Although the Pietists could hardly be deemed tyrants, Francke's great enthusiasm to renounce and avoid things worldly did seem to get out of hand on occasion. The orphanage physician, Dr. Juncker, at one point demanded that Francke allow more free playtime for pupils.[84] Francke was hardly a lone pioneer in the propagation of the importance of being serious, however, for in Müller we find,

---

[79] Illustrative here is Francke's insistence that a believer may not partake of the Lord's Supper with the wicked, as this would be an offense to God, and tarnish the Christian's holiness. Believers should share regular meals with unbelievers, however, since this might lead to their conversion, and follows an example set by Jesus. *SFP*, p. 877.

[80] *WIA*, p. 386; Scriver lists a number of prominent figures who died while, or immediately after, dancing. Let that be a warning. *Gotthold*, pp. 511–514.

[81] *WIA*, p. 386.

[82] *WIA*, pp. 388, 389.

[83] Schmidt, *Pietismus*, p. 79.

[84] Wolf Oschlies, *Die Arbeits und Berufspädagogik August Hermann Franckes*, (Witten-Ruhr, 1966), p. 235.

> Better sad in God than happy in the world. Sooner
> tears with Jesus than laughter with the world. One will
> not find Jesus with laughter. Where have you read that
> he laughed? ...In the end the world will laugh itself into
> weeping.[85]

Müller goes on, "Yet you should not think that I am always sad.
I have a gracious God, that makes me glad."

Despite their seemingly rather narrow views in many areas of
life, the early Pietists were hardly inflexible tyrants. Francke, for
example, reminds the believer that he or she is not to despise the
worldly person, or think too highly of him- or herself, since
"there but for the grace of God go I."[86] He also points out that
"the ways of the servants of GOd are often different from one
another."[87] This means that each believer must be allowed to
operate as he or she feels led by God, "...Solus cum solo, that
is/one should see only/that one stands right with GOd/and not
trouble oneself about/how other people think of or judge our
behavior."[88]

Love of neighbor, avoidance of particularly wicked company
and circumstances, caution and consideration in society, and
watchfulness that God's glory, neighbor's good and one's own
sanctification be protected and promoted are the basic rules for
life in the world. "If I must have contact with the godless then, I
will watch myself, that he does not make me worse, and strive
that I may improve him."[89] And, finally, "The standard of the
Christian walk is not the customs of the world: rather Christ's
teaching and life.[90]

---

[85] *GE*, #20, p. 21; cp. *LR*, p. 21.

[86] "Let us then consider/if we perhaps see/that a thief is hung/that
someone is flogged/or is punished for some crime. Let no one then be proud
in his heart. Know/that no vice is too coarse/so horrible and atrocious/that
you could not wallow in it yourself/if GOd's mercy were not to hold you
back from it." *SFA*, II, p. 239.

[87] *SFA*, III, p. 229, Marginal note.

[88] *SFA*, III, p. 231.

[89] *GE*, #189, p. 221.

[90] *HLK*, II, xi, p. 744.

WORK

A person's life is like an iron tool, if one uses it,
it shines, if one leaves it lying still, rust devours it. If
you love the shine and wish to be honored, then love
the work, too.[91]

It is in God's order that people work.[92] One must work because
it has been so ordained by God that one obtain his or her bread
by the sweat of his or her brow (Gen. 3:19; 2 Thess. 3:10), that
one is to show love to one's neighbor by serving him or her
through work, that one can thereby earn money to share with the
needy, that one may not offend one's neighbor,[93] and that one
may provide for one's own needs.[94] Besides this, working is
healthier than remaining idle.[95] Thus work is a fundamental part
of human life, and touches upon every area of life.

"Idle life, shameful life."[96] Activity is in the very essence of
creation. Heavenly bodies are in constant motion, bees are ever at
work, ants busily lay up stores for the winter. "Is it not then a
shame that a person, the noblest creature of God, should be
lazy?"[97] Idleness is not only abominable, it is also spiritually
dangerous for a person.[98] Scriver points out that one's need to
work in order to survive and get ahead is actually a blessing,
because the idle person is on the road to hell, "*For it is impossi-
ble/that a lazy person would not do evil/because idleness is the
school in which one teaches and learns the doing of evil...*"[99]
Müller also writes, "Idle life, sinful life."[100] Both Müller and

---

91 *GE*, #191, p. 225.

92 "This is the divine order, that, if we want to eat, we should also
work." *CP*, P. 491; cp. *SFA*, II, pp. 176, 177.

93 *SFA*, II, p. 176.

94 *LR*, p. 99.

95 *SFA*, II, p.244; cp. *SFA*, II, p. 176.

96 *GE*, #191, p. 223.

97 *GE*, #191, p. 223.

98 "For idleness is a very atrocious and shameful matter/and a person is
always in danger/that Satan will ensnare him; or if he is already trapped in
Satan's snare/that he cannot be saved from it/as he is idle." *SFA*, II, pp. 176,
177.

99 *Gotthold* , p. 302.

100 *GE*, #191, p. 223.

Francke call idleness a puddle[101] in which one finds all manner of worms and vices.

The Christian must work to provide for the poor.

> Say not/I do not need/to work/even if I sit with
> my hands in my lap/I have enough to live. I hope/a
> heathen would speak more reasonably/for such slug-
> gards are harmful to the common good. If you have no
> reason to work/Paul gives you one: Work and create
> with your hands (not something careless/useless/vain/
> lustful or out of boredom/but rather) something good/
> so that you have something to give the needy.[102]

This applies particularly to the wealthy who, by refusing to work, both deprive the poor of what they need and ignore God's order.[103] "Ah, mine, when you sit at table, eat and drink, what do you find in your bowls and mugs? Truly nothing other than the sweat and tears of the poor."[104] Not only does the idler fail to provide for the needy, but he or she lives off the labor of others[105] and thus is nothing less than a thief.[106]

Positively seen, work fulfills God's order established since the Fall, provides for the poor, and keeps the worker from idleness and spiritual disaster. As the world is so disorderly and perverse, the Christian is of great value because he or she is by (his or her new) nature faithful and honest in his or her vocation, and thus brings an element of stability to society.[107] To this end, the believer must carry out every task, however small, with diligence and vigor.[108]

---

[101] *SFA*, II, p. 188; cp. *GE*, #191, p. 223.

[102] *LR*, p. 106; cp. *SFA*, II, p. 55.

[103] *CP*, p. 491.

[104] *GE*, #191, p. 224.

[105] "Whoever will not work, must live off the sweat and blood of other people." *GE*, #191, p. 224.

[106] "Live idly, live like a thief." *GE*, "191, p. 224; So Francke: "But if your work is not pleasing to God and profitable for humanity/you steal the bread from people." *LR*, p. 99.

[107] "Therefore one sees that Christianity brings the world a great profit and advantage, because a Christian is faithful and honest in his calling, and returns all that is out of order and misbegotten to its proper order." *LP*, VII, p. 189.

[108] *LR*, pp. 105, 106.

But not just any sort of work is acceptable. If it does not lead to God's glory and neighbor's good, it must be given up, even though to do so may appear to the Christian to be as difficult as Christ's command to the rich young man. The Christian must trust that God will not let him or her starve (although it is better to starve to death in holiness than to live well, only to die in sin).[109] If one is about to begin a vocation, one must first be sure that it is not contrary to the will of God. Before starting, the Christian is to call upon God for God's blessing not only upon the work, but upon the believer's motives and intentions as well.[110] Should the job be acceptable, two things must happen: the believer's attitude must change, and Christ must become part of the work. "Even in an otherwise good profession if you do not have the sincere aim of God's glory/and the neighbor's best/you must change your disposition."[111] This means that success is no longer to be determined by profit, but by the degree to which God is glorified and neighbor served. It also means that God's will, rather than the job itself, must determine whether and how the work is to be done. To absolutize the job, and to make plans which cannot be changed is to reject the leading of God.[112]

The feeling that one earns his or her keep by working, or that it is absolutely necessary for a Christian to work in order to survive at all (Gen. 3:19 and 2 Thess. 3:10 notwithstanding), reflects the attitude that God is not reliable and provident. Those who trust in their own labor rather than believe Matt. 6:33 have greedy and untrusting hearts:

> Indeed they say/I do not see/a fried dove flying
> into someone's mouth/I do not see/someone giving me

---

109 *LR*, pp. 99–101.

110 "Should the work of your head, your heart, and your hands be blessed, do something which is good, and be about nothing but what God has either commanded or permitted in his Word. How can you do something in Jesus' name which is contrary to him?...Begin nothing until you have first called upon God, that he would not only bless your work in Jesus, but also sanctify the plans in the work..." *GE*, #294, p. 377.

111 *LR*, p. 99; "Likewise [as with the ruling class] is it so with the other classes/that the person should use his profession only to the honor of God/and the good of the neighbor; but everything/that is drawn into our vain mind and arrogance/that is nothing but the work of the devil..." *SFA*, I, p. 598.

112 *LR*, pp. 104, 105.

> something/when I have nothing. This amounts to/
> slapping the LOrd JEsus in the face...[113]

Experience teaches that not everyone who works hard has a lot.[114] Everything depends on God's generosity. One person may plow, a sheep may give milk and wool, and a bird may fly, sing, raise its young—each has its appropriate task—yet it is the earth which brings forth the plants which nourish them all. That with which one works and that which one's labors appear to provide, exist only because God first puts it there.

> You must labor and do something, but it is not
> your labor which supports you, but rather divine
> blessing. Where God puts nothing you will find
> nothing, whether you seek or work yourself to
> death.[115]

Physical labor, likewise, does not automatically bring spiritual blessing. From the story in Luke 3, of Peter fishing all night, we learn that hard work will not earn an individual salvation.[116] Indeed, however great the dangers inherent in idleness, there is equal peril in over-emphasizing, to the neglect of the soul, one's vocation and its responsibilities.

> Now here they have no excuse/which say; their
> position and vocation require that/they remain stuck in
> it/they cannot let it drop/they must consider their
> vocation. For dear person/you have *two vocations/one*
> has to do with your soul/the *other* has to do with your
> body: Which then is the main one? You excuse your-
> self/that you cannot attend to the vocation of your
> soul/on account of your outward vocation: How then

---

[113] *SFA*, II, p. 181.

[114] "But that you have sustenance and abundance, is not to be ascribed to the work, but to the goodness of God. Many a person works mightily and yet has little bread to eat; another works slowly and it flows to him." *GE*, #208, p. 248.

[115] *GE*, #208, pp. 248, 249.

[116] "Behold/you should indeed learn this from this/what the harmful error of the people is/which lay hidden in their hearts/that they think: they will obtain the blessing of GOD with their work/with their industry/with their cheerfulness/with their diligent attentiveness/and concern: that must be taken completely out of your heart/you will gain nothing thereby." *SFA*, II, p. 185.

can that be a good excuse/that you neglect the soul/and pay attention to the body?[117]

Too much work also endangers the soul by overburdening the mind with thoughts of nothing but one's job, which tend to crowd out thoughts of God, and which then too frequently cause the preoccupied person to become ambitious and greedy.[118]

The solution is not, however, to abandon one's work for what would appear to be a good reason, that is, to devote more of oneself to God. Rather, the solution is to do everything in faith, and thus make all of one's life, including one's vocation, a path to God.[119] The Christian is to make room in his or her work for the leading of Christ, and then do everything to God's glory and neighbor's good. If he or she does this, the good and acceptable job the believer does will remain in eternity.[120] The basic advice of both Müller and Francke was the motto of St. Benedict—pray and work. "*Ora & labora, caetara Deo commenda.*"[121] "The welfare of Christians consists in prayer and work....Beg and dig, pray and work, mouth open, hands

---

[117] *SFA*, II, p. 187.

[118] *LR*, pp. 102, 103.

[119] "But if it is the opinion/that you should abandon your work/and not remain in it; but rather your calling must only have a different aim/than it has had to this point: Everything must be directed to GOd's honor/and the neighbor's profit/you must seek GOd in all you do/all/that you intend/must come out of faith/and your whole life/being and doing/must be a path to GOd." *SFA*, II, p. 709; "I am not saying that one should not carry out one's profession, insofar as it is not sinful. I desire only that everything be done in proper order, with true composure of the soul [*Gemüth*], and in faith and obedience to our Savior, so that the sweet presence of this our best friend may not be hindered, but rather that the heart may always remain united with him." *SFP*, p. 43.

[120] "If one is in an outward vocation/and carries out his work in it/he thinks/what does this have to do with faith and eternal life; for example a servant or maid/when they do their work in a house/think about nothing further: but the one who knows what truth is/will know/that everything/he does/even in an outward vocation/must and can be so done/that it might remain in eternity; not as concerns the outward work in itself/but the good heart/that GOd has worked in the person/that remains/and what one seeks in his work/which is GOd's honor and the love of neighbor/belongs to the imperishable." *SFA*, I, p. 603.

[121] *SFA*, II, p. 244.

on."[122] Unfortunately, people are generally too concerned with earthly things, and thus ignore God's order.

> God has given us body and soul/the body/which is earthly/the soul/which is spiritual and heavenly: so then surely may our hands work; but our heart should not remain bound up with outward matters/but rather live in and with GOd in heaven. Where it is so ordered/that is the right path.[123]

Thus we see that work is a crucial element of the person's life in the world, and of his or her spiritual well-being. The Christian's vocation comes under the same scrutiny as other areas of life and calls for the same balanced approach in which neither the spiritual nor physical dimension is ignored or emphasized to the detriment of the other. Nonetheless, one's vocation as an outward activity must take its direction and meaning from one's inner life. Work, like everything else, must be done in the name of Jesus (Col. 3: 17), and to the glory of God (I Cor. 10:31).

MONEY AND MATERIAL POSSESSIONS

In discussing human life in the world the Pietists referred frequently to money and possessions. These are the desired, but not always desirable, products of the person's labor. Avarice, selfishness, ostentation and worry about one's own well-being are the main objects of Pietist wrath. Money and possessions are inextricably linked not only with one's relationship with neighbor, but with one's inner being as well. Francke says,

> Now as long one has such a mind/that he also wants to do something good for neighbor/but make a profit by it; he will gladly serve his neighbor with his possessions/but for the sake of some advantage/in such a way/if he can get some of his neighbor's money with his own/and use his in such a way/that he always has a profit by it/and thinks as well/what a service he has done for his neighbor/when in fact his heart is false/ which looks only to its *own profit*: a person has a

---

[122] *GE*, #294, p. 376.
[123] *SFA*, II, p. 179.

> publican's mind/in that he wants revenue from every-
> thing.[124]

This sort of thinking is sinful in that it places the self in the center of life, relegating both God and neighbor to lesser and support-ing roles. Both Müller and Francke remind people that they cannot serve God and Mammon, that this divides a person and defiles the gift that otherwise would be an acceptable offering to God.[125] They also lament the same sins and evil methods in-volved in getting rich.

> You should go to church, hear God's Word to
> your comfort, [but you] stay at home because there is a
> *Gulden* [money] to be made....You seek to get rich
> through cursing, lying, deception.[126]

The greedy person has forsaken the living God and has placed his or her trust in a god which is completely powerless.[127] Indeed, such a one's courage and outlook on life rise and fall with the amount of money and possessions he or she has stored up.[128] This means that faithless people seek to gain and keep as much as possible, not only for themselves, but because they are worried about the welfare and wealth of their children and grandchildren. To this end they frequently use dishonest means, and thus bring a curse upon the stored-up possessions, thereby ensuring that they will never make it to the third generation. "Behold! that must first be done away with/that will not come to the third generation/rather it will go/in the manner it was gained."[129] Material possessions simply are not reliable,

---

124 *SFA*, II, pp. 615, 616.

125 *GE*, #184, p. 214ff; cp. *SFA*, II, p. 521ff.

126 *GE*, #163, p. 179; Francke says, "Many a person has gained much money and possessions through dishonesty. For example, Many a person has profaned [Sunday]/and has increased his money and possessions thereby. Another has gained his through gambling/with deception/with lying/with false friendship/unchristian trade/with cursing/and swearing/or otherwise through theft." *SFA*, II, p. 62; cp. *GE*, #184, pp. 214, 215.

127 *GE*, #163, p. 180; cp. *SFA*, II, p. 519.

128 "You seek only after gold, if you have possessions you have courage, for your god lives; should your possessions disappear your courage disappears, for your god is dead." *GE*, #163, p. 179; Francke says quite similarly, "If he has something in storage/he is content and blesses himself: but when his stores are used up/he is fearful and afraid." *SFA*, II, p. 519.

129 *SFA*, II, p. 62; Over thirty years earlier Müller had written,

although they tend to be seen as a form of social security, particularly in times of personal instability.

> For when people do not know/how they should conduct their State/they fall out of pride [and] into greed. And there is greed and worry about one's belly among the rich as well as the poor.[130]

Among many Lutherans usury was still considered an ungodly activity, and was condemned as contrary to the love of God. Charity, however, was seen as "Christian usury" which will be repaid in enormous amounts because it is lending to the Lord.[131] Indeed, godliness, or faithfulness, in handling goods and money brings spiritual blessings which, in like manner, are to be used faithfully in their own way.[132] The thinking behind this is that material goods are simply not as important as spiritual things, and the proper use of money and possessions is a sign of the reality of one's conversion.[133] Discernment and change in this area, however, are particularly difficult since "It is hard to bring greedy people to the knowledge of their greed"[134] because of the number of excuses handy; one has to work, pay the authorities, provide for one's family, consider the future, etc.[135] People tend to think and act as though their money and goods actually belong to them. This is due to a primarily spiritual misunderstanding arising out of ignorance of the will and ways of God and God's world. Everything always remains God's. One is only given something temporarily, and for a purpose. To

---

"Sometimes the curse of God is upon it/if it is gained or possessed dishonestly/it eats it away/like rust iron/or a moth clothing/that it may not reach the third generation." *GLF*, II, x, p. 843.

[130] *SFA*, I, p. 34; Both Müller and Francke stress particularly the duties and selfishness of the wealthy.

[131] "Usury is unchristian/when one lives off his neighbor's sweat and blood thereby/or lends his money to the poor and needy at great interest: Such usury and interest is completely contrary to Christian love: But it is Christian usury/when one lends his money to a neighbor/from whom he has nothing to hope/or gives alms to the poor and needy/such a person will receive not 5. 10. or 100. but rather a thousand per cent interest: *For whoever gives to the poor*/says the wise teacher/*he lends to the LOrd.*" *Gottlob*, pp. 62, 63.

[132] *SFP*, p. 1283.

[133] *SFP*, p. 1280.

[134] *SFA*, II, p. 518, Marginal note.

[135] *SFA*, II, p. 518.

fulfill this purpose is to repay God, or, to repay God is also to fulfill God's purpose.[136] The unregenerate person does not recognize that to cling to goods and money is to squander them, while to give them away is to save them. Müller writes, "What one saves on God is secured with the devil. The poor are God's treasure chest, [they] can best preserve your goods for you."[137] Were people to understand that material goods are only shadows, they would handle them properly, and concern themselves more with the grander things of the Spirit. The "child of light" must learn and practice the truth that temporal goods are something foreign, as compared to the treasures of the grace of Christ which one is to regard as true and real. The Pietists' basically Platonic understanding of reality is well illustrated in their attitude toward earthly goods.

> Mammon, or all goods which a person possesses in temporal things, is nothing other than a mere shadow, and may not be be considered as something true...[138]

In the end, one's use of and attitude toward money and possessions is a matter of faith.[139] A concern to amass great wealth and a reluctance to share one's possessions betray a fundamental lack of trust in God. In a sermon on just this subject in 1697, Francke recites the lines of a hymn,

---

[136] "You wealthy are God's debtors. God has not given you his goods, but only loaned them, and wishes to be repaid in his needy children." *GE*, #240, p. 293; "God has not appointed you master over his gifts/he remains LOrd himself/you are only a manager/that others might be cared for through you." *GLF*, II, x, p. 832.

[137] *GE*, #35, p. 35; Also, "What one keeps for himself, that is lost, what one gives to the poor, that is preserved." *GE*, #267, p. 337; cp. *GLF*, II, x, p. 843; So Francke, who says that just as it is foolish for a person to keep seed where he or she can see and look at it rather than plant it, "So is it also foolishness/when people have temporal goods/and will not distribute them to their neighbor to do good thereby; but rather will sooner let them lie in a coffer/that they can walk by often/and see/what it looks like." *SFA*, II, p. 350; Scriver also stresses the concept of giving as saving, and quotes Müller as a supporting authority. *Gotthold*, pp. 1004, 1005.

[138] *SFP*, p. 1281.

[139] Francke writes, "Greedy people do not believe the Word of GOd." *SFA*, II, p. 181, Marginal note.

He will always nurture us/preserve us, body and
soul/He will prevent all evil/no suffering shall befall
us/He cares for us/protects and watches/all is within his
power.[140]

He then impresses upon his listeners that they had just sung
those very lines:

But should mouth and heart oppose each other/in
most hearts there would be a great contradiction to
these words. For the unbelieving world considers GOd
the LOrd as a laughing-stock/and it respects his glorious promises much too little/to trust them/and not
burden its heart with worries about sustenance.[141]

This sin of over-concern with self-preservation through acquisition is just as bad, and requires as much vigilance, as the sin of
epicureanism.[142] Indeed, "Greed is even worse than gluttony
and wine-bibbing."[143] Francke reminds the greedy that, despite
all their excuses today, they will have to give an account on
judgment day of what they have done with their earthly
goods.[144] Müller predicts that those who serve Mammon, and
thus the devil, will end up in hell.

'God will not have hypocrites in heaven.... You
are the devil's with body and soul; you serve the one
who pays you. Such work merits such pay."[145]

Here, as in any Pietist discussion of the important things in life,
heaven and hell loom large.

---

140 *Er wil uns allzeit ernehren/Leib und Seel auch wohl
bewahren/allem Unfall wil er wehren/kein Leid sol uns wiederfahren/Er
sorget für uns/hütet and wacht/es steht alles in seiner Macht.*
141 *SFA,* II, p. 409.
142 "Those who fret about their sustenance always think they are better
than such Epicureans who lived in gluttony and drunkenness; but do not
consider that their [miserly] concern about sustenance is nothing but
disbelief, with which they offend GOD as much as those [the Epicureans]
with their excess. Therefore we should guard ourselves against the one as
much as against the other." *SFP,* p. 43; cp. *SFA,* II, p. 511.
143 *SFA,* II, p. 512, marginal note.
144 *SFA,* II, p. 49.
145 *GE,* #184, p. 215.

The disposition of money is determined by simple rules: keep enough to live on, and give the rest away. Francke's sermons, particularly to the wealthy, apparently struck a number of his listeners as a bit too radical, for Francke felt obliged to defend his stance in another sermon. He stated that he had been accused of claiming that Christians must have all things in common, when actually he had stressed that greed is the root of all evil, and that people will have to account for how they keep or get rid of the goods which God has loaned them.[146] Believers should not lord it over others or deprive others. The equality of all believers is fundamental for Müller as well, and is basic to his rather startling statement, "Our neighbor, above all as he is pious, has as much right to our possessions as we ourselves, and perhaps a greater [right]."[147] These Pietists were hardly Christian communists. They did, however, emphasize frugality with self, and generosity with others, and demanded that, while keeping enough to maintain health and well-being, one should give eagerly and often.

Even in the realm of hard cash and material goods, the spiritual world is present and evident. A person's concrete gifts to others and his or her use of earthly possessions are intimately bound up with his or her spiritual condition and destiny. Indeed, one's possessions are significant only in light of how they fit in God's will. They receive their actuality, as it were, from the actuality of God. As ends in themselves or as means to eternal life they are totally pointless. Thus, apart from their use in the service of God and neighbor they are at least meaningless, and can be dangerous, since their false "reality" tempts one to rely upon them rather than upon God. Money and goods, in the same manner as labor, receive both substance and value insofar as they are used to glorify God, serve neighbor, and promote the believer's sanctification.[148]

---

146 *SFA*, II, p. 246.

147 *HLK*, II, ix, p. 709.

148 Here a brief discussion of Pietist social-economic thought seems appropriate. Much has been written about the financial programs of the Halle institutions. See C. Hinrichs, "Der hallische Pietismus als politisch-soziale Reformbewegung des 18. Jahrhunderts", in *Zur neueren Pietismusforschung*, hrsg. von Martin Greschat, (Darmstadt, 1977), pp. 243–258; G. Bondi, "Der Beitrag des hallischen Pietismus zur Entwicklung des ökumenischen Denkens in Deutschland", in the same, pp. 259–293. For a rather negative treatment of Pietism (in spite of the author's claims): Martin Scharfe, *Die Religion des Volkes*, (Gütersloh, 1980), pp. 141–143; Most of this material draws attention to the rejection of wealth and ostentation by the Halle

TIME

Closely related to work and money is time, in that it, too, is something which belongs to God, and can be used for good or wicked purposes. Müller writes, "Lord, this time is mine and yours....World, you are excluded. Should I serve you? I have no time for that. The time is mine and my God's."[149] Just a few lines after this he amends his statement and further narrows the ownership of time, "Time is not mine, but my God's. Not one moment is in my hands....The day belongs to God."[150] Because time is something which can be possessed, as it were, its use will be judged by God. People will have to render an account of they used the time allotted to them. Francke tells just how specific this judgment will be:

> Now then each person shall go back into his life/and consider/in what foolishness he was from youth on/and how much time slipped by him/which he did not employ for God's glory. How will he stand then/when it comes to a reckoning/and it will be: *Give an account* of the time/which you lived/see/there stands in your life: on this and that day I was in this company/where one spoke useless words/where one cheated his neighbor/where one was a glutton and a sot/where one ruined his health/and did other useless things; this and that hour I wasted my time with games/with dancing and leaping about/and with other worldly desires?[151]

Pietists while they were at the same time involved in establishing a wholesale operation which received and sold the very luxury items which they so roundly condemned, such as Italian and Hungarian wines, furs, coffee, tea and tobacco. Even while buying and selling jewelry, Francke asked the wealthy person to consider "that to this point he has either let his jewelry, pearls, precious stones, rings, chains and other adornments lie about unused or else has worn them in mere vanity and ostentation, that he has locked away a lot of gold and silver tableware in a drawer without God and people being the least bit served thereby..." *GA*, pp. 158, 159; Francke also came to loan money at interest. This is certainly a contradiction. Nonetheless, this economic activity was seen as promoting God's glory and serving the needy.

[149] *GE*, #11, p. 11.

[150] *GE*, #11, p. 12.

[151] *SFA*, II, p. 337; Müller, too, presumes that the wicked use of time will result in damnation. *GE*, #11, p. 11.

Here we see that one's sins are compounded by the concomitant sin of wasting time. While the wicked use of time is condemned, the proper use of time—such as work well done—follows one into eternity and brings a reward.[152] Therefore, any activity takes on a double value; it is doubly sinful or doubly salutary, in that it is an act *per se* (and thus shall be judged), and it is simultaneously the use of (God's precious and unrepeatable) time.

Because diligence in one's vocation serves neighbor directly and earns more money for charity, it is extremely important that one use time wisely. Thus the individual always should be punctual[153] and should always be active. "For this reason [that the loss of time means the loss of souls], the Christian is duty-bound to ceaseless activity."[154] Church attendance, charitable works, prayer, diligence on the job, and punctuality, for example, all are godly uses of time, and should not be avoided or postponed. "Would you wait until tomorrow [to love and serve God]? Who knows where I will be tomorrow? Today I walk on the stone, perhaps tomorrow the stone will cover my bones."[155] To be idle or to waste time in the lusts of the world is not really a valid option for a person. People are intended always to use their time for God's purposes. Müller dismisses the world's competition for the Christian's time with a rather cavalier statement: "World, the time is not mine, I cannot serve you, ask my God if he will grant me a leave of absence. If not, leave me in peace."[156]

---

[152] *SFA*, II, p. 878; cp. *RGZ*, p. 29.

[153] "The connection between the consciousness of time, worth, and responsibility was strengthened the most by the vocational ethos of the Reformation. Vocation is a divine task, my specific form of cooperation in the establishment of the kingdom of God. This thought finds its most radical practical expression in German Pietism where August Hermann Francke developed his very strict ethic of punctuality and thrift from the Christian understanding of the concept of time." Ernst Benz, *"Zeit, Endzeit, Ewigkeit"*, special reprint from *Eranos 1978*, vol. 47, p. 13.

[154] Klaus Deppermann, *Der Hallesche Pietismus*, p. 94. Although Deppermann correctly cites the treatment of the orphans at Halle as an example of carrying this idea too far, his inclusion of prayer and edification in the category of *"pausenlose Aktivität"* seems to stretch the point a bit.

[155] *GE*, #11, p. 11.

[156] *GE*, #11, p. 11.

CHAPTER 8

DEATH AND THE AFTERLIFE

A major preoccupation of Pietism, and a strongly recommended preoccupation for the person who would be saved and sanctified, is death, particularly a peaceful "blessed death"[1] and how to be sure that one attains to it.[2] Arndt points out that, "Our whole life is nothing other/than a constant passage to death and to the grave."[3] He writes of three kinds of death: "spiritual death" in which one dies to carnal desires, arrogance, etc., "natural death," and "eternal death."[4] Here we are concerned only with "natural" and "eternal" death. Francke speaks of these two types of death as well. If, after dying outwardly, giving up the ghost, departing this temporal life, one "sees" and "tastes" death, then one has passed from simple, natural death into that eternal death in which one is damned forever.[5]

Many things in life may be uncertain, but death is absolutely inescapable. Indeed, life aims at it. "Human life is nothing other than a quick course to death, we go from one grave into the other, from the womb into the earth."[6] And, "Ah yes/it [life] is only a passing through/you may indeed esteem it and use it/but

---

[1] That is, while everyone must die, the Christian need not fear death, "but rather can anticipate it with joy/and thus pass out of this world in peace." *SFA*, III, p. 53.

[2] Fritsch gives a little rhyme: "Was nicht nach dem Tod ist nütz/Das ist lauter Narren=Witz." (What is of no use after death/is nothing but foolishness.) *Gottlob*, p. 61.

[3] *Wahres Christenthum*, p. 322.

[4] *Wahres Christenthum*, p. 67.

[5] According to Francke, to "see death" has two meanings in Scripture, and thus in one's life: "For sometimes it means as much/as to taste death/ that is/*to experience and feel death as a judgment and punishment of GOd/* and thereby be swallowed into the second death as it were/that one not only die outwardly before people's eyes/give up the ghost/and depart temporal life; but also pass through death into damnation. Scripture tends to call this/ *seeing death/tasting death.* But where this does not occur/one does not see death/even if one dies physically and naturally." *SFA*, III, p. 56; A Christian neither "sees" nor "tastes" death, however, and so has nothing about which to worry.

[6] *HLK*, I, xxiii, p. 561.

not keep it."[7] In fact, God determines the end of one's life even from before one's birth.[8] Thus life is, so to speak, simply a life-long journey to a predetermined rendezvous with death.[9] This applies not only to wicked or faithless people, but to believers as well.[10] For the true Christian death is a necessity in order that the believer may finally be rid of sin,[11] and, as Francke points out, that the soul finally may be free to look directly upon her Savior and Bridegroom, an impossibility so long as a person is trapped in his or her body in this world.[12] As already noted, one's life is a journey to death. It is a death, however, which does not simply await one down the road, as it were. It also accompanies the person on his or her earthly pilgrimage. Müller compares death with a murderer who joins up with a traveller, walks with him, then kills him along the way.[13] The moment of death itself is by no means happenstance, but is actually the culmination of a gradual, life-long process.[14] Scriver compares death with a woodworm which can be heard in the night, gnawing away in a beam.[15]

One reason that death is always present is that, as we have seen, sin is always present in a person's life. Along with sin, the Law, the devil and the world, death appears as one of humanity's

---

[7] *GLF*, I, xxiii, p. 625; "Thus nothing is more certain than death/life is not given to us/but rather is loaned." *HLK*, I, xxv, p. 602.

[8] "The love of GOd gives our life a goal, and before we are born, it determines us for death." *HLK*, I, xxiii, p. 545; "Indeed no person dies by coincidence/GOd is a LOrd of your life. He has determined your life's time and hour." *Wahres Christenthum*, p. 708.

[9] "A person's nature rushes back to the earth/from which the person was taken/and from the first moment of birth already begins to die/that is/to rush to death." *GLF*, I, xxiii, p. 601.

[10] "Now it comes to this/that we all must overtake this goal/and die/ the godless as well as the pious." *GLF*, I, xxiii, p. 601.

[11] "Now this enemy remains even with those who participate in the redemption of Christ through faith, for body and soul must part, so that the body may perish and thus the soul become free, but the arm of the enemy is cut off." *HLK*, I, vi, p. 58

[12] *SFA*, III, p. 57.

[13] *GLF*, I, xxiii, p. 608.

[14] "From day to day your life diminishes/so you die gradually. As soon as the child comes into the world/one wraps it in linen cloths/from which one also makes gravecloths." *GLF*, I, xxiii, pp. 619, 620.

[15] *Gotthold*, p. 74.

enemies, "which hangs on sin like the apple on the tree."[16] Original sin contributes to one's death; "the poison of original sin dwells in all our flesh/which eats up our bodies/like a worm an apple."[17] Actual sin also plays a role in the shortening of one's life:

> And not only is this life in itself short/but GOd also shortens [the life] of the wicked/often before they intend. For as often as they commit a sin/with words or deeds/through anger/unchastity/intemperance etc., so often must something be lost from their life/just like a tree/the closer to it something poisonous dwells/the sooner it withers. As often as they sin/so often they shorten their life.[18]

Sin not only contributes to one's death directly, but indirectly as well. On account of a person's sin death can come to him or her as a rescuer, as a good friend who prevents the person from losing everything.

> Had you a good friend/who gambled the whole night through/lost all his money/and won nothing but blows/you would indeed put out the light/so that the gambling would be prevented.[19]

The fact that death can come to a person as a rescuer indicates the basic Pietist view that life does go on beyond the grave and that, at least for the godly person, life is better there than it is here. Müller, too, asserts that there are good reasons, such as the need of rescue, for the apparently early death of apparently godly people.[20]

---

[16] *HLK*, I, vi, p. 58; "Where sin is invited as a guest, it brings death there with it, like one good friend the other." *HLK*, I, vi, p. 58.

[17] *GLF*, I, xxiii, p. 601.

[18] *GLF*, I, xxiii, p. 607; cp. *HLK*, I, xxiii, p. 550.

[19] *HLK*, I, xxiii, p. 574; cp. *GLF*, I, xxiii, p. 635; Francke stresses as well that a believer's death may be a necessary preventative measure by God which is in no way contrary to God's love: "But if our Savior thought it not good that he leave a person who placed all his trust in him in this world longer; but rather in his omniscience knew that such would attain to his destruction; he would do nothing contrary to his omnipotence or love if he removed the sick person from this world." *SFP*, p. 1454.

[20] These reasons are: 1) that the believer has come as close to perfection as he or she can in this life, 2) that the believer may not be

Albeit that death is certain, and that it accompanies a person throughout life, "As certain as death is, so uncertain is the hour of death."[21] Fritsch reminds his readers that, "Daily experience teaches us/that human life is very weak/fragile and uncertain."[22] Scriver gives accounts of the sudden and unexpected deaths of a man at a wedding dance, a pallbearer who falls into the grave he is digging, a servant girl who tumbles into a vat of boiling water, a man who is buried alive, etc., and warns the reader that "similar cases are not rare."[23] A subtitle of one of the *Geistliche Erquickstunden* is "Today red, tomorrow dead." Müller then goes on, "Today rich, tomorrow sick; today....."[24] One tends to deceive oneself, assuming that it is in old age that life first begins to fade, when, in fact, one may not necessarily be intended to live into "old age."[25]

The suddenness and unexpectedness of death is good reason for one ever to be prepared. Indeed, God keeps people ignorant of the moment of death so that they may be moved to penitence, watchfulness, and holy lives, lest death catch them in a bad moment.[26] Fritch's Gottlob comes across a man burnt "coal black," struck dead by a bolt of lightning. To the crowd gathered around the charred corpse, Gottlob says, "Dear people! Do not think/that this happen by chance."[27] This all happened in God's good order. The lesson to be learned is that this poor fellow did not take the time to repent, and now would never have the opportunity. Scriver laments people's foolish attitudes in the face of life's uncertainty, and he promises to remain faithful:

corrupted by evil; 3) that God likes to have God's beloved nearby; 4) that the believer might be saved from impending misfortune (*HLK*, I, xxiii, pp. 533, 534); and 5) that the world might be punished, since the loss of a Christian means the loss of a great blessing. *GLF*, I, xxiii, p. 609.

[21] *GE*, #164, p. 181.

[22] *Gottlob*, p. 75; Müller concurs, "We know that our life is like a fragile glass." *HLK*, I, xxiii, p. 561; cp. *GE*, #164, p. 181.

[23] *Gotthold*, p. 268.

[24] *GE*, #164, p. 181.

[25] "You think of an old man and wither in the bloom of your years. Not all shoulders are strong enough to bear the old man. Not all heads are worthy to wear the crown of honor of gray hair. One bears more calfskins to market than cowhides. Death gives no advance notice of when it will come; in a twinkling it takes up its sickle and cuts you down. You are never too green for its granary."*GE*, #164, p. 181.

[26] *Wahres Christenthum*, p. 352.

[27] *Gottlob*, p. 88.

> Similar cases [sudden deaths] are not rare/and
> nonetheless we pay little regard: We stand on the tip of
> eternity/and eat/drink/and are self-assured! My GOd/I do
> not know/how/where and when death/at your command/
> will make an end of my life/but this I know/that it will
> not fail to appear: thus my pact in faith with you is
> now and ever/my God/that I live unto you/die unto
> you/and living or dead be and remain yours.[28]

In seeing death all around, the person is reminded that his or life is little more than a puff of smoke, and thus, caring for his or her soul, he or she treats each day as if it may be his or her last.[29] Francke speaks of unsuspecting, and uncaring, people as oxen being fattened for the slaughter, oxen for whom the day of slaughter seems far off, and to whom all threat of death is irrelevant. Thus one needs to turn to Christ in order to flee the wrath and judgment of God.[30] Scriver warns that, contrary to one's expectations, death may be lurking just around the corner, and that, hidden or not, it is like a sharpshooter who never takes aim from the target. This should be sufficient to inspire a person to keep death in mind and be ready for it.[31] It only makes good sense to be prepared. "Then because death is certain, let us always be prepared to die."[32] One way in which the nonbeliever may be moved to a saving faith, and the believer to a more steadfast faith and perseverance in true Christianity is through the constant awareness and contemplation of death. People should find reminders of death everywhere: in the hooting of an owl which the superstitious normally consider a sign of misfortune or

---

[28] *Gotthold*, pp. 269, 269.

[29] "Whoever knows/and considers/that a person's life is like/the grass/ steam/smoke/shadows and wind/will constantly carry his soul in his hands/ and consider every day of his life/as his dying day." *Gottlob*, pp. 76, 77.

[30] "See/as long as an ox is in the stall/as long as it will be led to the meadow/it seems to have it quite good. But it is fattened/for the slaughter. And so it is with the godless and unrepentant as well...a day of slaughter will come/namely the great slaughter day of GOd/when they will see/for what they were fattened in their temporal life of ease/and how all the threats of GOd and his severe judgment will fall upon them." *SFA*, I, pp. 116, 117.

[31] *Gotthold*, pp. 174–176.

[32] *HLK*, I, xxiii, p. 561; Francke says, "My most beloved/if you do not struggle/to get in such a condition/that in every moment you could appear before the judgment seat of Christ/indeed that you could stand before the face of GOd with joy: you are truly not upon the right path." *SFA*, II, pp. 772, 773.

death. "Even though I do not endorse the common superstition/it is not offensive to me/that this bird reminds me of my mortality..."[33] Reminders may also be found in common things such as an hourglass whose sand is running out, the earth which will one day be one's grave, water as it is absorbed by the earth, and the prayers said in church for the sick and dying.[34] It is not enough that a person be led by coincidence to contemplate death; he or she should also take positive steps to keep death in mind.[35] Why? Because "thoughts of death are like wormwood/very bitter/ but very healthy and good for the soul."[36] Meditation upon death heightens one's consciousness of the fleeting nature of human life and turns one from wicked things to higher pursuits.[37] Müller lists several reasons to contemplate death:

> Such contemplation of death is very salutary/for it drives out the desire to sin/like a bitter purgative the bad vapors ....Think often of death/and you will be safe from deadly sin....Above all this contemplation dampens love of the world in us ....The contemplation of death is a salutary textbook for you. It teaches you to despise the world's splendor/for how does great glory suit you in the grave?...The contemplation of death is also a golden book of comfort for you. For in death all affliction must die with you.[38] It teaches us to set earthly things aside...It teaches us to flee temporal lusts...It teaches us to walk carefully and care for our souls.[39]

As we have seen, the best and only adequate preparation for a blessed death is faith in Jesus Christ. It is an either/or situation for the person, as Francke says,

---

33 *Gotthold*, pp. 379, 380.

34 *GLF*, I, xxiii, pp. 623, 624.

35 Scriver describes a person who made a pomander in the shape of a skull, "that he might constantly remember his mortality." *Gotthold*, p. 102; He describes yet another fellow who kept a coffin nearby for the same reason. *Gotthold*, p. 536.

36 *Gotthold*, p. 537.

37 "But the one does cleverly and wisely/who constantly thinks of the transitoriness of his human life/scorns all temporal/earthly/transitory things/ and considers [them] as bad and of little worth/but loves/treasures/longs for/ seeks/and strives for the eternal and heavenly/with complete sincerity and diligence." *Gottlob*, p. 105.

38 *GLF*, I, xxiii, pp. 624–628.

39 *HLK*, I, xxiii, p. 568.

> As long as the ascent to the heights does not
> appear to a person/he still has his paths/which he
> takes/but they are paths to *hell/which lead one down
> into death's chamber.* Prov. c.VII, 27.[40]

People must realize that there is more to life than what meets the
eye. Müller condemns what today would be called materialism
(in the philosophical sense of the word):

> Indeed nature has put eyes in the head, but only in
> the wise do they attain the goal she seeks, they look
> into [and take account of] the future. The worldly fool
> is blind, or has eyes only in [his] feet, that is, he sees
> only what he walks on with his feet, what is earthly.[41]

If a person has not "seen Christ," that is, if he or she has not
turned to Christ in faith, before death, he or she can neither
rejoice nor be comforted in the face of death.[42] This "seeing
Christ," which requires an openness to spiritual reality, and the
reductionistic, materialistic perspective of the "worldly fool" are
mutually exclusive. Thus it behooves worldly people to concern
themselves with that spiritual experience without which there is
no chance for a blessed death,[43] and which will no longer be
possible in the afterlife. "For after death there will be no time or
place for repentance. Hic enim aut vita amittiur, aut retinetur."[44]
The "infinite mercy" of God is not so infinite that it extends
beyond the grave to those who choose to die in unbelief.[45] "For
as GOd finds you/so will he judge you. Therefore you should be
in your life/as you wish to be in your death."[46] For this reason,
for example, Francke warns against speaking only soothing

---

[40] *SFA*, III, p. 147.

[41] *HLK*, I, xxiii, p. 562.

[42] "This then is the thing/of which the departure into peace/or a blessed
death/consists/namely not to see death/unless one has seen Christ the LOrd
first. For as someone has seen death/and has not seen Christ the LOrd/he has
no blessed end in which to rejoice and take comfort." *SFA*, III, p. 56.

[43] "It is then this *spiritual seeing of Christ/without which it is
impossible*/that one *can die with a true/divine joy*. Thus one must take great
pains/that one experience such in his soul." *SFA*, III, p. 59.

[44] *Wahres Christenthum*, p. 353; Francke preaches, "Therefore dear
people, while you are still healthy and fresh, make yourselves well
acquainted with the LORD JESUS." *SFP*, p. 729.

[45] *Wahres Christenthum*, p. 353.

[46] *Wahres Christenthum*, p. 352.

words and quoting only comforting verses of Scripture at an unbeliever's sickbed. Comforting the unrepentant with sweet verses may make the sinner feel better for the moment, but it fails to take into account the next world and the clear entrance requirements of heaven, of which repentance is one. "And in such a way many 1000 people are comforted by false prophets into hell."[47]

The same severe differentiation between born-again and unregenerate people applies here as much as in all other facets of human existence. The believer and the unconverted person approach old age and death in radically different ways. The devout Christian sees that old age and its attendant infirmities are simply more obstacles which are unavoidable and are to be met with Christian faith and resolve.[48] The nominal Christian, on the other hand, sees no need to consider the future or to look after the condition of his or her soul. Indeed, the worldly person perceives his or her advanced age and years of religious custom as a sort of buffer against the spiritual demands of Christ as presented by the Pietist.[49] As a result, the unregenerate person not only feels a diminished need to turn to Christ, but transfers more energy to worldly concerns.

---

[47] *SFA*, II, p. 293.

[48] Gottlob picks up several different quill pens and tries to write with each. None writes clearly, however, because each is old and dull, and it suddenly occurs to Gottlob, "...when I consider my increasing age/when understanding and memory begin to become dull/the eyes dark/the hands tremble/the otherwise well-sharpened quill can no longer work right....There is no art/to always writing with a good pen/one must also learn/as one has the time and opportunity/to use dull pens/and not throw such away out of impatience; endure/what one cannot change/and improve/and do as much/as GOd and one's nature/grant the ability to do." *Gottlob*, p. 15.

[49] "Thus it happens/because so many among you tend to say: Now I am already old/should I now be converted and become different? Should I now learn/how I must become a Christian/even though I was born and raised in Christianity and have been to confession and to the Lord's Supper so many times in my life? and so forth. Many think this/just because/they are old and grown/they need not trouble themselves with conversion and growth in Christianity/and assume/that it is surely right. But I say to you: There is many a person 60/70/80 years old/and yet who is not in the state of the new birth/and thus is not to be called a true child of God; but rather if he would be saved/he *must* just as CHrist said to Nicodemus/Joh. III. 3.5.6. *turn about* and *be born anew*." *SFA*, I, p. 162.

...we see as well/that such an age is not without hindrances. Indeed such is all the greater/because concerns about sustenance tend to increase/and the person is drawn for the most part into outward matters of the household/so/that/if he is not yet converted to God/such is surely not a little in the way.[50]

Müller echoes Francke's sentiments, "The older the colder....The older the weaker," and encourages his aging readers, "The older the more enthusiastic....The older the stronger."[51] Recognizing and fully accepting the debilitating and difficult character of old age, even calling it "a common grave" and "the dregs of our life,"[52] he sees two possibilities for a person. The first is the sorry end of the unbeliever who has put off his or conversion and growth in holiness too long.

Therefore, my heart, do not save your piety for old age. Then everything is a cold, decayed, dead thing;...We should increase in spiritual things with time, we decrease; we should become ever more zealous in good works, we become ever more dull.[53]

The second possibility, the way of the Christian, is progress in faith and zeal, and growth in piety and love.

Christianity consists not of decrease but rather of increase, not in retreat but rather in progress. A tree must always grow....What I am not, I will through God's grace make an effort to become, and what I cannot become, yet would I gladly become.[54]

So we see that for a person in old age basically nothing has changed spiritually, while physically life is more difficult. The

---

[50] *SFA*, I, p. 418.

[51] *GE*, #158, pp. 173, 174.

[52] "If a lamp has no oil, a fire no more wood, straw or coals, it goes out; when food and drink no longer taste good, the body's vital warmth is consumed. [Old] age is like the winter of our life....When nature reaches its goal in growth, it decreases in strength gradually, just as it grew; if it ceases to go uphill, it begins to go downhill. [Old] age is like a common grave, in which all the weaknesses of the human body are poured. The last days are the dregs of our life, they ever seek the bottom." *GE*, #158, pp. 173, 174.

[53] *GE*, #158, p. 174.

[54] *GE*, #158, p. 174.

same need for repentance, sanctification, etc., is present at every age, and takes on a bit of urgency with time because of one's waning ability to become zealous for Christ, increased hindrances to faith through greater preoccupation with physical needs, and the greater likelihood that death will overtake one before one can repent. In growing old, a person's spiritual condition is no small matter, for it determines where he or she spends eternity, and affects his or her attitude in this life toward dying.

One's understanding of, and attitude toward, death is determined by whether one is a worldly person or a godly person. "Whoever will not die gladly/with this one things are not yet right."[55] One element of the worldly person's approach to death is made up of repression, illusion or delusion, in that,

> The life of the self-assured, worldly person is a
> dreamed or pictured immortality: He builds houses,
> plants fields, gathers treasure; worries about temporal
> things as if he would possess them forever.[56]

Francke points out that while the Christian may be ready to greet death gladly, the worldly person invites death out of completely different, and bad, motives:

> The fleshly unconverted *worldly person* says yes
> in the same way from time to time: Why would I not
> die gladly; but it comes to him generally in good times
> out of fleshly security/but in the bad times out of
> impatience and a desire to flee affliction/which thus is
> indeed very different from the longing of the child of
> GOd.[57]

Nor can blustery pronouncements about not fearing death dispel death's bitterness, for what one says now cannot change the reality he or she will encounter on his or her deathbed.[58]

---

[55] *SFA*, I, p. 563, marginal note.

[56] *HLK*, I, xxiii, p. 559; Also, "A wise person considers the future/the worldly fool does not do this." *GLF*, I, xxiii, p. 621.

[57] *SFA*, III, p. 66.

[58] "How many a child of the world looks upon death with impudent boldness, and says like Agag (I Sam. 15: 31): I am not the least bit afraid of death; but is making a big mistake. The bitterness of death will not be driven away in such a manner. Death is not that sort of visitor. You do not know

Despite any bold statements, fantasies, etc., the unregenerate person can only anticipate with terror the moment of death.

> It could not be other/than that fear and terror be in
> us before death/where one has not first seen and ac-
> cepted in faith the power of God.[59]

The Christian, on the other hand, can face death not only without fear, but with joyful anticipation and even longing. Fritsch sees no good reason why a person should regard death as such a "foreign, strange and unusual thing, as we commonly tend to do," but rather one should become accustomed to the idea of death and accept it, and thus be able to let go of life will-ingly.[60] As in everything concerning person's fate, there are two arenas of activity. The objective act of God in the incarnation which has destroyed the power of death, and the person's sub-jective response of faith have changed the person's condition from that of *posse non mori* to that of *non posse mori*. This makes it possible for the believer to anticipate a joyful and peace-ful death.[61] When the Christian thinks on this and adds to it both the daily examination of his or her conscience and sincere repen-tance for the wickedness found therein, he or she feels no anxiety or distress at all.[62] Indeed, the Christian comes to regard death in

---

him. You are like a blind person who walks into a gruesome ditch which he does not see. Is not sin the sting of death? Do you not serve sin? O do not be so audacious, the sting is still there. I say, you are lying in the throes of death, the number of your sins will come before, you will also see what sin brings along, namely eternal curse, eternal; damnation. Hell opens its abyss, death will push you in, you will find no comfort against your sin. Tell me, how would you find courage? Would you not taste the bitterness of death? Would you not feel its sting? The bite and terror of sin in your conscience is the bitterness of death. O woe to the one, who shall taste it!" *GE*, #233, p. 284.

[59] *SFA*, III, p. 68.

[60] "We are indeed no better/than our fathers. Death was the way of all flesh before us/and will remain so as long as the world lasts..." *Gottlob*, p. 11; So Arndt as well: "So many glorious and holy people have gone before you/all the patriarchs/prophets and many thousand faithful/why would you not follow them?" *Wahres Christenthum*, p. 707.

[61] "Whereupon then follows/that this too is a *fruit of the birth of Christ*/that we/we who believe in the name of the only-begotten son of GOd/*no longer* have to *fear death*/but rather can anticipate it with joy/and thus depart this world in peace." *SFA*, III, p. 53.

[62] *GLF*, I, xxiii, p. 615; *cp. HLK*, I, xxiii, p. 557.

a radically new way: "Faith considers death as much as nothing ...Indeed faith holds death to be a particular grace of God."[63] Death has a new appearance to the believer. As it is now seen as a pathway to God and a gateway to heaven, the Christian can actually rejoice in it.[64] Francke, who along with Müller also sees death as the person's gate to an eternity with Jesus, the angels and the elect,[65] says,

> Well then! since my JEsus went to his Father, I
> now have no death before me, but only a departure to
> the Father. Here I am not yet in my fatherland, but
> travel on in my pilgrimage; but how glad I am, that the
> end of it will finally come, and I will enter my true
> fatherland! will go to my Father."[66]

With this in mind, the Christian gladly invites death. With fear no longer a factor, the believer is anxious to cast off his or her wretched carcass, and finally attain to true beauty.[67] The believer, in fact, will await this transforming moment with longing sighs and aching. The exchange is well worth dying for.[68] If we remember here the Pietist's aversion to the things of this wicked world, it becomes clear why the journey from this (wicked) world to the (glorious) next is considered a wholesome escape, and why death can be called not only "the Lord's angel," but even "my Redeemer."[69] Both Müller and Scriver advocate that one not only anticipate death joyfully, but, in the manner of

---

[63] *HLK*, I, xxiii, pp. 547, 548.

[64] "If we consider, that death is only a path to the Father, and a door to heaven, truly we would die with joy." *HLK*, I, xxiii, p. 575.

[65] *SFP*, p. 314.

[66] *SFP*, p. 666; So Müller, "Fatherland, sweet land." *GE*, #250, p. 305.

[67] "As long as I feed and adorn this carcass, so long do I create only wretchedness, but if you destroy this carcass, then will I first be ready for true beauty." *HLK*, I, xxiv, p. 589.

[68] "If a great king promises a poor peasant/that he/as soon as his straw hut collapses/will dwell with him in his royal palace/the peasant would not weep/but would await the collapse of his hut with sighing and aching....How gladly we throw away the old, tattered rags/when beautiful new clothing is given to us..." *GLF*,I, xxiii, p. 635.

[69] "Through birth we enter life, enter suffering; through death we leave life, leave suffering....death comes, the angel of the Lord, and leads me out. I follow out of life with joy...death, my redeemer, is there and summons me out." *GE*, #254, pp. 312, 313.

the mystics, know death well enough to call it a friend and, as we have seen in the case of affliction, welcome and embrace it when God sends it.

> It [one's constant meditation upon death] teaches us to laugh at death. For no one is happier to die, than the one who interacts often with death. One does not fear a good friend.[70]

For the Pietist it is quite understandable that a person would perceive death with either fear or rejoicing, depending upon the state of his or her soul. Death actually is different for the two types of people. Since in this life one will never reach holiness, there remains an element of the natural or worldly person in even the most pious Christian's meditation upon death. This natural person within the believer sees death from the front, or from this side of eternity, whereas the Christian part of the person sees a completely different side of death. Indeed, the "holiest, wisest, most courageous people in the world" have feared death. "But the fear which you feel as a human being, you must overcome as a Christian."[71] To the Pietists, Satan and his demonic forces were very real beings. Thus the deathbed circumstances of the wicked and the godly are contrasted in light of spiritual realities. The worldly person is tormented at the approach of death by the devil who reminds him or her of his or her many wicked thoughts, words and deeds, and with images of a severe judgment, eternal flames and the like.

> The closer the moment of death/the busier is the devil/for he knows/that he has little time. Were your eyes to be opened/that they could see spirits/you would see many thousand demons around the beds of the godless.[72]

Francke points out that people may not expect things to go so easily on their deathbeds if they have spent their lives in the pursuit of earthly things.[73] In contrast to the worldly person's

---

[70] *HLK*, I, xxiii, p. 568; cp. *Gotthold*, p. 380.

[71] *GE*, #6, p. 6.

[72] *GLF*, I, xxiii, p. 612.

[73] "Now if you should some day die, you must prepare yourselves early, that you then are able to enter eternity with joy. You dare not think, when your soul [*Gemüth*] is laden with earthly and temporal things, and are unacquainted with the LOrd JEsus, that it will go so gently with you on your deathbed." *SFP*, p. 729.

final moments, the Christian's are full of angels and comfort.

> But for the pious, GOd is in the final moment of
> death. Their bed is surrounded by h[oly] angels as by a
> crown. Should the devil wish to frighten them through
> sin, Christ stands at their side, speaks kindly to them:
> Be comforted, dear child, I have come into the world,
> that I might save sinners, I have shed my blood so
> generously, that it should cleanse you of all sin.[74]

From his or her deathbed one goes on to judgment:

> For his dying day will indeed be for a person his
> judgment day: For it *is given to a person to die once,*
> *and thereafter comes judgment.* (Heb. 9, 27)[75]

Judgment day is yet another reason for a person to live in a godly
manner, and it is to be remembered at all times. Fritsch quotes
St. Jerome, "*sive edo, sive bibo, sive sto, sive sedeo, ubicunque*
fuero, semper in auribus meis sonat vox illa terribilis, surgite
mortui, venite ad judicum."[76] Judgment is also a good reason to
test oneself and repent, for one's behavior "in physical life" plays
a role in how one fares at judgment.[77] The implication is that
judgment is reserved particularly for the wicked. All people must
appear before the judgment seat of God, but the wicked seem to
tarry there to receive the full brunt of the Law, while the godly
are pardoned and move on to glory. In this sense the wicked
"arise to judgment," that is, to a terrible judgment, while the
faithful arise to eternal, glorious life. Thus Christ appears in
different ways to people depending upon their spiritual condition
at death.[78] Following judgment one goes on to eternity, or to
everlasting heaven or hell.

Judgment is inescapable. Pietist language seems to indicate
that there is a time of sleep for the dead, during which, as in
earthly life, time apparently loses meaning and from which the

---

[74] *HLK*, I, xxiii, p. 557.

[75] *SFP*, p. 1683.

[76] *Gottlob*, p. 122.

[77] "For we all must be revealed/before the judgment seat of CHrist/
that each one may receive/according to how he behaved while alive/be it good
or evil." *SFA*, I, p. 31.

[78] "Christ wakes only the pious, as a savior of his spiritual body, but
the godless, as a judge of the dead and the living." *HLK*, I, xiv, p. 585.

dead are awakened by "the final trumpet."[79] Presumably this will occur with the return of Christ to judge the living and the dead,[80] a return which will terrify and destroy creation. Francke sees historical precedent for this in biblical prototypical events:

> For GOD has already made many great and partic-
> ular judgments in the world indeed; as at Sodom and
> Gomorrah/over Jerusalem and the Jewish nation: But he
> has not poured out his wrath/as he will reveal it on the
> great day of wrath/which in H. Scripture is called in
> particular the day of the LOrd.[81]

This day of judgment is God's final weary answer to the increasing wickedness of humanity, and to creation's longing to be rid of the curse which humanity has brought upon it.[82] Thus the person plays a role in the necessary destruction of creation. No one will escape the coming of Christ,[83] and, as with the judgment of the dead, the judgment of the living will be a joyful and comforting experience for the faithful, and "completely horrifying and terrible" for the wicked.[84] There is a pecking order, as it were, in the judgment of the wicked. The first to go through this awful experience will be

> those who call themselves by his name, but have
> not lived worthily of it; as which will feel first his
> judgment and punishment, as they have by the abuse of
> his huge and glorious grace merited such ahead of the
> others.[85]

---

[79] "The resurrection to eternal life will occur at the time of the last trumpet. Then the trumpet will sound/and the dead shall rise incorruptible." *GLF*, I, xiv, p. 653.

[80] *SFA*, I, p. 23.

[81] *SFA*, I, p. 28.

[82] "Ah, how full of wickedness is the earth!...humanity scorns everything, acts contrary to God and his Word, however he can. Creation is troubled with such evil, and will bear the curse, which crushes it in the service of vanity, no longer. How long, do you think, will God sit still? He must finally hear the fearful longing of creation and give it a rest. He must finally grow weary of mercy, burst in with the day of judgment and preach hellfire to the world." *GE*, #260, p. 323, 324.

[83] "This day will be a great day/when all the nations will be gathered in the presence of the great king." *SFA*, II, p. 864; cp. *SFP*, *pp. 1291, 1292.*

[84] *SFA*, II, p. 870.

[85] *SFP*, pp. 1296, 1297.

Thereafter follow the less arrogant, less self-assured sinners.

Whatever the order, however, and whatever the experience, one does indeed face judgment, either arising to it from the grave or encountering it while yet alive at the sudden return of Christ. It is somewhat difficult to understand thoroughly the Pietists' concept of the judgment, since they rarely spoke of it *per se*, but rather mentioned it in the context of exhortations and warnings intended to to inspire people to accept Christ and/or to persevere in holiness. We learn from this warning of Francke's, for example, that people will be frozen as they are, so to speak, at the unpredictable irruption of Christ into the world: "The earthly-minded will be in a wretched state."[86] Thus it behooves people to be ever on their best behavior.

Because the Pietists did not demythologize Scripture, we must here consider heaven and hell, for in Pietist thought one indeed continues on past the moment of death into circumstances which are in some ways radically different from this life, and which in other ways are rather similar to those of temporal existence. As we have seen, hell is the final destination for those who have not seen Christ, that is, have not truly been born again and seek to live in ways pleasing to God.[87] Scriver repudiates universalism, and at the same time gives a theological justification for the necessary existence of hell:

> Indeed there have been people/who were of the opinion/that the mercy and infinite goodness of GOd would not allow/for him to cast his creation into torment and pain for all eternity: And/I would say nothing else against this/if it were possible/that there could be repentance and faith in hell/I would also say that mercy would be there: But how can something good be there/where demons/rule according to their will/in body and soul? Indeed the teachers have decided/that he who dies in sin and deliberate wickedness/will remain therein forever and always/for if GOd's grace is of no help/how can he be other than evil?[88]

---

86 *SFA*, I, p. 35; Francke points out that worldly people want just the opposite. They wish to wallow in the filth of this world until the trumpet sounds, "but then they want to be canonized, and one should call them blessed or saint." *LP*, VII, p. 458.

87 "On Christian Perfection", Appendix, *LR*, p. 120.

88 *Gotthold*, p. 672.

And hell is a terrible place for one to find him- or herself. Hell is full of everything that is dreadful and is empty of anything that is good.[89] As concerns a wicked person's fate, "Hell is a land of eternal death. The damned lie in hell like sheep to be slaughtered/death gnaws at them/and their worm does not die."[90] The damned, as Francke points out, will be tormented by a heart with no hope of rescue, by a bad conscience, and by constant discomfort. This anguish is only compounded by the sight of one's companions in damnation.[91] Scriver speculates further on the horrors of hell, emphasizing that the agony will only increase with the passing of time, time that will go on forever. His protagonist, Gotthold, sees a wasp in his study, catches it, cuts it into three pieces, and notes that the sections live on: the jaws bite, the wings flutter, the abdomen attempts to sting. He goes on to say that he cannot explain how body and soul will be divided after death, but he does know that

> the godless and damned will be in eternal death in hell/yet will live eternally: Who would doubt/that the demons will not do their worst/with those who have been handed over to them? I believe they will rip them several times a day/and tear them in many pieces/not to help them out of their torment with a final death/but rather to increase it....And thus they will ever and never die/but rather live eternally in death.[92]

The other post-death possibility is heaven, which is reserved for the born-again believer. Müller writes, "It is easier to say/ what will not be in eternal life/than what will be there."[93] Among those things lacking in heaven will be sin and reason to sin, toil, affliction, *Anfechtung*, pain and death.[94] Müller's claim to the contrary, there is much descriptive material on the state of things

---

89 "What is hell but a house, with eternal sadness without joy, eternal hate without love, eternal fear without hope, eternal anxiety without comfort, eternal torment without rest?" *HlK*, I, ixx, p. 451.

90 *GLF*, I, xxv, p. 680; cp. *KLH*, I, xxv, p. 615.

91 *SFA*, II, p. 57.

92 *Gotthold*, p. 671.

93 *GLF*, I, xxv, p. 656.

94 *GLF*, I, xxv, pp. 656, 657; cp. Arndt, "In the new imperishable being will be no more sin/no more death/no more suffering..." *Wahres Christenthum*, p. 702; cp. Francke, "Here it must vary from affliction/to suffering and sorrow; but there [it will be] without vagary/without change/without vexation and disgust..." *SFA*, I, p. 380.

in heaven. The stark contrasts that characterize life on earth exist in heaven as well, but no longer in tension, rather in presence and absence.

> There is health without aches/excess without lack/pleasure without vexation/wisdom without ignorance/joy without pain/peace without sorrow/light without darkness/wealth without poverty/glory without disgrace/life without death/eternity without end.[95]

Heaven is different from life on earth in that the concerns of temporal life such as food and clothing, a place to live, etc., will be eliminated because God, who is all in all, meets every need, indeed is whatever anyone may desire.[96] While the unpleasant aspects of earthly life are lacking in heaven, and every need and desire is obviated because it is already met, the joys of heaven are nonetheless similar to temporal joys, but in an infinitely larger amount and for an infinitely longer time.[97] Francke refutes those who envision eternity as a period of unrelenting boredom:

> For how is it possible/that the time will be boring for a soul/when it with all its desires is wrapped up in the word of CHrist/and is ensnared, as it were, in his love? Thus even the unending eternity of the elect will not be boring/because they constantly *will be with the LORD*/with whom there can be no discontent.[98]

Heaven is just the opposite of hell. As those in hell are tormented in every way, so heaven's citizens find their senses sharpened, and rejoice in every aspect of their new existence.[99] While in hell the tormented will have their anguish increased through being forced to look upon their suffering companions, in heaven the resurrected believers will see and know each other and the patriarchs, prophets, apostles, martyrs, angels, et al.[100]

---

[95] *GLF*, I, xxv, p. 661.

[96] *GLF*, lxxv, p. 659.

[97] Things are such in heaven "that the person tastes sweetness and kindness for all eternity/and yet will not become satiated therewith/but the more he has of it/the more he will be filled with ecstasy." *SFA*, I, p. 380.

[98] *SFA*, I, p. 763.

[99] "In sum/as with the damned all the senses will be tormented/so with the saved will all the senses rejoice." *GLF*, I, xxv, p. 679.

[100] *GLF*, I, xxv, p. 675; cp. *Wahres Christenthum*, p. 704.

And, of course, while hell is the land of eternal death and torment, heaven is the realm of eternal life and joy.[101]

We have seen that death is described as a sleep which lasts until the final trumpet is blown. This view is challenged, however, by Francke's refutation of any sort of post-death existence in which the soul can somehow go astray or wander into the wrong place, since, according to Francke here, it is immediately in God's hands.[102] He also stresses the immediacy of the believer's conscious presence with God:

> Yea the faithful soul knows very deeply and certainly, that from the moment that it departs this temporal life paradise and the realm of heaven stands open to view, and that accordingly it need not wait until the second coming of CHrist; rather may enjoy it here already in *faith*, there immediately in sight; as Paul 2. Cor. 5,7. connects the two with each other and puts no third thing between them.[103]

There appears to be no satisfactory resolution of this conflict of the idea of a sort of "soul sleep" with that of the immediate presence of the believer's soul with God. Müller asserts that the body sleeps until it is resuscitated to be rejoined with the soul.[104] This does not resolve the tension, however, and only demonstrates further the homiletic, devotional concerns (as contrasted with the systematic) of the Pietists.

However great the difference between earthly and heavenly existence, there is a certain continuity as well. One's understanding in heaven will be touched and deepened in order that he or she may fathom those doctrinal incomprehensibles which were insoluble on earth, such as the essence of God, the nature of the Trinity, how Christ can be fully human and fully divine at the

---

101 *HLK*, I, xxv, p. 615.

102 "You know, that you need not worry about being lost, and that your souls will not stray for even an instant, or go to the wrong place; rather that when the separation from the body happens, it comes immediately into the hands of your heavenly Father and shall be preserved there faithfully." *SFP*, p. 665.

103 *SFP*, p. 658.

104 "Therefore death is called a sleep, in that the body, which has been laid to rest in the grave as in its bed, shall be reawakened." *HLK*, I, xxiv, p. 586.

same time, etc.[105] Furthermore, a person will retain a sense of personal identity in that he or she will have memories of his or her earthly life. This must necessarily be the case, since in heaven one will see the providential workings of God in the events of his or her temporal life.

> We will understand the causes and ways of the
> divine reign, which is hidden from our eyes in this life,
> there we will confess, that in the world GOd guided us
> wondrously, indeed blessedly, there we will thank him
> for our affliction and say: *He has done everything well*;
> Marc. 7. v.37.[106]

Not only personal matters such as intellectual enlightenment and continuation of the person *via* memory appear to carry over into celestial existence, but so do some social customs. One is the reward system; another is a sort of class structure within equality. In solid Lutheran fashion (despite clear messages about the significance of a holy life), the Pietists stress that a person may in no way trust in any good works to attain eternal life, but must rely in faith solely upon the merits of Christ, and immerse him- or herself in Christ's holy wounds.[107] Once the river of death has been crossed, however, the believer's deeds play a role in determining how much heavenly light, joy, etc. he or she is to receive. Basically, only the status symbols have changed: as on earth the powerful and wealthy receive glory and honor, so in heaven those who were the most Christ-like in the world are elevated to the highest levels.[108]

A major difference, then, between heaven and earth is that no one envies or resents the joy and well-being of his or her neighbor, indeed everyone is equal, in that each is completely satisfied. The similarity to earthly experience is that the absolute amount of heavenly joy and glory dispensed and received is based upon one's performance while on earth.[109] We must again

---

[105] *HLK*, I, xxv, p. 604.

[106] *HLK*, I, xxv, p. 604; cp. *GLF*, I, xxv, p. 684.

[107] *GLF*, I, xxiii, p. 637.

[108] "We need not think/the rich/the mighty/the great in this world will shine in that life in the greatest brightness and glory: Rather those/who have been like the poor/the afflicted/the scorned JEsus; for they will also be most like him in eternal salvation." *SFA*, I, p. 978.

[109] "The most delightful thing of this fellowship will be/that no one will resent the other's glory. The main treasure will be one/for they all

remember that this sort of apparently contradictory, or at least convoluted, thinking is found in sermons, etc., and thus it was intended less to instruct and describe than to inspire godly living among the listeners and readers. Indeed, the danger of falling into works-righteousness is ever present in Pietist doctrine, as the following quote from Francke indicates. Here we see clearly both the *quid pro quo* economy and the social distinctions which obtain in heaven:

> Therefore the elect of GOd have always desired/that they may die a martyr's death/and have thirsted/that their blood may be spilled for the sake of the name of JEsus CHrist/because they knew well/ what a crown and honor would rest upon it in heaven.[110]

A final, and crucial, element of the afterlife is the resuscitation of the corpse, that is, resurrection. Resurrection is the process by which the believer's dead body is restored to life, a very different sort of life. All this is taught to humanity in nature, in Scripture and in the Catechism.[111] The very creation of humanity is prototypical evidence for resurrection.[112] Besides

---

without distinction will see God face to face/as he is. In this vision each will experience full satisfaction/and desire no more. Yet the coincidental joy and glory will vary/in the one greater and more abundantly than in the other/ according as the one had done more good/had suffered more evil/than the other. They will all be illumined by one light/yet with different radiance. They will all drink one sort of milk from one of God's breasts/and be satisfied thereby/yet the one will drink more than the other/according as his spiritual mouth and stomach is larger than those of the other.[a] Each will receive his reward according to his work. Each will be followed by his works....No drink of cold water will go unrewarded. ...In the wine cellar there are different vats/whole/half/and double/which are all filled with the best wine/yet according to their measure and size/each has as much/as it needs and can hold. The elect are in the wine cellar of God/some large/some small/ some medium-sized vats/yet all filled with God/who makes them spiritually intoxicated. The smallest is according to its capacity as full of God as the largest/and cannot hold more/thus it does not envy the one/which has a greater abundance/for it has as much as it could want/and complete satisfaction."

[a] (according as...the other) is found in *HLK*, I, xxv, p. 619.

110 *SFA*, I, p. 978.

111 *GLF*, I, xxiv, pp. 640–643.

112 "The creation shows you/that your resurrection is not impossible.

this, it only makes good sense.[113] Because the Pietists took seriously the concept of the indwelling of the Holy Spirit (they espoused not only *Christus pro nobis*, but *Christus in nobis*), they could conclude on theological grounds that the body would be resurrected.[114] Müller stresses the continuity which here obtains:

> Not only does GOd show his love for the pious,
> in that he awakens them, but that he also calls forth
> their bodies, which have fallen into the dust of death,
> back out of the dust. It would not be right, that a
> different body should suffer torment in hell than the one
> that had served sin here, so would it also be no love, if
> a different body should wear the crown there, than the
> one which struggled here, and another receive the
> *Groschen* (money), than the one who worked here.[115]

And this body will be far better.[116] The resurrected body gains its glorious qualities from the soul. As one is transformed from glory to glory (I Cor. 3: 18), "There we will be grasped by GOd/as by fire be changed and participate in his divine nature."[117] It is from this glory of the soul that he body of the believer receives its glory. As in its earthly existence, the heavenly body is still compared with clothing for the soul.[118] Body

---

Indeed God created a human being out of the earth/and breathed a living spirit into him." *GLF*, I, xxiv, pp. 643, 644.

[113] "Who would let a beautiful house/on which he has spent so much/ indeed even his own blood/collapse and not rebuild it: Should a rich man's old house collapse/he rebuilds a much grander one." *GLF*, I, xxiv, p. 644.

[114] St. Paul writes in Rom. 8: 11 that the Spirit of God dwells in a person. Müller writes, "If you sense, that GOd has made you inwardly beautiful, alive, righteous and blessed, he will not leave behind the body, which is the tabernacle and house of the living Spirit, but because the Spirit is already resurrected here from sin and death, the tabernacle and corruptible mantle, namely flesh and blood, must also be raised again out of the dust, because it is the shelter and dwelling of the Spirit in this life it must also remain for ever." *HLK*, I, xxiv, p. 648.

[115] *HLK*, I, xxiv, p. 586; cp. *GLF*, I, xxiv, p. 648.

[116] "Precisely the body/which here is so empty/so frail and wretched/ will there be so beautiful and glorious....It is even greater love/that GOd makes your body go forth again much more glorious and beautiful/than it was [when] laid in the grave..." *GLF*, I, xxiv, pp. 648, 649.

[117] *GLF*, I, xxiv, p. 667.

[118] "From this radiance of the soul the bodies of the elect too will

and soul receive joy together.[119] Müller surmises further in delightful, almost fantastic bursts of speculation (despite the earlier disclaimer that heaven can hardly be described) that the transfigured body will take on spiritual characteristics:

> But the transfigured bodies have power/they feel no sickness/because there is no sin there/which gnaws at and stings them/they are strong and capable of doing/ whatever they merely think and desire/the least among them could easily smash the planet earth/roll like a ball from one place to another....A natural body is one/that eats/drinks/sleeps/puts on and loses weight/has children/feels hunger/thirst/cold and heat/is heavy and coarse and impotent. All this shall disappear from the transfigured bodies. Like a spirit or angel/they will need no food/drink/sleep/clothing/marriage/and the like; They will be fast as lightning/which flashes in a moment across the sky; light and agile/that they too can move across the heavens and go in an instant/ wherever they want.[120]

As we have seen, for the Pietists heaven and hell are not simply outdated religious ideas which are useful homiletic devices. The afterlife constitutes a very real and exceedingly important element of human life, a component more important than one's temporal existence, since damnation or salvation lasts for eternity. This reality casts its significance back into a person's earthly life, since it is during this period that one's eternal condition is determined, both by the grace of God and the deliberate response of the person. The importance of the afterlife cannot be overstated. Heinrich Müller's deathbed statement reflects well the meaning of death for the Pietist:

---

receive a greater glory....The light with which their soul is illumined, will pour its radiance through their bodies, as on Mount Tabor Christ's radiance shone forth through the clothing." *HLK*, I, xxv, p. 607.

[119] "Body and soul together will feel their joy from this beatific vision of GOd." *HLK*, I, xxv, p. 608; Francke prays, "Receive then even in the hour of death our spirit, and bind it in the bundle of the souls of the elect, until body and soul are again united and transfigured before your face, and we then enter into the joy, which you have gained for us through your death on the cross." *SFP*, p. 668.

[120] *GLF*, I, xxiv, pp. 650, 651; *HLK*, I, xxiii, pp. 658, 659.

> Not I, but my wretchedness and suffering will die.
> I do not know, that in my whole life I have had a truly
> happy day in this world; after this life the joy of my
> heart will truly commence. Unhindered by the body of
> death I will pray before the throne of the lamb with
> great power for my sons, for you, my dear confessor,
> for all my little sheep, especially for my benefactors.
> So all of you be comforted. I know without any pre-
> tense and airs and anguish that quite soon I will depart
> this life.[121]

Indeed, no element of Pietist theology or anthropology can be
understood apart from heaven and hell and the nature of death
that is the gateway to one of them. One would do well to remember these words from Ahasverus Fritsch, *"Non potest male mori,
qui bene vixit."*[122]

---

    121 *AP*, xi, xii; This can be found in slightly different versions in
Klaiber, *Evangelische Volksbibliothek*, p. 237 and *GE*, p. vi.
    122 *Gottlob*, p. 88.

CONCLUSION

The Pietist view of the individual is characterized by division and tension within unity. That is, taking their cues from Platonism and the mystics, the Pietists considered the material realm—or at least fallen creation—as both wicked and unreal. Thus, the individual, as he or she lives in this world and is fallen, is seen as less than a worm and as a shadow and smoke in comparison with that ultimate human being, Jesus, who is glorious and real. At first glance we might assume, then, that Pietism would be a renewal movement characterized by a rigorous asceticism, escapism and hatred for the world. While these elements are present to some degree, here, however, is where the integrity or unity of the individual plays a role.

Despite the bifurcation of the person into soul and body, or inner and outer, and despite the emphasis upon the greater importance of the inner person, the Pietists regarded the individual as a whole. However subservient the body may be to the temptations of an evil world, of the devil, and of its own desires, and however much it requires discipline (not necessarily understood as punishment), it is still a *sine qua non* of humanity. A person can only be regarded as such when taken as a whole. A soul without a body or a body without a soul is, humanly speaking, a *non ens*. A person must care for every part of him- or herself, or else he or she endangers every part of him- or herself.

The person lives in tension. He or she is ever pulled in one direction by the world's and his or her own fallen lusts and desires, and in the opposite direction by the love of God and the remnant of the *imago Dei* in his or her soul which seeks to return to unity with the Creator. This tension is manifested in constant struggles between the inner and outer person, faith and unbelief, godliness and worldliness, the indwelling Christ and the old Adam. Sin, flesh, world and devil are ever active. The person, thus, must persevere in watchfulness and faithfulness in true Christianity lest he or she stumble and fall. One must press on in sanctification because, "Every standstill is already a step backward,"[1] backsliding being a constant threat to one's salvation. This tension—and source of no small anxiety—is mitigated to some degree by the indwelling Christ. Insofar as the believer is

---

[1] E. Peschke, *Studien*, I, p. 105; See *SFA*, I, pp. 637, 920.

surrendered to Jesus Christ, he or she is capable of resisting the world.

There is providential involvement, too, which offsets Satan's power in people's lives. While the Lutheran Pietists rejected the rigid predestinarian views of some orthodox Calvinists (thus the very high valuation of and emphasis on one's will), they reported that the believer frequently made an *ex post facto* realization that God had been guiding and helping him or her in certain matters.

As we have seen, no area of human life is free of struggle. This constant, fateful struggle calls for a response of some sort. We have seen that a person's prayers are disrupted by untimely thoughts, which are influenced by worldly ideas, which are rooted in the desire for the wrong things, which the person would use wrongly in any case, *ad infinitum, ad nauseam.* It is the unity of the individual which precludes escapism or harsh asceticism, for it is in the care of the whole person, and in the person's (godly) engagement with the world that God's glory, neighbor's good and one's own holiness may be advanced. *Absonderung* (Separation) from and renunciation of worldly things and people are not to be interpreted as escapist, but rather as means of self-preservation and of protecting, as it were, God from dishonor. The believer is to remain apart from the wicked world, yet be ever active in it. He or she must be about transforming the world while avoiding as much as possible unchristian activities and circumstances.

The tension of life is increased by the high demands of Scripture as interpreted by the Pietists. Were it possible for a person to overcome his or her natural desires, or to renounce forever worldly ways, he or she would nonetheless have to contend with the discrepancy between his or her present state and the spiritual, moral, and ethical demands made by his or her Pietist instructors. This tension is inescapable. Emil Brunner, while hardly a Pietist, captures the essence of this tension:

> The contradiction...is not simply 'something contradictory' in man, but it is a contradiction of the whole man against the whole man, a division within man himself. And this division...can only consist in the fact that man, who was originally created to decide in accordance with the divine determination, has decided against this determination, so that, just as the original determination gave him true life, this hostility to it

robs him of his true life, and allows him to fall prey to
an unreal life.[2]

Two basic problems arise from people's condition of being lost:
on the one hand, with only themselves to rely upon, they become
arrogant, thereby dishonoring God and offending neighbor; on
the other, they become anxious and full of "*Bauchsorge*" (worry
about their bellies), thereby repudiating God's providential
goodness, "slapping Christ in the face" and harming neighbor
through selfishness, deception and even theft. Thus the person is
caught in a vicious circle which leads to hell. At the very center of
this wretchedness is unbelief. This is the source of people's sin,
error, and susceptibility to the enticements of the world and the
devil, as well as to the anxiety inherent in their own finitude.
Only as one repents and surrenders to Christ is the process of
overcoming human false pride, sinfulness, self-estrangement,
and anxiety begun.

God is always the starting point of Pietist anthropology. That
is, it is simply impossible to speak of humanity without men-
tioning God directly or indirectly: people are by nature sinful,
they persevere in holiness, they are repentant, they are born
again, they are backsliders, etc., all these terms having meaning
only in reference to God. When explicitly theological terms are
not used, the language is nonetheless laden with theological
significance: to ignore the needy is to sin, to work diligently is to
honor God and contribute to God's creation, and so forth.
Scripture, and the Pietist interpretation thereof, is the clear standard against which a person's condition and all his or her behavior are measured. To the degree—and only to that degree—in
which a person has, and pays heed to, the mind of Christ, can he
or she know what is good and real and true. By instruction of
Scripture, the aid of the submitted human will, and the guidance
of the Holy Spirit, the believer can and must then live out his or
her Christianity.

This view of the person explains Francke's virulent response
to the "new" ideas of Christian Wolff, that unaided human reason
can attain to moral truth. Such thinking leaves God out of the
picture and puts human reason in God's place. Theologically it

---

[2] Emil Brunner, *Man in Revolt*, tran. Olive Wyon, (London, 1947[3]),
p. 118. Again, while Brunner cannot be put willy-nilly alongside Müller and
Francke, this statement captures the Pietist view well, including the words
and concepts of real and unreal, and hostility to God.

mitigates the need for conversion and the imitation of Christ. Anthropologically it runs counter to the Pietist view that people are by their fallen nature disobedient to God, and that the natural will must be broken and submitted to Christ before enlightenment can come. Here Pietism presents a view of the person which was soon overtaken and discarded by much of western society as people began to regard themselves as unique sorts of beings rather than as creations of God with inherent limitations and corruption which require outside (read divine) assistance.

The popular modern view that people are basically good and need only to get back in touch with themselves and grow is antithetical to the Pietist view. Indeed, the Pietists emphasized self-awareness, but in the service of repentance, conversion and sanctification. The Pietist conventicles, like modern small therapy groups, sought to facilitate the unburdening and the upbuilding of the suffering soul through confession, forgiveness, sharing, chastisement, encouragement, and the prayerful reading of Scripture and devotional materials. The modern T-group, while similar in structure and, to some degree, technique, omits the divine component and encourages the emergence of the essentially good person within the individual. The Pietists dealt instead with a struggling sinner trapped by worldliness, sin, death and the devil, who needed less of self and ever more of Jesus. Whereas modern people may be perceived to be whole, but perhaps misguided or ill or wounded or unfulfilled because they are out of touch with their true selves, the Pietist individual is seen as less than whole and can be fulfilled only in Christ.[3] In any case, in Pietism the struggle for personal fulfillment had more than this-worldly consequences.

If a person is by nature characterized by tension and struggle, this conflict is finally resolved at death. As we have seen, to the Pietists the afterlife was real, and thus provided for a person both a fitting end to his or her earthly existence, and the answers to the questions inherent in human finitude. Death ends the tension one way or the other, through an eternity of torment or of complete joy.

---

[3] For a brief description of how theology connects with the modern view of the person in the conventicle or therapeutic setting, see H.-M. Barth, "Partnerzentrierte Seelsorge als Herausforderung an die Systematische Theologie" in *Anthropologie als Thema der Theologie*, hrsg. von Hermann Fischer, (Göttingen, 1978), pp. 203–212.

Werner Georg Kümmel describes the anthropology of the New Testament as follows:

> Man is seen solely as the one who stands before God. He is created by God and is duty bound in obedience to his Creator. He tries to set himself up against God and thus becomes a sinner in the sight of God. His sin does not have root in his natural bodily existence. Rather, man is essentially a *unity*, whose whole being stands over against God and is therefore ripe for His final judgement. Only God's sending of Jesus Christ has given him the possibility of salvation from the condemnation which awaits him. This picture of man within history is the outcome of a judgement of faith, of belief in the historical act of salvation by God in Christ, and can therefore only really be understood and affirmed through such a judgement of faith.[4]

Assuming that Kümmel is correct, we must say that the Pietists held a biblical view of the person with, however, an accretion of Platonic, typically mystical elements which are worked into standard biblical concepts. For example, the immortality of the soul is held alongside the concepts of resurrection and a judgment day. In their desire to gain converts and encourage and exhort the faithful, however, the Pietists did not, for the most part, concern themselves with whether these concepts were compatible. Rather, they simply interwove the seemingly contradictory, or at least incongruous, traditions which they received, and preached them.

Our concern here is not to decide whether the Pietist view of the individual is correct. It has been to lay out that view as rather consistently presented by Heinrich Müller and August Hermann Francke. The reader must decide for him- or herself if the Pietists were right.

Although we cannot determine whether their understanding of the individual was correct, we can see that the views of Reform orthodoxy and Pietism, as they appeared in northern Germany, are virtually identical as concerns the person. They were concerned with, and spoke to, the same individual. We have examined particularly the works of Heinrich Müller and August Hermann Francke as representatives *par excellence* of

---

[4] Werner Georg Kümmel, *Man in the New Testament*, trans. J. J. Vincent, (London, 1963), p. 83.

their respective movements, and have discovered time and again striking similarities in language, themes, images and basic pre-suppositions about the nature and destiny of the individual. Normally, Reform orthodoxy and Pietism are presented by historians as two different movements, although occasionally, as we have seen in Klaiber's *Ev. Volksbibliothek*, thinkers from these two movements are brought together in one group.

These historical divisions are helpful, in that they help us identify groups. The idea of Reform orthodoxy, for example, is normally applied to those theologians active mainly in northern Germany, in Kiel and Rostock (although they were also found in Strassburg), whereas the term Pietism generally covers a wide range of thinkers in various geographical locations and confessions. These divisions are also harmful, however, in that they mask the intimate connection of Reform orthodoxy and, especially, Pietism as found in Brandenburg-Prussia. This problem is manifested in the case of Spener. He was in correspondence with, and a personal friend of, men such as Scriver, Fritsch, Sandhagen, von Seckendorff and Müller—all traditionally numbered among the Reform orthodox. Perhaps Spener is considered a Pietist because his *Pia Desideria* gave rise to that term. So Francke, who clearly relied upon the works of Arndt and Müller, is also called a Pietist, although with his northern German origins, his education under Rostock- (and Müller-) trained teachers, and his obvious affinity for the Arndtian piety which characterized Reform orthodox thought, he could easily be considered a Reform orthodox theologian were it not for the appearance and spread of the name Pietist.

Indeed, that the name Reform orthodox is rarely, if ever, used of anyone with pious tendencies after the late 17th century has, in my opinion, less to do with the passing of that movement than with the fact that it and Pietism in northern Germany actually constituted one movement, the name of which has been changed by the events of history and by historians. Thus, as pointed out in the introduction, we have used the term Pietism to cover the thought of both Müller and Francke in this study of the individual.

I hasten to remind the reader that I use the term Pietism in this way only for this work on the individual in the thought of Müller and Francke because of the clear and overwhelming evidence for the unity of the thought of these two men. I would not use such an approach, for example, in a comparison of J. A. Bengel and

Müller, despite their similarities. As far as concerns Reform orthodoxy and the Pietism of Brandenburg-Prussia, however, it would be very fruitful to see if the congruence of thought which is so evident in the realm of anthropology is equally consonant in other areas as well.

BIBLIOGRAPHY

Primary Sources and Abbreviations

August Hermann Francke

AWC   *Schrifftmäßige und gründliche Anleitung zum Wahren Christenthum.* Halle, 170(?)

BF I–II   *Buß=Predigten.* 2 Teile. Halle, 1706.

CP   *Catechismus=Predigten.* Halle, 1729.

EP   *Predigten Über die Sonn= und Fest= Tags= Episteln.* Halle, 1729.

Erfahrung   *Die Erfahrung der Herrlichkeit Gottes.* Halle, 1716.

EU   *Einfältiger Unterricht/ Wie man die H. Schrifft zu seiner wahren Erbauung lesen solle/ Für diejenigen/ welche begierig sind/ ihr gantzes Christenthum auff das theure Wort GOttes zu gründen.* Halle, (No date)

Fußstapfen   *Segens=volle Fußstapfen des noch lebenden und waltenden liebreichen und getreuen GOttes.* Halle, 1709.

GA   *Der Große Aufsatz.* hrsg. von Otto Podczek. Berlin, 1962.

LP I–VII   *Lectiones Paraeneticae.* 7 Teile. Halle, 1726ff.

LR   *Schrifftmäßige Lebens=Reglen/ Wie man so wohl bey als ausser der Gesellschafft die Liebe und Freundligkeit gegen den Nechsten/und Freudigkeit eines guten Gewissens für GOTT bewahren/und im Christenthum zunehmen soll.* Leipzig, 1695.

Manuductio	*Manuductio ad lectionem Scriptura Sacrae,* Halae, [No date]
Methodus	*Methodus stvdii Theologici.* Halae, 1723.
PS	*August Hermann Franckes Pädagogische Schriften.* hrsg. von G. Kramer. Langensalza, 1876.
RGZ	*Der rechte Gebrauch der Zeit.* Halle, 1713.
Rührung	*Die Göttliche Rührung des Hertzens.* Halle, 1716.
SFA	*Sonn= Fest= und Apostel= Tags= Predigten.* 3 Teile. Halle, 1704.
SFP	*Sonn= und Fest= Tags= Predigten.* Halle, 1724.
Timotheus	*Timotheus zum Fürbild Allen Theologiae Studiosis dargestellt.* Halle, 1695.
WIA	*August Hermann Francke: Werke in Auswahl.* hrsg. von Erhard Peschke. Berlin, 1969.
WWD I-III(IV)	*Oeffentliches Zeugniß vom Werck/Wort und Dienst GOttes.* 3 Teile. Halle, 1702ff.

Heinrich Müller

AP	*Heinrich Müller: Ausgewählte Predigten.* hrsg. von Gustav Leonhardi. Leipzig. 1891.
DA	*Geistlicher Danck=Altar/ Zum täglichen Lobe=Opffer der Christen.* Franckfurt am Mayn, 1694.
GE	*Geistliche Erquickstunden.* Hamburg,1855.

GLF   *Göttliche Liebes=Flamme oder Auffmunterung zur Liebe Gottes.* Franckfurt am Mayn, 1694.

HLK   *Himmlischer Liebes=Küß.* Hof, 1738.

TE   *Theologische Erörterung Zweyer Fragen.* Franckfurt am Mayn, 1694.

TSB   *Theologische Schrifftmäßige Bedencken.* Hof, 1738.

Others

Evangelische Volksbibliothek Selected sections. hrsg. von Dr. Klaiber. Dritter Band. Stuttgart, 1864.

Wahres Christenthum   Arnd, Johann. *Sämtliche Bücher vom Wahren Christenthum.* Franckfurt am Mayn, 1704.

Gottlob   Fritsch, Ahasverus. *Gottlobs Hundert sonderbare Zufällige Andachten.* Franckfurt und Gotha, 1684.

Gotthold   Scriver, Christian. *Gottholds Zufällige Andachten.* Leipzig, 1689.

The Practical Works of Richard Baxter. Grand Rapids, 1981.

Breward, Ian (ed.). *The Work of William Perkins.* Appleford/ Abingdon/ Berkshire, 1970.

Schicketanz, Peter (ed.). *Der Briefwechsel Carl Hildebrand von Cansteins mit August Hermann Francke.* (Texte zur Geschichte des Pietismus, III, 1). Berlin, 1972.

Secondary Sources

Aland, Kurt. *Hilfsbuch zum Lutherstudium.* Gütersloh, 1957.

_____. *Kirchengeschichtliche Entwürfe.* Gütersloh, 1960.

_____. *Pietismus und Bibel.* (Arbeiten zur Geschichte des Pietismus 9). Witten, 1970.

_____. *Spener-Studien.* (Arbeiten zur Kirchengeschichte 28). Berlin, 1943.

August Hermann Francke: Festreden und Kolloquium. Leipzig, 1964.

Barth, Karl. *Die protestantische Theologie im 19. Jahrhundert.* Zürich, 1947.

Bauch, Hermann. *Die Lehre vom Wirken des Heiligen Geistes im Frühpietismus.* Hamburg-Bergstadt, 1974.

Benz, Ernst. "Ecumenical Relationships between Boston Puritanism and German Pietism: Cotton Mather and August Hermann Francke" in *The Harvard Theological Review.* Vol. LIV. No. 3. July, 1961. pp. 159–193.

_____. *Endzeiterwartung zwischen Ost und West.* Freiburg, 1973.

_____. *Evolution and Christian Hope.* Garden City, 1968.

_____. "Symbole der Unio Mystica in der Barock-Mystik" in *Symbolon.* Neue Folge. Band 1. (Sonderdruck)

_____. *Der vollkommene Mensch nach Jakob Boehme.* Stuttgart, 1937.

Beyreuther, Erich. *August Hermann Francke und die Anfänge der ökumenischen Bewegung.* Hamburg-Bergstedt, 1957.

_____. *August Hermann Francke. Zeugnis des lebendigen Gottes.* Marburg, 1969[3].

_____. *Geschichte des Pietismus.* Stuttgart, 1978.

Bornkamm, Heinrich. *Mystik, Spiritualismus und die Anfänge des Pietismus im Luthertum.* Giessen, 1926.

_____. (ed.) *Imago Dei. Beiträge zur theologischen Anthropologie.* Gustav Krüger zum 70. Geburtstag am 29. Juni 1932 dargebracht. Giessen, 1932.

_____. Friedrich Heyer and Alfred Schindler (eds.). *Der Pietismus in Gestalten und Wirkungen.* Martin Schmidt zum 65. Geburtstag (Arbeiten zur Geschichte des Pietismus 14). Bielefeld, 1975.

Brehier, Emile. *The History of Philosophy: The Seventeenth Century.* trans. Wade Baskin. Chicago, 1966.

_____. *The History of Philosophy: The Eighteenth Century.* trans. Wade Baskin. Chicago, 1967.

Brown, Dale. *The Problem of Subjectivism in Pietism.* Ph.D. diss. Northwestern University. Chicago, 1962.

_____. *Understanding Pietism.* Grand Rapids, 1978.

Brunner, Emil. *Man in Revolt.* trans. Olive Wyon. London, 1947³.

Clouse, Robert. *The Church in the Age of Orthodoxy and the Enlightenment.* St. Louis, 1980.

"Contemporary Perspectives on Pietism: A Symposium" in *The Covenant Quarterly.* Vol. XXXIV. Nos. 1 & 2. February/May, 1976.

Deppermann, Klaus. *Der hallesche Pietismus und der preußische Staat unter Friedrich III.(I.).* Göttingen. 1961.

Deeter, Alan. "Pietism, Moralism, and Social Concern" in *The Covenant Quarterly.* May, 1975, pp. 19–39.

Dillenberger, John and Claude Welch. *Protestant Christianity.* New York, 1954.

Filhaut, E. (ed.) *Johannes Tauler: ein deutscher Mystiker.* Essen, 1961.

Fischer, Hermann. (ed.). *Anthropologie als Thema der Theologie.* Göttingen, 1977.

Gass, Wilhelm. *Geschichte der protestantische Dogmatik in ihrem Zusammenhang mit der Theologie überhaupt.* Bd. I–IV. Berlin, 1854–1867.

Gerdes, Egon. "Pietism: Classical and Modern" in *Concordia Theological Monthly.* No. 39, 1968.

_____. "Theological Tenets of Pietism" in *The Covenant Quarterly.* February/May, 1970, pp. 25–60.

Greschat, Martin. (ed.). *Zur neueren Pietismusforschung.* (Wege der Forschung 440). Darmstadt, 1977.

Henningsen, Jurgen. "Leben entsteht aus Geschichten. Zu August Hermann Francke" in *Neue Zeitschrift für systematische Theologie.* 19. 1977, pp. 261–283.

Hartmann, R.J. *August Hermann Francke.* Stuttgart, 1897.

Hinrichs, Carl. *Preußentum und Pietismus: der Pietismus in Brandenburg-Preußen als religiössoziale Reformbewegung.* Göttingen, 1971.

Hoffmann, Bengt. *Luther and the Mystics.* Minneapolis, 1976.

Holborn, Hajo. *A History of Modern Germany: The Reformation.* New York, 1961.

_____. *A History of Modern Germany: 1648–1840.* New York, 1964.

Hubatsch, Walther. *Deutschland zwischen dem dreißigjährigen Krieg und der Französischen Revolution.* (Ullstein Deutsche Geschichte 2/III). Frankfurt/M., 1974.

Jungst-Stettin, J. *Pietisten.* Tübingen, 1906.

Kantzenbach, Friedrich. *Orthodoxie und Pietismus.* Gütersloh, 1966.

Koepp, Wilhelm. *Johannes Arndt und sein 'Wahres Christenthum'.* Berlin, 1959.

_____. *Eine Untersuchung über die Mystik im Luthertum.* Berlin, 1912.

Kramer, Gustav. *August Hermann Francke: Ein Lebensbild.* Bd. I–II. Halle, 1880–1882.

_____. *Beiträge zur Geschichte August Hermann Francke's.* Halle, 1861.

_____. *Neue Beiträge zur Geschichte August Hermann Francke's.* Halle, 1875.

Kümmel, Werner Georg. *Man in the New Testament.* trans. Jay Vincent. London, 1963.

_____. *Römer 7 und das Bild des Menschen im Neuen Testament.* München, 1974.

Lang, August. *Puritanismus und Pietismus. Studien zu ihrer Entwicklung von M. Butzer bis zum Methodismus.* Neukirchen, 1941 (Darmstadt, 1972).

_____. *Der Wortschatz des deutschen Pietismus.* Tübingen, 1969.

Leppin, Günther. *Carl Hildebrand Freiherr von Canstein.* Giessen, 1967.

Leube, Hans. *Kalvinismus und Luthertum im Zeitalter der Orthodoxie. Der Kampf um die Herrschaft im protestantischen Deutschland.* Leipzig, 1928/1966.

_____. *Orthodoxie und Pietismus. Gesammelte Studien.* ed. D. Blaufuß. (Arbeiten zur Geschichte des Pietismus 13). Bielefeld, 1975.

_____. *Die Reformideen in der deutschen lutherischen Kirche zur Zeit der Orthodoxie.* Leipzig, 1924.

Mahrholz, Werner. *Der deutsche Pietismus.* Berlin, 1921.

McNeill, John. *Modern Christian Movements.* Philadelphia, 1954.

Memoirs of August Hermann Francke. Philadelphia, 1831.

Mirbt, Carl, Friedrich August and August Nebe. *Zum Gedächtnis August Hermann Franckes.* Halle, 1927.

Nagler, Arthur. *Pietism and Methodism.* Nashville, 1918.

Niehbuhr, Reinhold. *The Nature and Destiny of Man.* Vols. I–II. London, 1941–1943.

Nussbaum, Frederick. *The Triumph of Science and Reason. 1660–1865.* New York, 1953.

Obst, Helmut. *Der Berliner Beichtstuhlstreit.* (Arbeiten zur Geschichte des Pietismus 11). Witten, 1972.

Oehl, J. F. *The Inner Mission.* Philadelphia, 1950.

Oschlies, Wolf. *Die Arbeits- und Berufspädagogik August Hermann Franckes.* (Arbeiten zur Geschichte des Pietismus 6). Witten, 1969.

Peschke, Erhard. *August Hermann Francke.* Berlin, 1981.

_____. *Bekehrung und Reform. Ansatz und Wurzeln der Theologie August Hermann Franckes.* (Arbeiten zur Geschichte des Pietismus 15). Bielefeld, 1977.

_____. "Kirche und Welt in der Theologie August Hermann Franckes" in *ThLZ* 88. 1963. pp. 241–258.

_____. *Studien zur Theologie August Hermann Franckes.* Vol. 1. *Die Ordnung Gottes - die Kinder Gottes und die Kinder der Welt.*Berlin, 1964. Vol. 2. *Die Heilige Schrift - das Studium der Theologie.* Berlin, 1979.

Pietismus und Neuzeit. Ein Jahrbuch zur Geschichte des neueren Protestantismus. Im Auftrag der Historischen Kommission zur Erforschung des Pietismus. ed. M. Brecht *et al.* Vol. 4: *Die Anfänge des Pietismus.* Göttingen, 1979.

Pinson, Koppel. *Pietism as a Factor in the Rise of German Nationalism.* New York, 1934.

Richard, Marie. *Philipp Jacob Spener. August Hermann Francke.* Philadelphia, 1897.

Ritschl, Albrecht. *Geschichte des Pietismus.* Bd. I–III. Bonn, 1880–1886.

Rotermund, Hans-Martin. *Orthodoxie und Pietismus. Valentin Ernst Löschers 'Timotheus Verinus' in der Auseinandersetzung mit der Schule August Hermann Franckes.*(Theologische Arbeiten 13). Berlin, 1959.

Sachsse, Eugen. *Ursprung und Wesen des Pietismus.* Wiesbaden, 1884.

Sattler, Gary. "August Hermann Francke and Mysticism" in *The Covenant Quarterly.* Nov. 1980. pp. 3–17.

_____. "Getting a Heart of Wisdom: The Christian and Life. Ahasverus Fritsch's *Gottlobs Hundert sonderbare Zufällige Andachten*" in *The Covenant Quarterly.* May, 1983, pp. 3–14.

_____. *God's Glory, Neighbor's Good: A Brief Introduction to the Life and Writings of August Hermann Francke.* Chicago, 1982.

Scharfe, Martin. *Die Religion des Volkes. Kleine Kultur- und Sozialgeschichte des Pietismus.* Gütersloh, 1980.

Schmalenberg, Gerhard. *Pietismus - Schule - Religionsunterricht.* (Theologie und Wirklichkeit 2). Frankfurt/M, 1974.

Schmid, Heinrich. *Die Geschichte des Pietismus.* Nördlingen, 1863.

Schmidt, Martin. *Pietismus.* (Urban Taschenbuch 145). Stuttgart, 1972.

_____. *Wiedergeburt und neuer Mensch. Gesammelte Studien zur Geschichte des Pietismus.* (Arbeiten zur Geschichte des Pietismus 2). Witten, 1969.

_____. and Wilhelm Jannasch (eds.). *Das Zeitalter des Pietismus.* (Klassiker des Protestantimsus 6). Bremen, 1965.

Sellschopp, Adolf. *Neue Quellen zur Geschichte August Hermann Franckes.* Halle, 1913.

Söhngen, Oskar. (ed.). *Die bleibende Bedeutung des Pietismus.* Witten und Berlin, 1960.

Spener, Philipp Jakob. *Der neue Mensch.* Stuttgart,1966.

_____. *Von der Wiedergeburt.* Stuttgart, 1963.

Stahl, Herbert. *August Hermann Francke: Der Einfluß Luthers und Molinos auf ihn.* Stuttgart, 1939.

Stoeffler, F. Ernest. *Continental Pietism and Early American Christianity.* Grand Rapids, 1976.

_____. *German Pietism during the Eighteenth Century.* Leiden, 1973.

_____. *The Rise of Evangelical Pietism.* Leiden, 1965.

Sträter, Udo. "Pietismus und Sozialtätigkeit: zur Frage nach der Wirkungsgeschichte des 'Waisenhauses' in Halle und des Frankfurter Armen- Waisen- und Arbeitshauses" in *Pietismus und Neuzeit.* 1982, pp. 201–233.

Tanner, Fritz. *Die Ehe im Pietismus.* Zürich, 1952.

Traditio - Krisis - Renovatio aus theologischer Sicht. Festschrift Winfried Zeller zum 65. Geburtstag. ed. B. Jaspert und R. Mohr. Marburg, 1976.

Underhill, Evelyn. *Mysticism.* New York, 1961.

Urner, Hans. *Der Pietismus.* Gladbeck, 1952.

Wachter, Moritz. *Das psychologische Moment in der Erziehung und Unterrichtsmethode A. H. Franckes.* Kulmbach, 1930.

Wächtler, A. *August Hermann Francke als Pastor zu St. Ulrich 1715–1727.* Halle, 1898.

Weber, Max. *The Protestant Ethic and the Spirit of Capitalism.* trans. Talcott Parsons. New York, 1958.

Weigelt, Horst. *Pietismus-Studien.* Teil 1: *Der spener-hallesche Pietismus.* (Arbeiten zur Theologie II 4).Stuttgart, 1965.

Wieser, Max. *Der sentimentale Mensch.* Gotha/ Stuttgart. 1924.

Williams, Edward. *Christian Life in Germany.* Chicago, 1897.

Winter, Friedrich Julius. *Johann Arndt, der Verfasser des Wahres Christenthums.* Leipzig, 1911.

Zeller, Winfried. *Frömmigkeit in Hessen. Beiträge zur hessischen Kirchengeschichte.* Marburg, 1970.

_____. *Theologie und Frömmigkeit.* Gesammelte Aufsätze. Vol. 1. (Marburger Theologische Studien 8). Marburg, 1971.

_____. *Theologie und Frömmigkeit.* Gesammelte Aufsätze. Vol. 2. (Marburger Theologische Studien 15). Marburg, 1978.

_____. (ed.). *Der Protestantismus des 17. Jahrhunderts.* (Klassiker des Protestantismus 5). Bremen, 1962.